Critical Discourse Analysis and Language Cognition

To Lisa

Critical Discourse Analysis and Language Cognition

Kieran O'Halloran

Edinburgh University Press

© Kieran O'Halloran, 2003

Edinburgh University Press Ltd
22 George Square, Edinburgh

Typeset in 11/13 Monotype Ehrhardt
by Servis Filmsetting Ltd, Manchester
Printed and bound in Great Britain by
Antony Rowe Ltd, Chippenham

A CIP record for this book is available from the British Library

ISBN 0 7486 1828 7 (paperback)

The right of Kieran O'Halloran
to be identified as author of this work
has been asserted in accordance with
the Copyright, Designs and Patents Act 1988.

Contents

Acknowledgements vi

1 Introduction 1

SECTION A: THE INTERPRETATION STAGE IN CDA

2 CDA and Manipulative News Text 9
3 Symbolicism 35
4 The Symbolicism of CDA 56

SECTION B: NEWER APPROACHES TO LANGUAGE COGNITION: IMPLICATIONS FOR CDA

5 Connectionism 85
6 Cognitive Linguistics 111
7 Psycholinguistic Evidence for Inference Generation 134

SECTION C: THE IDEALISED READER FRAMEWORK

8 Constructing the Idealised Reader: Compatibilities between Connectionism, Cognitive Linguistics and Psycholinguistics 169
9 Further Constructing the Idealised Reader: Compatibilities with Relevance Theory 197
10 Detecting News Text Likely to Mystify in Reading for Gist 223
11 Conclusion 252

Bibliography 262
Index 273

Acknowledgements

This book has its roots in my PhD thesis. Thank you to the Institute of Education, University of London for the bursary they gave me. Many thanks also to Guy Cook who supervised me – I had a thoroughly good time and had my mind expanded. I am grateful also for all his subsequent support and encouragement. My examiners, Michael Hoey and Henry Widdowson, were very kind in giving me ideas for improvements to the book. I am grateful to both for that as well as for their support. Others have read this book through, made penetrating comments and basically created headaches for me by not saying it was ready. Thank you to Caroline Coffin, Elisabeth Leue, Theresa Lillis and Peter R. R. White. By making me think really hard, everyone of the above saved me from some real idiocies, the remaining ones being my own work. Thanks also to Melanie Coote, Ann Hewings, Bill Hicks, Simon Phillips and Richard Whatmore . . . Elisabeth Leue suffered my absences during the writing. This book is fairly obsessed with looking for absences when it was me all along. Since this is an acknowledgements section, I would like to acknowledge this selfishness. Finally, thank you also to Norman Fairclough for his generosity. He suggested that Edinburgh University Press explore the possibility of taking this book.

The author and publisher are grateful to the following for permission to reproduce figures and texts from copyright material:

Atlantic Syndication Partners for the articles and photograph from the *Evening Standard*

David Burges for the photograph accompanying the article reproduced from *The Daily Telegraph*

Guardian Newspapers Limited for the article from *The Guardian*, © Alex Bellos

The MIT Press for the figure from David Rumelhart, James McClelland and the PDP Research Group *Parallel Distributed Processing: Explorations in the Microstructure of Cognition, volume 1: Foundations*, p. 320

Pearson Education Ltd for the figure from Norman Fairclough, *Critical Discourse Analysis: The Critical Study of Language*, p. 98, and to Norman Fairclough for agreeing to minor additions to the figure

Telegraph Group Limited for the article from *The Daily Telegraph*

Andrew Testa for the photograph accompanying the reproduced article from *The Guardian*

Thomson Publishing Services for the figure from Michael Eysenck and Mark Keane, *Cognitive Psychology: A Student's Handbook*, 3rd edition, p. 11, © Psychology Press.

CHAPTER 1

Introduction

1.1 CRITICAL DISCOURSE ANALYSIS AND THE ANALYSIS OF MYSTIFICATION

This book is concerned with how news texts can mystify what is being reported, whether intentionally or not. By 'mystify' I mean reducing the reader's understanding of the events and participants being described. This may be highly significant if the rationale for the actions of one group of participants is mystified in a news text when this is not the case for another group of participants. Let us say a particular news text reports a clash between two groups, for example, environmental protestors and police. Let us say also that it does not fully explore the rationale for the protest but is quite explicit on why there was a need for police action. For someone who is reading only for gist, the following may be the case. Given the effort to notice the absence of rationale for the protest, reading of the news text may contain a negative bias with regard to the protestors since the text mystifies their rationale but not that of the police.

In focusing on mystification in news text, this book follows in the tradition of Critical Discourse Analysis (CDA). This is a branch of linguistics that is concerned, broadly speaking, with highlighting the traces of cultural and ideological meaning in spoken and written texts.[1] News texts, specifically, have been a staple in CDA as a result of their salience in modern culture. Over the last twenty years CDA has established itself internationally, and is now one of the most popularly embraced forms of discourse analysis. It has been used increasingly by practitioners in disciplines other than linguistics, such as media studies, geography and law.[2] CDA has a number of techniques for uncovering language mystification as well as language manipulation more generally which, in an age of political spin and soundbites, gives it an obvious appeal. Two main stages in CD analysis of text are as follows:[3]

1. *Interpretation*: CDA interprets texts on behalf of readers who do not take up a critical position to indicate how such readers can be manipulated unwittingly by the text *or* positioned into a particular reading because of the social values they carry. Analysis of mystification in news text is situated in the interpretation stage of CDA since the latter is concerned with the analysis of the relationship between readers and the texts being read. In the interpretation stage, there has been some focus on the cognition of texts. By cognition, I mean the mental processing involved in reading and understanding texts.
2. *Explanation*: CDA explains connections between texts and the wider social and cultural context *and/or* explains how wider social and cultural contexts might shape the interpretation of a text.

Recent developments in CDA have seen it create a dynamic space for interdisciplinary work in linking linguistic analysis with sociocultural analysis.[4] As a result of these more recent developments, analysis in CDA has been largely explanation-stage analysis. And because of this focus in recent years, relatively little attention has been given to cognition in the interpretation stage and so there has been relatively little cognitive focus on how text can mystify for readers the events being described. Indeed, there has been little development of this area in CDA since the end of the 1970s. This is because many of the assumptions for how CDA still detects mystifying text result from two seminal books published at the end of that decade: *Language and Control* (Fowler et al. 1979) and *Language as Ideology* (Kress and Hodge 1979). The general approach to cognition which pervades these two books and underpins how mystification is detected and analysed is called *symbolicism* in cognitive science. Symbolic modelling of the mind is based on the idea that mental processing consists of the activation of symbols in accordance with a rule-governed system. It was the dominant cognitive paradigm from after the Second World War until the 1980s. But the symbolicism in Kress and Hodge (1979) and Fowler et al. (1979) is taken for granted and almost unrecognised. This is understandable since symbolicism was the accepted view of cognition when these books were written and so would have seemed natural in the absence of any competing paradigms. However, symbolicism has been challenged and shown to be problematic in developments in cognitive science from the 1980s onwards (connectionism, cognitive linguistics, new evidence in the psycholinguistics of reading, and relevance theory). Since the way in which CDA highlights mystification is based on symbolic assumptions, these challenges to symbolism are significant for CDA.

It is safe to assume that critical discourse analysts spend quite some time in the analysis of text and that this must involve a much higher degree of effort than that invested by, say, readers who are reading for gist. This is particularly the case if analysts are pointing out absences from a sentence which, for them, mean the event being reported is mystified for the gist reader; analysing absences from a sentence in a text is not part of reading for gist. But this all begs the following question, one which is seldom addressed in CDA: how can analysts be sure that the absences from a sentence that they detect would not be generated as inferences anyway by a gist reader via other information in the text? This leads on to more general questions. For example, to what extent is the interpretation a critical discourse analyst makes from a text on behalf of a non-analyst dependent on the longer amount of time and thus larger amount of effort the analyst invests? How do analysts know that they are not *over-interpreting* on behalf of readers who, in reading only for gist, would not invest the same amount of effort? It is not surprising that such questions do not usually occupy critical discourse analysts. Because developments in CDA over the last fifteen years or so have been largely related to linking linguistic analysis with sociocultural analysis, anything to do with cognition in the interpretation stage has not received comprehensive scrutiny. Assumptions in CDA for how readers operate are largely intuitive or undeveloped. Indeed, CDA is largely unaware that it possesses a number of tensions with regard to how it treats the cognition of texts.

1.2 MY AIMS

I want to redress the balance and look at the interpretation stage of CDA from a cognitive point of view.[5] To do so, I introduce the newer approaches to cognition from the 1980s onwards in order to construct the innovation of a reader framework, crucially one based on reader effort. In line with the strong tradition in CDA of examining news text for language manipulation, my data focus in this book will be predominantly news text too. The reader framework constructed in this book is used to show how more systematic and reliable prediction can be made as to whether or not a news text is likely to be mystifying for a gist reader through what is absent in the report; helps to enhance the interpretative authority of the analyst; and can be used to help prevent over-interpretation of news text on behalf of a gist reader.

More generally, the book brings together linguistic and cognitive approaches which usually do not communicate; shows how the contemporary frameworks – connectionism, cognitive linguistics, psycholinguistic evidence for inference generation, relevance theory – challenge symbolic notions of cognition in CDA; and goes on to highlight the implications of these challenges for assumptions of language cognition in CDA, as well as how CDA highlights language manipulation.

The cognition of causal relations (for example, who or what caused an action or event) and how causal relations can be mystified in news text will be a central focus of this book. The generation of inferences in reading with regard to the understanding of causal relations will also be a major focus. But by-products of these cognitive foci mean that cognition in CDA more generally can also be brought up-to-date and made more consistent. While my focus in this book is cognitive, this should not be taken as any kind of implicit denigration of how the socioculturally focused explanation stage has motivated CDA work more recently. Rather, my focus is cognitive because of its relative neglect in the interpretation stage. The constraints of the book mean anyway that I will not be able to explore the explanation stage and thus will not attempt any serious bridging of the interpretation and explanation stages via my cognitive focus.

1.3 THE STRUCTURE OF THE BOOK

The book is divided into three sections. Section A covers the interpretation stage in CDA. In Chapter 2, I introduce CDA and its techniques for analysing language manipulation in the interpretation stage. A key focus of Chapter 2 is to outline a host of assumptions used in CDA for highlighting a particular kind of manipulation: how news text can mystify the nature of the event being described. In Chapter 3, I outline symbolicism, and in Chapter 4 I show how symbolicism not only underlies much of CDA but also influences what CDA locates as mystifying text.

Section B describes the newer approaches to language cognition and their implications for CDA. In Chapters 5, 6 and 7, I outline newer approaches to language cognition (connectionism, cognitive linguistics and psycholinguistic evidence for inference generation, respectively) so as to show how they present a direct challenge to symbolicism. In demonstrating how these cognitive approaches are in conflict with symbolicism, I also show that there are problems with highlighting mystifying text in CDA. After doing this, I argue that what is needed is a way of locating mystifying news text that is *not* based on symbolicism, and that such an approach should also make a distinction between the level of effort invested in reading by analysts who search for absences from a text and that invested by readers who, in reading for gist, do not.

In order to do that, I go on to construct an idealised reader framework in Section C. In Chapter 8, I construct the basis of the reader framework in highlighting compatibilities between the three paradigms outlined in Section B. In Chapter 9, I add a more obvious pragmatic dimension to the reader framework by filtering relevance theory though the compatibilities of Chapter 8. Chapter 10 sees the reader framework comprehensively used to analyse a complete news text so as to get a richer sense of how it is likely to mystify, for a gist reader, through what is absent from the text.

Although my focus is mainly on one part of CDA – mystification analysis in its interpretation stage – I often use the term CDA to refer to practitioners who have been involved in such analysis. Let me be clear that this use of the reference term CDA is only for the sake of convenience. I am certainly *not* dealing with the whole of CDA. However, the book does have ramifications for the interpretation stage more generally. In trying to take the interpretation stage forward from a cognitive point of view, inevitably I will offer criticisms of previous work in CDA. Given the relative neglect of language cognition in CDA, my criticisms are very much in the spirit of raising awareness. They are meant to be constructive; constructive so as to provide, I hope, some enrichment of the interpretation stage, attempting to move it forward in theorising the reader. Indeed, many of these criticisms merely flow from the advantages of hindsight and developments in cognitive science that did not exist when the seminal ideas used in Fowler at al. (1979) and Kress and Hodge (1979) were first formulated.

NOTES

1. The following are a number of books which have helped to establish the field: Fowler, Hodge, Kress and Trew (1979), Kress and Hodge (1979), Fairclough (1992), Hodge and Kress (1993), Caldas-Coulthard and Coulthard (1996), van Dijk (1997a, 1997b), Chouliaraki and Fairclough (1999), Fairclough (1989/2001).
2. See Chouliaraki and Fairclough (1999).
3. In laying out these two stages, I follow the framework in Norman Fairclough's (1989/2001) *Language and Power*. Now in its second edition, this is the seminal work on CDA (Cook 2003: 122), Fairclough being a highly significant figure in this field (Trask 1999: 63). His framework is a standard one in CDA and its influence stretches to the structure and content of introductory textbooks, for example Goatly (2000). Aside from being one of the most cited books in CDA, *Language and Power* is probably the most cited CDA source in sociolinguistics and discourse analysis more generally.

4. Chouliaraki and Fairclough (1999) is a significant advance in this direction.
5. To be clearer, I should say this book focuses on the process of interpretation rather than the process of production (see Figure 2.1). One text production focus of CDA has been on how official texts (such as government documents) are transformed in the tabloids' reporting into a colloquial format with corresponding changes in emphasis and sometimes even meaning (see Fairclough 1995a). But text production has not really received the emphasis in CDA that interpretation has. So when I talk about the interpretation stage of CDA in this book I am talking only about interpretation of texts by non-analysts and analysts, and not about the production process.

SECTION A

The Interpretation Stage in CDA

CHAPTER 2

CDA and Manipulative News Text

2.1 INTRODUCTION

This chapter provides detail on how CDA highlights manipulative news text, news text having been something of a staple in CDA given its salience in modern culture. As Goatly (2000: 286) writes: 'For many people, newspapers are probably the only regular leisure reading, and are the most widely circulated print medium.' Three types of news text manipulation, whether intended or not, dealt with by CDA are highlighted in this chapter. But there is a strong focus on only one particular type of manipulation: how news text can mystify the nature of the event being reported or who was responsible for actions associated with the event. Part of this chapter involves outlining actual mystification analyses in CDA. To begin with, however, let me provide more detail on what CDA is and where mystification analysis fits into it.

2.2 CRITICAL DISCOURSE ANALYSIS

2.2.1 Orientation

In the Introduction I indicated two major standpoints with regard to text: *interpretation* and *explanation*. Figure 2.1 shows in more detail how the interpretation stage and the explanation stage relate to each other.

The other stage – *description* – involves systematically describing what linguistic features are in a *text* (such as news reports, menus, train departure boards or advertisements) as well as highlighting features which are not. A text need not be a string of sentences. Indeed, it could consist of one word or even one letter, for example 'W' on a toilet door. For reading,

10   CDA AND LANGUAGE COGNITION

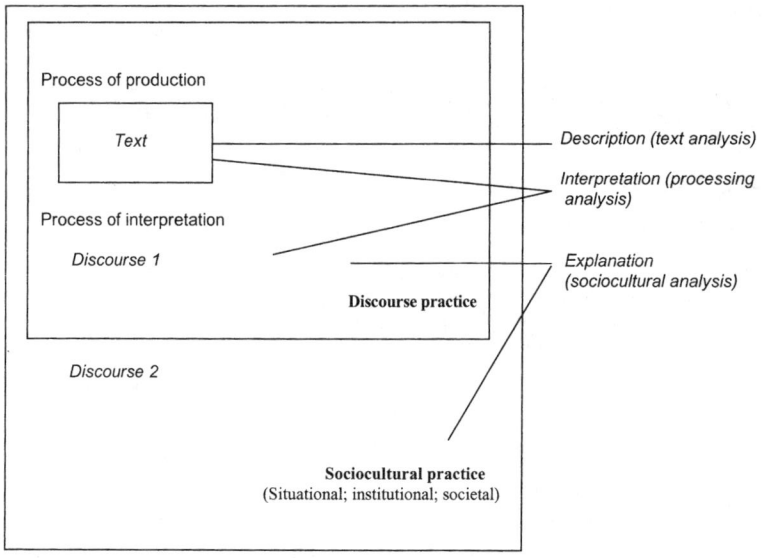

Figure 2.1 Source for original figure: Fairclough 1995b: 98. Some very minor additions have been made. Used with the permission of Pearson Education Ltd.

discourse practice refers to the activity of reading a text, and making a coherent understanding of it in line with the context (for example, reading purpose, spatial location, background knowledge, the nature of the participants). *Discourse* is the result of this: the interaction between text and context. So the discourse a man is likely to make from 'W' on a toilet door is likely to be different from that of a woman since men will normally understand this to mean they should not enter.

Because of the way a particular text, say a news text, is constructed and organised, it may be mystifying of the events being reported. Let us return to the example in the Introduction about the news text which reports a clash between two groups, environmental protestors versus police. As before, suppose that the rationale of the protest is absent from the news text but the text is all the same quite explicit on why there was a need for police action. Now consider a reader who is reading for gist and so is not reading the text in the same way that an analyst would. That is, consider a reader who does not search for absences from a text. I refer to this reader later in this book as the 'non-critical reader'. Of course, I am not saying that people cannot be critical readers, but that any reader, including critical discourse analysts, who analyses a text for its absences will take more time and effort to do this than if reading quickly for gist. So my notion of a non-critical reader here is more akin to a state of low(ish)-effort investment on a continuum of reading states which move from low to high effort of investment. (Because 'non-critical reader' is bound up with an effort investment only necessary for extracting gist from a text, it could indeed refer to an 'off-duty' critical discourse analyst.) Returning to the news text example, because the above readers do not expend the effort to notice absences, the discourse they produce from the news text could inadvertently contain a negative bias with regard to the protestors since the text mystifies their rationale but not that of the police. Figure 2.1 shows that it is the *interpretation stage* which is concerned with analysis of the relationship between the discourse practice of readers and the texts being read and thus where analysis of such mystification would be situated. As 'processing analysis' in Figure 2.1 would suggest, in CDA there has been some focus on the cognition of texts in the interpretation stage. Some focus on cognition of text in CDA has been in relation to highlighting mystifying text.

As I said in the Introduction, work on the relationship between language and cognition in linguistic manipulation has not been a major focus of development in CDA in recent years.[1] Where development has taken place in CDA is in linking linguistic to sociocultural analysis. Indication of this greater focus in CDA can be seen in van Dijk's (2001: 352) recent definition:

> Critical Discourse Analysis (CDA) is a type of discourse analytical research that primarily studies the way social power abuse, dominance, and inequality are enacted, reproduced, and resisted by text and talk in the social and political context. With such dissident research, critical discourse analysts take explicit position, and thus want to understand, expose, and ultimately resist social inequality.

A number of key thinkers from the twentieth century are drawn upon or referred to in CDA, namely, Althusser, Bakhtin, Gramsci, Habermas and Volosinov. Furthermore, in isolating how power abuse, dominance and inequality are enacted, CDA makes particular use of the concept of discourse developed by the French social theorist and philosopher Michel Foucault.

2.2.2 Foucauldian Discourse

Foucault (1972) characterises discourses as systematically organised sets of statements that give expression to the meanings and values of an institution. For him, discourses define and delimit what is possible to say and not possible to say (and, by extension, what to do or not to do) with respect to the area of concern of that institution. For example, different religions have their own discourses which delimit explanation of natural behaviour. Catholicism now accepts that the universe began with the 'Big Bang' (scientific discourse) but believes that the Christian God initiated it (mix of scientific and religious discourse). In 2.2.1, I mentioned the concept of discourse in the context of the phrase 'discourse practice'. It has become an unfortunate fact of life that discourse analysts have to use the term 'discourse' to refer to at least two different phenomena. Discourse (1) refers to the coherent understanding the reader makes from a text. It can include how the values of the reader, the reading context and so on affect the reading of the text in the production of coherence. 'Foucauldian discourse', or discourse (2), refers instead to the way in which knowledge is organised, talked about and acted upon in different institutions. To go back to Figure 2.1, while discourse (1) is associated with the *discourse practice*, discourse (2) is associated with the *sociocultural practice*. While discourse (1) is bound to a particular reading context, discourse (2) is bound to a particular sociocultural context. Discourse (2) is then the more general notion and, as Figure 2.1 indicates, can affect discourse (1) especially as the values a reader carries will affect his or her interpretation of a text. With regard mainly to discourse (2), Fairclough and Wodak (1997: 271–80) isolate a number of common tenets in CDA:

1. CDA addresses social problems
2. Power relations are discursive
3. Discourse constitutes society and culture
4. Discourse does ideological work
5. Discourse is historical
6. The link between text and society is mediated
7. Discourse analysis is interpretative and explanatory
8. Discourse is a form of social action.

Despite Foucauldian discourse theory being commonly drawn upon, CDA is not a unitary theoretical framework. In highlighting its diversity, Fairclough and Wodak (1997) also usefully provide outlines of approaches which fall under CDA (Critical Linguistics, Socio-Cognitive Studies, Social Semiotics, Sociocultural Change and Change in Discourse, Discourse-Historical Method, Lesartenanalyse, Duisberg School, French Discourse Analysis). Since my focus is on mystification analysis in CDA which derives from ideas in Critical Linguistics, I will provide an outline of Critical Linguistics (see 2.2.3). There is not the space to look at any of the other strands here (although I gloss 'sociocognition' below) so I refer the reader to Fairclough and Wodak's (1997) very useful overview.

The development of sociocultural analysis in CDA has been in line with the use of Foucauldian discourse theory. Work on sociocultural analysis in the explanation stage of CDA (see Figure 2.1) has informed the interpretation stage, and it was in drawing on Foucauldian discourse theory that CDA introduced a socio-cognitive angle into the interpretation stage. This was done so as to detect a different way in which texts can manipulate readers: socio-cognitive manipulation. Fairclough (1992) indicates how readers can be manipulated socio-cognitively as follows: they can be positioned by texts because they are drawing upon a particular discourse (2) without necessarily realising that this discourse (2) sets limits on their reading. The purpose of socio-cognitive analysis in CDA is to expose how discourses (2) can set such limits on someone's reading (that is, their discourse (1)). For example, teenage girls reading advertisements for cosmetics may be drawing on a certain discourse of femininity which emphasises the need to strive for physical perfection. In turn, this could affect their reading of the advertisement. Inadvertent drawing-upon this discourse of femininity can help to reproduce unequal relations of power between men and women (in the absence of a corresponding discourse of masculinity which also emphasises the need to strive for physical perfection to the same extent). This is what Fairclough and Wodak (1997) mean when they state that discourse (2) can do ideological work because 'ideologies are particular ways of representing and constructing society which reproduce unequal relations of power, relations of domination and exploitation' (Fairclough and Wodak 1997: 275). Being critical in socio-cognitive analysis means being critical of ideological processes in discourse (2):

> There is a strong case to be made for a mode of language education which emphasizes critical awareness of ideological processes in discourse, so that people can become more aware of their own practice, and be more critical of the ideologically invested discourses to which they are subjected.
> (Fairclough 1992: 90)

Socio-cognitive analysis, then, is a form of critical discourse (2) analysis. A critical discourse analyst who places emphasis on the 'cognitive' in socio-cognitive analysis is Teun van Dijk. Van Dijk is explicit that discussion of the relationship between discourse (2) and social structure cannot fruitfully take place without consideration of how these phenomena are linked to the cognition of individuals (van Dijk 2001).

From what I have outlined in this chapter so far, CDA as a whole cannot be considered an homogenous research project. But aspects of it which relate to cognition *do* have a certain homogeneity, especially as regards discourse (1). For example, much of CDA suffers from a paucity of appreciation of language cognition, and psycholinguistic evidence is rarely cited. Moreover, the concept of the 'reader' and how they cognise is undeveloped in CDA. These are homogeneities in CDA which I address in this book. I also examine another homogeneity in CDA: the way in which contemporary CDA detects mystifying text is still based on the critical linguistic work of the 1970s and many of these assumptions are grounded in the symbolic paradigm of cognitive modelling (see Chapters 3 and 4). So, given the focus of this book on mystification analysis, I need to provide an outline of Critical Linguistics.

2.2.3 Critical Linguistics

Critical Linguistics is the name used to describe the application of a particular set of linguistic procedures to texts with a view to uncovering concealed ideological meanings, whether or not intentional (see definition of 'ideology' in the last section). A key assumption in Critical Linguistics is that ideology is encoded in texts and that this can manipulate the reader and/or mystify textual subject matter. The critical reader is one who is vigilant to the prospect of reader construction, and seeks to expose 'the ideological level of meaning in texts that are manipulative of their readers and/or mystifying of their subject matter. To read innocently, non-analytically, is to be manipulated and mystified . . .' (Richardson 1987: 146–7).

With regard to mystification analysis, Critical Linguistics has had a strong analytical focus on how responsibility for particular actions can be backgrounded in texts. The principal source books for Critical Linguistics are Fowler et al. (1979) and Kress and Hodge (1979). Hodge and Kress (1993) is the second edition of Kress and Hodge (1979). It contains the same chapters as Kress and Hodge (1979) together with a new final chapter. All the authors of the two books worked at the University of East Anglia during the 1970s, and these books represent the culmination of thinking during that period. The books were highly original and taken up enthusiastically by students and practising academics of the time. Their originality lay in what they offered: a set of linguistic techniques for the analysis of language manipulation. Such is their impact that both Kress and Hodge (1979) and Fowler et al. (1979) continue to be referred to in CDA and continue to be recommended as further reading in introductory books (for example, Freeborn 1993; Montgomery et al. 2000; Stockwell 2002) as well as having analyses reproduced from them in introductory books (for example, Graddol et al. 1994; Montgomery 1995). As Fairclough and Wodak (1997) indicate, Critical Linguistics can be considered a branch of CDA.[2] But while CDA has absorbed Critical Linguistics – and thus its techniques for analysing how texts can mystify the responsibility for a particular event – there has been little development of these techniques since its absorption.

Critical Linguistics draws on a number of thinkers. Two principal figures are the American linguist Benjamin Lee Whorf, and the British linguist Michael Halliday, the latter having been influenced to some extent by the former. Whorf's articles were mostly written in the 1930s and early 1940s but many of them became more widely known when published posthumously in a book anthology in 1956. The works of Halliday relevant to Critical Linguistics date from the 1960s.

Whorf

Crucial to how Critical Linguistics is grounded is the Whorfian hypothesis.[3] This hypothesis is usually framed as follows: 'differences of linguistic structure cause the speakers of different languages in some sense to "see the world" in different ways' (Fowler 1991: 30). So, for example, Whorf regarded the non-Indo-European language Hopi as being bound up with a different world-view to that of English. For Whorf, time in Hopi is a different notion altogether to time in Western culture, and this is explained by differences in linguistic structure between Hopi and English. Since Critical Linguistics is interested in how language can manipulate thought, Whorf is cited as an important source of validation for the enterprise (Fowler et al. 1979). The Whorfian hypothesis is actually adapted in Critical Linguistics along the following lines: differences of linguistic structure in the same variety of English (such as in different news reports) can cause readers to see the world being described in different ways. (On the adaptation of the Whorfian hypothesis, see Fowler et al. (1979).) Here, for example, is a critical linguist using the Whorfian hypothesis:

> A central question in text linguistic research into media is: how can ideology be established through structural analysis of texts ... In essence this is a particular application of the Sapir-Whorf hypothesis about the relation between language and world-view: how is the world-view of journalists of a given newspaper reflected in the text?
>
> (Renkema 1984: 17)

Halliday

Various facets of Hallidayan functional linguistics (see Halliday 1994) are also drawn upon in Critical Linguistics. The working premise in Halliday's work is that 'language is as it is because of its function in the social structure' (Halliday 1973: 65). For Halliday, language serves three overarching functions:

1. *ideational* – to represent people, objects, events, and states of affairs in the world
2. *interpersonal* – to express the speaker's attitude to these representations
3. *textual* – to array 1. and 2. in a cohesive and appropriate manner.

Since a major concern of Critical Linguistics is how linguistic representations of events can be manipulative, particularly in mystifying events and/or responsibility for events, Halliday's ideational function is a crucial focus. Halliday's focus is indeed somewhat 'Whorfian', making his work particularly suitable as a theoretical source in Critical Linguistics:

> it is through this [ideational] function that the speaker or writer embodies in language his experience of the phenomena of the real world . . . We shall in no sense be adopting an extreme pseudo-Whorfian position (I say 'pseudo-Whorfian' because Whorf himself was never extreme) if we add that, in serving this function, language lends structure to his experience and helps to determine his way of looking at things.
>
> (Halliday 1996/1971: 58)

Having given something of the scope of CDA and where mystification analysis would be situated within it, let me move on to outline some key concepts used in CDA for mystification analysis, which were absorbed from Critical Linguistics. One of these key concepts – *transitivity* – was itself absorbed from Hallidayan functional grammar. In 2.4, we shall see these concepts being used when I outline actual mystification analyses from CDA.

2.3 KEY CONCEPTS IN MYSTIFICATION ANALYSIS

I deal below with the key concepts of 'transitivity', 'passivisation', and 'nominalisation'.

Transitivity

This refers to the grammatical system by which ideational meaning is represented in the clause, and the type of process (for example, material action, mental, relational, verbal) and the type of participants (for example, agent, affected, senser, phenomenon, verbiage) which accompany the process. It is a semantico-syntactic concept (see Halliday 1994). Consider Table 2.1.

Table 2.1

	She	slapped	me	on the patio	ACTIVE VOICE
	subject	verb	object		
	agent	process	affected		

'She' is subject because it comes before the verb and 'me' is object because it comes after the verb. This is a syntactic description. In terms of transitivity, 'kicked' is a material action process ('material' because matter is involved, 'action' for obvious reasons). The process is realised as a verb in the example above but it need not be: it could be realised as a gerund for instance (the *slapping* I get everytime I'm on the patio is getting on my nerves). Back to the example above. 'She' is the agent of the slapping; 'me' is what is changed by the action and so is called the affected. Agent and affected are participants. They relate more obviously to meaning, unlike subject and object, and so are sometimes referred to as *semantic roles*. If we turn things around and make the object the subject – that is, if we passivise the sentence – the result is shown in Table 2.2.

Table 2.2

	I	was slapped	(by) her	on the patio	PASSIVE VOICE
	affected	process	agent		

While we have a different subject, notice that the referents for affected and agent remain the same. This is because while the syntactic arrangement of the sentence has changed, the ideational meaning has not, whether it is expressed in the active or passive voice.

Ideational Passivisation

A large number of passives in English text can help to create an impression of distance between the writer and the reader, and thus an impression of formality, since human participants can be omitted. This is common in scientific experimental write-ups where the experimentor is left out in sentences such as, 'The excess hydrochloric acid was drained from the test tube and the copper sulphate was then removed.' Since passives can increase formality, we can say that for scientific experimental write-ups the interpersonal function (following Hallidayan nomenclature) can be significant with a high frequency of passivisations in this context. The textual function is also significant with passivisation in this context since it allows the removal of information that is understood (the person who did the write-up is usually involved in conducting the experiment). But mystification analysis in CDA tends to focus on passivisations where the ideational function is more significant, particularly with news texts. Compare the sentences in Table 2.3.

Table 2.3

Police agent	shot dead	10 people today as violence again flared in Jerusalem. affected
10 people affected	were shot dead today as violence once again flared in Jerusalem. (no agent)	

In the first sentence in Table 2.3, it would be grammatically unacceptable to leave out the agent but when the sentence is turned in to the passive, it is acceptable to do so. Mystification analysis in CDA often focuses on these kinds of sentences because passivisation can be ideationally significant if the representation excludes the agent. So with the second sentence in Table 2.3, it can be argued that it is mystifying because responsibility for the action is absent.

Ideational Nominalisation

Nominalisation refers to the process where a verb or another part of speech such as an adjective is changed into a noun. In a way similar to passives, agents are removed in nominalised clauses. So to return to the scientific experimental example, a nominalised version might be as follows: 'The *draining* of the excess hydrochloric acid was followed by *removal* of the copper sulphate.' As with the example of interpersonal passivisation, there is a corresponding increase in formality owing to the deletion of the agent. Therefore we can say that the interpersonal function can be significant with a high frequency of nominalisations in this context. The textual function is also significant for similar reasons that the textual function is significant with passivisations in this context. Mystification analysis in CDA tends to focus on the ideational function of nominalisation, and again particularly with news reports. Consider the following:

> The *shooting dead* of 10 people today reminds us all of the extent to which the Middle East crisis has escalated recently.

As with the ideational passivised version, there is an accompanying loss of agency. This sentence is ideationally significant with regards to what is included and what is absent. A case, then, might be made that the sentence is mystifying because responsibility for the shooting is absent.

Where the application of Hallidayan functional grammar has been particularly strong in Critical Linguistics, and later in CDA, is in the comparative tracing of transitivity patterns in different news texts so as to highlight different ideational biases. Consider the following, for example, from Montgomery et al. (2000: 92–3):

> In the coverage of the 1983 miners' strike, for instance, the action of picketing was constructed in quite different linguistic ways by different newspapers, depending on their political perspective. The *Daily Mail*, which generally supported the government position, described events on the picket line in sentences such as the following:
>
> 41 policemen had been treated in hospital
> police horses and their riders were stoned
> five police horses were also injured
> pickets demolished a wall
> pickets bombarded the police
>
> Using the categories of transitivity . . . we find that in material action processes 'the police' figure in the accounts mainly in the role of the affected (of usually violent actions). Where 'picketing miners' appear in action clauses it is usually as agents, mostly of (violent) actions performed against the police.
>
> In contrast to the *Daily Mail*, a newspaper such as the *Morning Star*, whose support for the miners was unwavering throughout the strike, described events on the picket line in sentences such as:
>
> police attacked isolated groups of miners
> several miners were hit with truncheons
> one miner was pounced upon by other policemen
> the miners massed around the entrance
> 3,000 pickets yesterday gathered outside Cortonwood Colliery

Here, police become agents of (violent) actions by which the miners are affected. And whilst the miners are sometimes presented as agents, it usually involves processes of non-violent movement (as in 'the miners massed around the entrance').

This brief analysis shows that the actual events of the picketing are constructed in quite different ways through the transitivity choices adopted in the respective newspapers. The choices in the *Daily Mail* present the industrial dispute as one in which the police are defenders of civil order in the face of a threat from the miners. The choices in the *Morning Star*, by contrast, present the dispute as working-class solidarity in the face of state provocation. These ideological viewpoints are not simply reflected in the language; they are produced and constructed through these different patterns of grammatical organization.

Using comparative transitivity analysis in this way helps us to see and articulate different biases in the lexico-grammatical patterns of the two newspapers (*lexico-grammar* refers to the interaction of vocabulary and grammar). It is possible also that comparative analysis may be done within a single text, that is comparing the lexico-grammatical realisations of different participants and their actions in the same news text. Either way, it is difficult to be specific about the relationship between bias in lexico-grammatical patterns and the cognition of a reader. In other words, it is difficult to gauge whether bias in a text could be taken into the discourse (1) of a reader. Because of this difficulty, it is best to refer to that kind of manipulation as *text bias*, this being a form of semantico-syntactic manipulation which only has the potential to manipulate at the discourse (1) level. Moreover, because we cannot know easily when this text bias is carried into discourse (1), this kind of bias analysis is better referred to as a form of *critical text analysis*. And since it is text analysis rather than discourse (1) analysis, it takes place in the description stage of analysis rather than the interpretation stage (see Figure 2.1 in 2.2.1). I should add a point about what is meant specifically by the term 'bias' above. Critical discourse analysis does not presuppose in its use of this term that there is such a thing as a value-neutral text. Likewise, in my use of the expression, 'text bias', I also do not presuppose there is such a thing as value-neutral text. All representations have their own slant or angle of telling. Trying to change a text so as to remove text bias and end up with a completely value-neutral text is difficult, if not impossible, to achieve.

This book does not focus on comparative text bias because I am interested in making fairly robust predictions as to the likelihood of a different type of manipulation: how absences from a news text may or may not lead to mystification, in discourse (1), of the event being described. In other words, my focus is a form of *critical discourse (1) analysis*. In contrast with critical text analysis, we might more clearly make a case for predicting manipulation in discourse (1) as follows: because of the effort required to detect it, an absence of agency in a sentence, other things being equal, can transfer into an absence of agency in the discourse (1) of a reader who is reading for gist. Critical discourse analysis makes a number of assumptions about text cognition in relation to how a text can mystify, but it is much less strong on this issue than it is in highlighting text bias. This is because, as this book will show, many of its assumptions about language cognition are problematic. Moreover, while Hallidayan functional grammar is legitimate for revealing (comparative) text bias, an implicit cognitive assumption in his work lends support to how CDA has problematically identified text which mystifies the events being described. I will return to this in Chapter 4.

Having laid out some key concepts for mystification analysis in 2.3, in 2.4 I outline actual examples of mystification analysis in CDA with a view to indicating the assumptions of cognition on which critical discourse analysts operate. Given that mystification analysis in CDA continues especially to take its bearings from Fowler et al. (1979), Kress and Hodge (1979) and Hodge and Kress (1993), some examples derive from these books. In Fowler et al. (1979), this is especially the case with a chapter by Trew (1979), one of the most regularly cited and key works in CDA.[2] Other examples of mystification analysis in CDA will be featured elsewhere in this book. In 2.4 (and 2.5), I flag where CDA explicitly uses the notion of a reader, undeveloped as it is. At other times in these sections, the notion of a reader in CDA is merely implicitly understood.

2.4 ASSUMPTIONS ABOUT COGNITION IN MYSTIFICATION ANALYSIS

2.4.1 Inferences are Weak Representations

In CDA, inferences generated in textual comprehension are often regarded as weaker mental representations than mental representation of the 'surface' sentential structure. Let us consider some examples. The following is an extract from Trew (1979) who examines news reports of the same event which appeared on 2 June 1975 in *The Times* and *The Guardian*. Trew's analysis is also referred to later in this book, not only as it has attained the status of a classic, but because of its continuous citation (and often reproduction) in introductory textbooks to linguistics, sociolinguistics and so on (for example, Graddol et al. 1994: 220–2; Montgomery 1995: 238–40; Montgomery et al. 2000: 348) and reproduction and endorsement in less introductory works (for example, Toolan 2001: 208–9; Simpson 1993: 105–6; Lee 1992: 97–100). Here now is Trew (1979: 98–9):

> *The Times*
> RIOTING BLACKS SHOT DEAD BY POLICE AS ANC LEADERS MEET
> Eleven Africans were shot dead and 15 wounded when Rhodesian police opened fire on a rioting crowd of about 2,000 . . .
>
> Not only is it [the *Times* report] in the passive, but the syntactic agent is deleted ('Eleven Africans were shot dead by . . .') **and is identified only weakly by implication** through the temporal conjunction with the police opening fire ('when police opened fire on a rioting crowd of about 2,000'). Looking at this in purely syntactic terms, with the deletion of the agent there is no longer any direct reference to who did the action and there is a separation of the action from whoever did it. [my bold]

For Trew, with the absence of agency in the clause 'Eleven Africans were shot dead', any inferencing necessary to link perpetrator and action is a *weaker* representation of the actual event. So with the agency of the police attenuated, textual mystification occurs. Hodge and Kress (1993: 26) hint at a similar assumption when they contend that in *passives* 'the link between actor and process is weakened, that is, the causal connection is syntactically looser'. ('Actor' is equivalent to the semantic role 'agent'.) A similar assumption that inferences are weaker representations can be found in Simpson (1993: 106, 170) and in Montgomery (1995: 240). Likewise, this notion is implied in Toolan's (2001: 209) commentary on the 'Rhodesia shooting' text when he says that in the *Times* report above, the agent 'has to be retrieved by inference from the subordinate temporal clause (*when Rhodesian police* . . .)'. Another supposition at work in the above is that inferences are separate from the processing of syntax. Finally, in Trew's analysis, there is implicit acknowledgement that in making sense of a text, readers rely on their knowledge of words and grammar (*bottom-up processing*). But at the same time, Trew has little focus on how readers draw on knowledge of the world (*top-down processing*).

2.4.2 A High Degree of Nominalisation Requires Extra Reading Effort

The following involves a discussion by Hodge and Kress (1993: 21) of part of a newspaper editorial (*The Guardian*, 20 December 1973) on the miners' overtime ban during the winter of 1972–3, and in particular of a sentence from the editorial: 'The Government knows that in early 1972 it was caught out by picketing of power stations which curtailed coal deliveries.' Here is the analysis:

> *Picketing* . . . curtailed coal deliveries
>
> If we asked speakers of English what the meaning of *picketing* was, they would probably explain it by describing the kinds of things involved: strikers, the action, a factory, or, in this case, a coal-depot. The noun is a contraction of a significant kind. The single word necessarily implies a particular kind of actor and a particular object of action. We might represent the process in this way:
>
> strikers picket a factory ⇨ picketing
> . . . there are two major effects associated with that transformation, which amount to a quite radical changing of the original form. First, although we know that there was an actor and an affected, the specific identities of both have been lost. We can guess about their identity but can never be certain. Second, in the resulting surface form the only thing that meets us is the verbal version of the action which was performed, and in this way our attention is directed to what is present and directed away from what is no longer there. So the focus of the expression has been altered by the speaker, our vision has been channelled and narrowed.

For Hodge and Kress, 'strikers picket a factory' is the 'deep' form (that is, it has the transitivity structure of agents-process-affected) which is absent from the report. It is supposedly needed for a better, more comprehensive understanding of the situation. Since the 'surface' or nominalised form here is 'picketing', to understand the situation the article is reporting the reader has to make more processing effort to recover the 'deep' form:

> As readers of this editorial we should have to be alert and willing to engage in mental exercise to get beyond the seductive simplicity

of the final form, with just three entities, and seemingly precise relations, where everything seems to be there on the surface . . . we can see that few commuters on the 8.05 from Brighton would have the energy to perform the mental gymnastics required.

(Hodge and Kress 1993: 22)

This time a reader is explicitly referred to, who might be captured by the expression 'non-energetic' reader. 'Non-energetic' readers will not recover the 'deep' structure of agents-process-affected and so for this reader the nature of the event and the participants involved are mystified. The reader's processing and thus appreciation of the event is shallow.

2.4.3 Excessive Nominalisation Distances the Reader from the Events being Reported

For CDA, nominalisations objectify the event being described and in doing so mystify the nature of the event. This is because the process nature of an event is then to some extent made absent. Mystification can occur because participants have also been made absent in nominalisation. Here, first, are Fowler and Kress (1979b: 208), on the 'objectification' effects of nominals:

> Two further effects of nominalization may be mentioned briefly. The first is objectification, the rendering of a process as an object: 'We still need lots of *contributions* to the jumble sale'; 'our new *development*, the 'Interference Absorption Circuit'; 'Now that you've had your first *look* at the new Record Saloon'. (Our italics in the last three examples.) This in turn affects lexicalization, the provision of words and phrases to code new concepts or consolidate existing ones: 'strict segregation', 'basic approach', 'school dinner services', 'people's trial', 'illegal detention'. Lexicalization fixes the object-as-process as a single habitualized entity.

The argument that nominal description of actions objectifies action and thus creates distance between the event and its appreciation by the reader (that is, ideational distance) is carried forward into CDA (for example, Kress 1989: 58; Fowler 1991: 80; Lee 1992: 95 (specifically flagging Fowler and Kress 1979b); Fairclough 1995a: 112). Here is an example from Martin (1989: 43) on how the killings of kangaroos and seals are respectively treated in different texts – in *Habitat* (June 1983) and *International Wildlife* (March–April 1983) respectively:

> Overall the [seal] article realises actions as nouns twice as often as the [kangaroo] editorial . . . Of particular interest is the way in which the two texts refer to the killing of seals and kangaroos. The [kangaroo text] tends to refer to the killing congruently, as a process: *the massive level of killing; the favoured killing of bigger, heavier male kangaroos; whose lives will be obliterated; killing 3 million kangaroos a year; when our prime wildlife is killed on this scale*. The [seal] text on the other hand tends to refer to the killing indirectly, using incongruent forms: *killing techniques, the whitecoat harvest, the slaughter of animals, the East Coast seal hunt, a slaughtering operation, killing methods, an almost instantaneous death, a humane death, the seal hunt*, and so on. In this way the [kangaroo] text focuses on the process of killing, while the [seal] text treats the killing as a kind of thing. This has the effect of *immobilising the most unsavoury part of the seal hunt* and helps draw attention away to other 'factual' considerations. [my italics]

For Martin, the high propensity of nominal forms in the 'seal' text is incongruous with the killing of seals since they diminish for the reader the fact that these are actions, and thus mystify 'the most unsavoury part of the seal hunt'. Martin's analysis receives a recent endorsement in Goatly (2001: 220) under the heading 'Traditional Critical Discourse Analysis'.

2.4.4 Readers Can Confuse Semantic Transitivity with Transitive Syntax

Another assumption about reading in CDA relates to the possibility that readers can confuse transitive syntax with semantic ('Hallidayan') transitivity. This assumption is found in Fowler and Kress (1979a: 42) but I focus on a more recent example. Consider the following from Kress (1993: 181–2), an analysis of the clause 'his parents could not afford a uniform', which features in a newspaper text (*Daily Express*, 3 May 1991):

> My interest here lies initially in the construction of the concept of poverty in the popular media . . . and my specific focus is the clause 'his parents could not afford a uniform' in sentence 1 . . . The cited clause in sentence 1 presents a syntactic ambiguity. What syntactic analysis/description do we give to *afford*? Overtly it looks to be a transitive verb, with *a uniform* as direct object, and *his parents* as subject. A syntactically analogous form to that

reading of this clause is 'His parents (could not) buy a uniform', which is clearly transitive. However, 'affording a uniform' is not clearly transitive; its subject noun is not clearly agentive: *His parents* is not an unambivalently agentive subject. *Afford* is a state of being, not a process under the control of an agent. And clauses which are not clearly transitive do not passivize easily: 'a uniform was (not) afforded by his parents' (and similarly with further tests, such as prenominalizing of the adjective), 'The afforded uniform ...'. **Yet many readers of the *Daily Express* may read across this clause in reading the text, and read it as fully semantically transitive,** which I shall call, following Hodge and Kress (1993), a 'transactive'. In support of that reading, these readers might say: 'We scrimped and saved, and we afforded a uniform for our children, so why can't they?!' [my bold]

Kress continues by arguing that if 'his parents' is read grammatically as a subject in 'his parents could not afford a uniform', it supports a reading of 'poverty as an event in which participants are caught up'; 'not afford' would be seen then in stative terms. However, if 'his parents could not afford a uniform' is read semantically as a result of 'reading across' this clause (by a non-critical reader), this can support a 'politically reactionary view' where the poor are responsible for their own poverty. 'Not afford' would be seen in dynamic terms since 'his parents' would be agents and thus *in charge* of the affording. In highlighting how a subject-verb-object clause can be 'read across', Kress indicates a type of shallow processing.

I move on in 2.5 to outline a few assumptions of cognition in socio-cognitive analysis and to make some contrast with assumptions in mystification analysis. In 2.2.2, I mentioned that socio-cognitive analysis seeks to show a different way in which texts can manipulate readers: how they can position readers to draw upon taken-for-granted discourses (2), which do ideological work, without readers necessarily being aware of this. We will see that there are a number of tensions in CDA between assumptions of cognition in mystification analysis and socio-cognitive analysis. These are tensions which have not previously been addressed and so, in order to clarify them, I summarise these tensions in 2.6. Given the book's focus on mystification, I am limited to how many examples I can include from socio-cognitive analysis. However, I choose examples from well-known sources in CDA.

2.5 SOME ASSUMPTIONS ABOUT COGNITION IN SOCIO-COGNITIVE ANALYSIS

2.5.1 Inferences are Strong Representations

In CDA, the notion that inferences make for weaker representations is not the only assumption around the issue of inference generation. Consider Fairclough's (2001: 44–5) commentary on the following newspaper text (*Daily Mail*, 1 June 1982) at the time of the Falklands/Malvinas conflict:

> THE PARAS' NEW LEADER: HE'LL DO HIS JOB WELL SAYS MAJOR'S WIFE [+ PHOTO OF MAJOR KEEBLE]
> The wife of the new CO of the 2nd Parachute Battalion spoke last night of her fears for her husband's safety.
> As she played in the sunshine with her four children, Jenny Keeble said she hoped her husband would not have to go into battle again.
> She said: 'I pray he and his men have done enough. But if they do go on I know that he is a man who will do his job to the best of his ability and I am certain he and the 2nd Parachute Battalion will succeed.'
> Major Christopher Keeble, a 40-year-old devout Roman Catholic, is to succeed Colonel Herbert Jones who died leading his men against an Argentine machine-gun post in the battle for Goose Green.
> Yesterday Jenny Keeble's family and friends gathered around in the garden of her old vicarage home – a rambling Tudor building at Maddington on Salisbury Plain – for a picnic afternoon as she tried to maintain an air of normility [sic] for the children's sake.

For Fairclough such a text helps to stereotype 'army wives', thereby placing limits upon the meanings that readers attach to such an individual as Jenny Keeble:

> Notice that at no point here (or in the rest of the article) is Jenny Keeble explicitly *said* to be 'a good wife', or an admirable person; **the process depends entirely on an 'ideal reader's' capacity to *infer* that from the list of attributes** – she expresses confidence in her husband's professional abilities, she is concerned for his safety, she 'prays' he has 'done enough', she

> tries 'to maintain an air of normality for the children's sake' . . .
> the process presupposes **an ideal reader** who will indeed make
> **the 'right' inference from the list, i.e. have the 'right' ideas
> about what a 'good wife' is**. Texts such as this thus reproduce
> sexists, provided that readers generally fall into the subject
> position of **the ideal reader**, rather than **opposing** it. [my bold]

This time the analysis explicitly mentions a reader, termed 'the ideal reader' by Fairclough. Now, compare the above with the supposition of CDA practitioners in section 2.4.1 that the inferences generated in reading are weaker mental representations than the mental representation of the 'surface' structure of a sentence. We find here quite the opposite. Indeed, for Fairclough, the inference itself is strong enough to lead to the reproduction of sexists. The final point is that, for Fairclough (2001: 139), there is no distinction between the process of interpretation made by an analyst and those made by a non-analyst (Fairclough's 'ideal reader' above). The analyst and the non-analyst do the same; 'it is only really self-consciousness that distinguishes' the analyst from the non-analyst since 'the analyst is concerned to explicate *what* she is doing'.

2.5.2 Inferencing as Work versus Automatic Gap-Filling

Consider the following extract from Fairclough (2001: 67–8; 1989: 81):

> There is no sharp dividing line between automatic gap-filling and
> inferencing, both because there is probably a scale from links
> which need no working out to links which need a lot of inferential
> 'work', and because a link which is supplied automatically by one
> person may need **inferential work** from another (or indeed from
> the same person on another occasion). Text 4.2 [a problem-page
> letter from a teenage magazine] would probably not require any
> inferential work from regular readers of the sort of magazine it
> comes from, but it might from other people. [my bold]

For Fairclough, there are, broadly speaking, two types of inferencing: 'automatic gap-filling' which requires minimum cognitive effort and 'inferences' which incur a higher than minimum amount of cognitive effort. The processing assumption in the above is that readers not familiar with the subject matter would still *work* to generate inferences to make coherence. Along similar lines, consider the following commentary on problem-page advice (*Sunday Mirror*, 17 January 1983) from Gough and Talbot (1996: 226) who adopt Fairclough's (1989) position on automatic gap-filling versus inferential work (Gough and Talbot (1996) is a chapter in a well-known anthology in CDA):

> 'Many heterosexual men have a passing curiosity about homosexuality, and that isn't such a bad thing. It compels you to make choices.'
>
> ... the **causal link** which is needed to coherently combine these two sentences is not cued by any formal element, and this is a point where **the reader's complicity** is required if the two sentences as they stand together are to make sense. **The 'missing link' we need to supply is that heterosexuality and homosexuality are separate sexualities and that interest in homosexuality is useful inasmuch as it reinforces this separate heterosexual identity.** For some readers it may require inferential work ... Following Fairclough's approach, this interpretation would be accounted for using the notion of automatic 'gap-filling' between explicit propositions. A reader who is unfamiliar with problem pages ... would need to engage in a good deal of inferential work to make this connection. [my bold]

The assumption in the text above is that the non-critical 'complicit' reader who is 'unfamiliar with problem pages' will work to produce the inference that 'interest in homosexuality (in this context, by adolescent males) is useful inasmuch as it reinforces this separate heterosexual identity'. In doing so, this reader becomes ideologically positioned. But there is a problem here. While we might suppose that a critical reader engages in more cognitive work, a complicit reader is surely someone who is *not* making such an effort. Indeed, in 2.4 when I was discussing mystification analysis, there was an assumption that readers do not make too much effort since they can end up 'reading across', for example.

2.5.3 Reading as Consumption

One term used to describe the reading process in the socio-cognitive angle of CDA is 'consumption'. The notion that texts are consumed by readers is particularly prevalent in the work of Fairclough (1992: 71–3, 78–9, 85; 1995a: 49–50, 57–9; (1995b: 9) but also in the work of others associated with CDA, for example Simpson (1993: 182): 'All this brings us on to the question of the position of the analyst relative to the interaction between producers and consumers of a text.'

2.6 TENSIONS BETWEEN THE EXAMPLES OF MYSTIFICATION ANALYSIS AND SOCIO-COGNITIVE ANALYSIS

There are a number of tensions between the examples of mystification analysis and socio-cognitive analysis:

1. Some of the mystification analyses are based on readers who do not make much effort, although these readers are never properly theorised. Readers are 'non-energetic' or 'read across' and so may not notice they are being manipulated. However, in the socio-cognitive angle examples, there is an assumption that while some inferencing will be automatic, other inferencing will require work that readers will be prepared to invest.
2. In mystification analysis, inferences in reading are weak representations. In the socio-cognitive analyses, inferences are implicitly strong representations since they can lead to ideological reproduction.
3. The reader is sometimes made explicit in the mystification analyses. The reader is made more explicit in the socio-cognitive analyses.
4. With regard to processing, the mystification analyses are bottom-up and the socio-cognitive analyses have more of a top-down focus.
5. In the socio-cognitive examples, readers 'consume' texts. In the mystification analyses, reading is more piecemeal, involving the 'recovery' at the sentential level of deep structure if sufficient energy is invested while at other times readers may 'read across' sentence structure.

In flagging these tensions there would seem to be shortcomings in how cognition has been conceived in CDA. Clearly these tensions cause problems for how critical discourse analysts operate within the interpretation stage. And indeed, the tensions I have drawn attention to are set against the background of other problems in CDA's interpretation stage that have been highlighted in the last few years. I outline some of the key ones below.

2.7 SOME CRITICISMS OF CDA IN RELATION TO THE INTERPRETATION STAGE

On criticisms[4] of CDA mainly with regard to interpretation, Stubbs (1997: 102) states that 'some sharp criticisms have been around for a long time, but remain unanswered'. One is that CDA lacks appreciation of how readers who are not analysts might interpret texts in different ways to the analyst; see Sharrock and Anderson (1981) for this criticism of Critical Linguistics, which is found in more developed form in recent criticisms of CDA by Widdowson (1995a, 1995b, 1996, 1997, 1998, 2000). Widdowson has probably been the most vocal dissenter from CDA in recent years. For him, any interpretation of a text is *partial*. Although critical discourse analysts may regard their socio-cognitive analyses as showing more generally how a dominant discourse (2) can delimit the interpretation of readers, Widdowson argues that critical discourse analysts merely confirm their own values, that is what they offer is merely a partial and thus subjective reading. A related criticism by Widdowson that is difficult to avoid is as follows: some CD analysts fix on certain aspects of a text and fit an interpretation of the text round these, going on to assume the text can manipulate readers along the line of this interpretation. But in doing so, these analysts often conveniently ignore other aspects of the text which do not fit their line of interpretation and indeed could support alternative interpretations (see Widdowson 1998).

There has been for some time a need in CDA to conceptualise the reader. Indeed, it is a while since Richardson (1987: 152–3) commented that 'little theoretical attention has been paid to the relation between lay and academic "readings"'. While there has been endorsement in CDA of using the idea of a 'lay-reader' in conducting analysis of a text (for example, Hodge and Kress 1993: 175) as well as calls for the reader to be conceptualised (for example, Fowler 1996a; Stubbs 1997), there has been little interest in taking this forward in developing a cognitive framework of a reader for use in CDA. A final criticism of CDA relates to cognition. Stubbs (1997: 106) criticises CDA for not making use of independent empirical evidence on the relationship between language and thought: 'If language and thought are to be related, then one needs data and theory pertinent to both. If we have no independent evidence, but infer beliefs from language use, then the theory is circular.'

2.8 DEVELOPING THE INTERPRETATION STAGE

An obvious reason for the tensions existing between the socio-cognitive and mystification analysis examples of 2.4 and 2.5 is that there has not been sufficient cognitive focus in CDA, nor has there been sufficient attempt to pull together the different strands of work in the interpretation stage. Another reason is that the concepts of reader in both angles of analysis have been fairly undeveloped, being largely based on intuition.

In subsequent chapters, I indicate one way in which the 'cognitive' in the interpretation stage can be taken forward both theoretically and practically through the construction of an idealised reader framework with an interdisciplinary cognitive base. Crucially, this reader framework will take account of the conditions under which mystification is more likely to take place; when reading effort is something akin to a minimum in line with general goals such as in reading for gist. This reader framework will help to highlight, *pace* Fairclough (2001: 139) (see 2.5.1 above), that the processing of a text by a non-analyst reading for gist is not likely to be completely the same as its processing by an analyst.

Moreover, since the reader framework's interdisciplinary source components will need to be consistent with one another, the construction of that framework will necessarily iron out inconsistencies between the 'cognitive' in mystification analysis and the socio-cognitive analysis examples given in 2.4 and 2.5. In constructing it thus, I echo commentators who have called for the conceptualisation of the reader (for example, Richardson 1987; Fowler 1996a; Stubbs 1997).

A crucial point that arises from the comparison between mystification analysis and socio-cognitive analysis is that there needs to be a richer appreciation of work in inference generation to avoid the conflict I outlined in 2.6. Indeed, there is little awareness in CDA of different types of inference. When inference theory *is* drawn upon in CDA, the age of the sources in discourse analysis (for example, Brown and Yule 1983) means that important experimental psycholinguistic work on inference generation which transpired in the late 1980s and onwards is absent. While this more recent experimental work is absent from reference books in discourse analysis, it is readily available in recent standard reference books in psycholinguistics and cognitive psychology (Gernsbacher 1994; Eysenck and Keane 2000; Harley 2001). The idealised reader framework I construct in this book is based to a large extent on this newer and readily available work in inference generation. I use this idealised reader framework in the critical discourse analysis of texts to make richer and more reliable predictions as to whether a particular text would be mystifying for a reader because of absences from the text. Since the idealised reader framework is based on empirical data on reading, I respond to criticism by Stubbs (1997). Moreover, since I show that different levels of effort can lead to different interpretations of the same text, Widdowson's (1995a) partiality of interpretation principle will also be demonstrated.

2.9 SUMMARY OF CDA AND MANIPULATIVE TEXT

To finish, let me summarise the three types of manipulation I have drawn attention to in this chapter. Let me also indicate how critical analysis means different things for each type of manipulation:

Description stage of CDA

1. text bias analysis – a form of critical text analysis.
   Critical analysis = comparative analysis of the lexico-grammatical patterns of texts (or within one text) which refer to the same event.

Interpretation stage of CDA

2. mystification analysis – a form of critical discourse (1) analysis

   Critical analysis = analysing a text for absences which lead to the events and participants referred to in the text being mystified in the reader's discourse (1); analysing a text for how its presences reinforce these absences from reading.

3. socio-cognitive analysis – a form of critical discourse (2) analysis

   Critical analysis = analysis of how the discourses (2) which readers habitually inhabit may channel reading of a text into a particular interpretation which in turn can lead to ideological reproduction.

Given that this book is concerned with the interpretation stage and mainly with a specific focus on mystification analysis, the way in which I use 'critical' will be for the most part akin to that used in 2. above. And because the seeking of absences from a news text is not a usual part of reading, especially if the reading is for gist, when I refer to the *non-critical reader* in this book as 'non-critical' I am referring to reading for gist which does not analyse a text for its absences.

Lastly, let me repeat the following and then elaborate upon it. Of course, people can be critical in the sense of 2. above should they want to expend the effort to notice absences from a text. You do not need to be a critical discourse analyst to be a critical reader. All the same, I want to suggest that there should be two key differences between being 'critical' in critical discourse (1) analysis and 'critical' in critical lay-reading. The former should be much more systematic than critical lay-reading in its detection of absences from a news text as well as of how the presences in a news text reinforce these absences. Creating a framework to enable such systematicity is one of the aims of this book. 'Critical' in critical discourse (1) analysis should mean also trying to avoid a subjective interpretation (for example, in line with the analyst's political values) so that prediction can be made of the extent to which absences from a news text would be mystifying for non-critical readers in general. This kind of generalisability would presumably be beyond the inclination of most critical lay-reading. Creating a reader framework which can generate reasonable generalisability is another aim of this book.

NOTES

1. Certain critical discourse analysts do acknowledge, however, that work on the relationship between language and cognition can inform analysis of discourse practice. So, for example, in focusing on discourse practice, Fairclough (1995a: 59) says 'one could also include here more psychological and cognitivist concerns with how people arrive at interpretations for particular utterances'.
2. Indeed, van Leeuwen (1996: 38) refers to Trew (1979), a work formerly part of Critical Linguistics, as being a classic article of CDA.
3. The Whorfian hypothesis is sometimes referred to as the Sapir-Whorf hypothesis; Sapir was a linguist whose work was along similar lines to Whorf's. It should also be mentioned that there are a number of problems with citing Whorf as a theoretical basis. There is actually no hypothesis mentioned in Whorf's posthumously published writings (Whorf 1956). When we read Whorf we find his writings indicate a more subtle appreciation of the relationship between language, thought and culture than that gleaned from the phrasing of the hypothesis. For Whorf language and thought are blended rather than separated as the hypothesis suggests. Indeed, as argued elsewhere (O'Halloran 1997), the hypothesis is an *ex post facto* distillation of his work via the logical empiricism (objectivism) which prevailed in the mid-twentieth century. However, while we might be suspicious that the 'hypothesis' would have had Whorf's approval, more charitably we might regard the 'Whorfian hypothesis' as a peg on which to hang the common intuition that use of language can naturalise particular perspectives. The 'Whorfian hypothesis' becomes a convenient citation point for those who feel this mimsy strongly.
4. Since my focus is on interpretation, I will not deal with those criticisms that relate to the explanation stage, a prominent one being Hammersley (1996).

CHAPTER 3

Symbolicism

3.1 INTRODUCTION

I have surveyed the general principles of CDA in its interpretation stage and indicated some tensions with regard to how cognition is conceived in it. As I said in the Introduction, much of how CDA detects mystification is based on symbolic assumptions which are problematic. However, the symbolicism in CDA is largely unrecognised since it has been inadvertently absorbed. The purpose of Chapter 4 will be to reveal the symbolicism within CDA. Section B (Chapters 5–7) will then show how this symbolicism is problematic, question assumptions of language cognition in CDA more generally, and in turn indicate the ways in which how CDA detects mystification are also problematic. But before I can show the symbolicism in CDA and indicate its problems, I need to describe in some detail what symbolicism is. This is the purpose of this chapter. I begin by giving a sketch of symbolic modelling in cognitive science. I also deal with related areas: logical empiricist philosophy of language, the classical theory of categories and 'syntax-first' approaches to processing. I deal with these related areas because, as I reveal in Chapter 4, they too have had some influence on how CDA detects mystification. I refer to the compatible assumptions in these areas, taken together, as *symbolicism*.

3.2 SYMBOLIC MODELLING

3.2.1 Orientation

Symbolic modelling of the mind within cognitive science is based on the idea that mental processing consists of the manipulation of symbols that can be transformed according to rules. In symbolic architectures of the mind, representations are viewed as semantically interpretable, structured objects consisting of symbols which have parts. As exemplification of this notion, here is Cooper (1996: 28):

> The symbol '34', for example, has parts (the symbols '3' and '4'), and the meaning of '34' is a function of the meaning of '3' in the tens position and '4' in the units position. The arabic representation of numbers, then, is a structured, semantically interpretable representation.

The provenance of symbolic modelling lies in the computational theory developed by John von Neumann (1947) and Alan Turing (1950) and has been incorporated into nearly all existing electronic computers. Sketching out the nature of what has become known as a *Turing machine* will help to understand the essence of symbolic modelling. A Turing machine is not an actual machine but an abstract model. It has an infinite memory in the form of an infinite strip of tape. It also consists of a typewriting device that can type a symbol on the tape, erase such a symbol, and move left and right along the tape. By specifying exactly what symbols the typewriter uses, and how it should respond to them as it passes along the tape, the Turing machine converts one set of symbols and spaces ('input') into another ('output'). For Turing, the machine was extremely powerful since theoretically it could transform any input into any output given some computable relation between them. That is, a Turing machine can execute any *algorithm*, an algorithm being a set of computable instructions. However, the power of the Turing machine lies in the abstract. The blueprint for most standard modern computers was in fact established by John von Neumann. Processing in a von Neumann machine is serially based on a fetch-instruction/execute-instruction cycle. The machine fetches the current instruction and then moves the instruction indicator to the next directive. It executes the instruction it has just retrieved, fetches the next directive and so on. In a strict sense, von Neumann machines are less powerful than a Turing machine because they have finite memory. However, in practice and particularly with modern computers, this is rarely a problem.

In symbolic modelling, the syntactic nature of thought is stressed. For example, the symbolicists Fodor and Pylyshyn (1988) maintain that structured symbols and computation that is structure-sensitive are key elements in mental cognition. Human cognition is wired to assemble complex symbols from rudimentary ones. On the basis of this notion, they hold that thought is *compositional*. So, for Fodor and Pylyshyn, a thought's meaning is regarded as a function of the meaning of its parts, molecular representations being formed out of its constituents. The thought that 'semolina is lovely' is, for instance, a function of the meaning of the thought 'semolina' and the meaning of the thought 'is lovely'.

3.2.2 Symbolic Modelling and Philosophy

The symbolic notion of a Turing machine has been influential in the philosophy of mind and cognitive science. One philosopher influenced by the concept of a Turing machine is Putnam (1975). For Putnam (1975: chs 18, 20, 21) mental cognition is understood in terms of the manipulation of symbols via the computation of a set of algorithms. And because mental states are algorithmic in symbolicism, there is no need to understand them in relation to the neurophysiology or 'wetware' of the brain. In many ways, the Turing machine is itself a distillation of well-known perspectives in logic and philosophy which view the mind most prominently in its capacity to reason and where reason is characterised as the algorithmic manipulation of abstract symbols (Bechtel and Abrahamsen 2002: 7). An example of an algorithm within logic is the simple inference rule *modus tollens*: from one proposition of the form, if p then q, and another of the form *not q*, we can infer the proposition *not p*. For instance: if I am playing tennis, I am happy; if I am not happy *then* I am not playing tennis. Within philosophy also, the idea that human cognition is based upon symbolic manipulation has been a recurrent one that cuts across the old division between empiricism and rationalism (Lakoff 1987a: 164). It is found in Hobbes ([1651] 1962: 41) who regarded reason as analogous to mathematical computation. Rationalists such as Descartes and Leibniz and empiricists such as Locke and Hume helped to further establish this view of cognition as consisting of rule-governed logical manipulation (Bechtel and Abrahamsen 2002: 9). Because the digital computer operates via symbolic manipulation, and because reason has been for many philosophers equivalent to formal deductive logic, the computer has been seen by many as possessing the capacity for reason.

One of the ancient 'problems' in philosophy is what is known as the *mind-body problem*. Reduced to its essence, the mind-body problem revolves around a dichotomy. Is the mind a 'ghost in the machine', composed of non-corporeal material, or do mental phenomena (beliefs, intentions and so on) have a physical basis? The positions that answer these questions in the affirmative are known as *dualism* and *materialism* respectively. Well-known dualists have included Plato and Descartes and more recently Eccles (1977) and Swinburne (1986). Prominent materialists have included Hobbes and more recently Skinner (1957, 1976), Quine

(1960) and Churchland (1988). As a consequence of a rigid separation between mind and body, dualists regard psychology as independent of neurophysiology since the latter is concerned much more with mental 'wetware' and much less with the mental phenomena it supports. Indeed, dualism is a commonplace assumption about the mind, supported by a folk-psychology vocabulary such as 'beliefs', 'attitudes', 'hopes' and so on. Since dualism is such a commonplace notion, it can make the study of mind in the absence of biological considerations or widely accepted evolutionary principles of selection or descent appear natural. I indicated that in symbolicism, mental states are algorithmic and so need not be implemented in brains. This ties in neatly with philosophical dualism and 'common-sense' dualism, naturalising the study of the mind independent of the brain's wetware. In turn, this reduces the importance of locating mental states with brain states.

I have given a sketch of what symbolic modelling is in cognitive science, and how it entails dualism and thus sanctions the study of mind independent of brain 'wetware'. Language cognition in symbolic modelling also involves a set of algorithms. These algorithms constitute a syntax, that is, a set of linguistic rules which formally specify a set of operations on linguistic symbols. But to understand language cognition in symbolic modelling we need to understand something of the philosophical position known as *logical empiricism*. This is because logical empiricism has exerted much influence on how linguistic mental representation has been cast within symbolic modelling. So in 3.3 below I give an outline of logical empiricism. Another reason for doing so is that I will indicate how it has influenced ideas in the Chomskyan paradigm which CDA has adapted for its mystification analysis.

3.3 LOGICAL EMPIRICISM

3.3.1 Orientation

Logical empiricism was a branch of philosophy mostly associated with members of the Vienna Circle of the 1920s and 1930s. Members included Rudolph Carnap, Otto Neurath and Moritz Schlick. It was so called since its practitioners sought to apply logical methods to the world of empirical experience. Thus, logical empiricism can be viewed as something of an amalgam of the traditional poles of empiricism and rationalism. Their criterion of verificationism – whether propositions could be empirically verified or not – adjudicated between scientific knowledge and the non-scientific ('metaphysics').

3.3.2 Russell

The heritage of logical empiricism lay in work on the interface of logic, mathematics and philosophy by Gottlob Frege, Bertrand Russell, Alfred North Whitehead and the early work of Ludwig Wittgenstein. The British philosophers Russell and Whitehead (1910) aimed to derive mathematics from the fundamentals of logic. Their end-product, the *Principia Mathematica*, was to exercise a large influence on Anglo-American-Austrian philosophy in the first few decades of the twentieth century. *Principia Mathematica* attempted to provide the basis of a perfect logical language, perfect because this logical language would mirror the structure of the real world. For Russell, the real world is made up of facts which are essentially *atomic* in nature, that is, they cannot be reduced. These atomic facts or propositions have a subject-predicate structure (the predicate of a clause is everything except for the subject). Atomic facts were largely analysed by Russell in terms of truth or falsehood. He held that for an atomic proposition to be meaningful, that is, to be true or false, the subject should denote an individual entity and the predicate refer to some quality of that entity. By these criteria, 'Tony Blair is prime minister of the UK' (Tony Blair = subject; is prime minister of the UK = predicate), uttered in 2002, is a valid atomic fact or proposition. But what of a sentence such as 'The present king of France is bald' uttered in 2002? The structure may be that of subject-predicate, but the subject does not have denotation and so the sentence cannot be treated in terms of truth or falsehood. Such a sentence poses problems for Russell since by his criteria it is not meaningful.

Russell thought that mathematical logic could provide philosophy with a set of techniques for clarifying such a sentence. He held that there was an underlying logical structure to the sentence 'The present king of France is bald' that, once revealed, would show that the sentence is meaningful after all. For Russell, the underlying logical form of 'The present king of France is bald' is quite complex and contains the following assertions:

There is an entity x, such that:
1. x has property K   [K = 'king of France']
2. there is no other entity y which is distinct from x and has property K
3. x has property B   [B = 'bald']

In logical form this becomes:

$$\exists x [\, Kx \ \& \ \sim\exists y (\, (y \neq x) \, \& \, Ky \,) \ \& \ Bx \,]$$

This can be paraphrased as the conjunction of three propositions, or in Russell's parlance, a molecular proposition consisting of three atomic propositions:

> There is a king of France *and*
> There is no one else who is king of France *and*
> The king of France is bald

In expanding 'the king of France' in its logical form to include the clause 'There is a king of France', Russell was able to claim that the sentence 'The present king of France is bald' was now meaningful. Why did Russell think this? In a truth table for the logical connector &, if one of the propositions is false, then the truth value for the whole conjunction is also false.[1] On Russell's analysis, since the first proposition ($\exists x\ Kx$) is false, the *whole* of the logical form of 'The king of France is bald' is also false. Because Russell viewed the meaning of a sentence to a large extent in terms of whether truth values could be ascribed to a sentence, he could then regard 'The present king of France is bald' as meaningful; (see Levinson (1983: 171) for more detail). Russell inherited the idea of a sentence being a fundamental unit from the German logician and philosopher Gottlob Frege and, indeed, in logical empiricism as a whole, emphasis was placed upon syntactic structure. This will become more apparent in the next two sections.

3.3.3 Wittgenstein

Russell's student, the philosopher Ludwig Wittgenstein, sought to develop his tutor's perspective in the *Tractatus Logico-Philosophicus* (1921). Wittgenstein too inherits from Frege the notion that the fundamental unit of meaning is not the word but the sentence. The basis of the *Tractatus* was a logical formalising of the correspondence between thoughts, sentences and objects in the world. As in Russell's work, there is a desire in Wittgenstein to clarify linguistic descriptions of the world by reducing them to their underlying propositions. These underlying propositions have a rudimentary logical syntax and are known as *simples*. For Wittgenstein, the logical structure of simples was concealed by the ordinary language form of a sentence. Another feature of simples was that they were logically independent of one another. In the *Tractatus*, Wittgenstein expressed the belief that if meaningful discussion was to transpire, then a sentence would not only have to represent reality, but the sentence and the state of affairs it represents must have a common structure. The corollary of this, for Wittgenstein, is that since the structure of the language must mirror the structure of the world, then it is possible to discern the structure of the world by analysing the structure of sentences. From this, Wittgenstein derived his 'picture theory of meaning', where language was a picture of how facts about the world were structured and so also a picture of how the world itself was structured.

3.3.4 Carnap

The philosophers of the Vienna Circle were heavily influenced by the *Tractatus*. Rudolph Carnap, for example, believed that much of philosophy was reducible to concerns of logical syntax. For Carnap, philosophy had to consist of the logic of science, which was itself identified with the logical syntax of a scientific language. Indeed, for Carnap, logical analysis of the language of a philosophical problem could allow a philosophical conundrum to be solved or at least shown to be insoluble (Carnap [1928] 1967). Carnap distinguished three kinds of sentence: *object, pseudo-object* and *syntactical*. An example of an object sentence is 'Babylon was a big town'. The corresponding pseudo-object sentence is 'Babylon was treated of in yesterday's lecture' and the corresponding syntactical sentence is 'The word "Babylon" occurred in yesterday's lecture'.

Carnap also made a distinction between *material* and *formal* modes of speech. Object and pseudo-object sentences were regarded as belonging to the material mode of speech and syntactical sentences to the formal mode. The point I want to highlight here is that for Carnap, pseudo-object sentences were so called because they were syntactical sentences misleadingly expressed as object-sentences; they were in fact syntactical sentences misleadingly expressed in the material mode. Translating them into the formal mode revealed their true syntactical character. It was Carnap's ambition to show that the respectable propositions of philosophy, as commonly formulated, were actually syntactical propositions of philosophy misleadingly expressed in the material mode; see Ayer (1982) for further discussion.

3.3.5 Compositionality

One prominent notion within logical empiricism that is a given with the above thinkers is that meaning is *compositional*. Within logical empiricism, the world is regarded as being constituted by objects with well-defined inherent properties and there are fixed relations between objects at any given time. A world constituted by well-defined objects can be ascribed discrete names. Since these objects have well-defined inherent properties, then each of these properties can be ascribed a predicate corresponding to each of those properties. And since the objects stand in fixed relations to one another, then a series of predicates can be ascribed so as to correspond to each relation. The natural consequence of such a perspective is to regard meaning atomistically, 'in building blocks', that is, compositionally. From the building-block view of meaning within logical empiricism arises a correspondence notion of truth. Here are Lakoff and Johnson (1980: 202) outlining how the logical empiricist perspective on objects, properties and relations relates to a correspondence notion of truth:

> Assuming that the world is this way and that we have such a language, we can, using the syntax of this language, construct sentences that can correspond directly to any situation in the world. The meaning of the whole sentence will be its truth conditions, that is, the conditions under which the sentence can be fitted to some situation.

3.3.6 The Removal of the Human Understander in Logical Empiricism

In logical empiricism, for a sentence to mirror or successfully correspond to a situation in the world, it must fully represent objects, properties and relations, independent of the contribution to processing of the human understander. Lakoff and Johnson (1980: 202–3) once more comment on logical empiricism:

> The meaning of the whole sentence will depend entirely on the meanings of its parts and how they fit together . . . every sentence of the language **must contain all of the necessary building blocks** so that, together with the syntax, nothing more is needed to provide the truth conditions of the sentence. The 'something more' that is ruled out is any kind of human understanding. [my bold]

Indeed, Carnap's attempt to produce a logical syntax that could be applied to the problems of philosophy consisted of these building-block properties with little consideration given to the contribution of the human understander.

I now go on to indicate how the thread of ideas that runs from Russell to the Vienna Circle has exerted an influence upon the symbolic paradigm in cognitive science.

3.3.7 The Influence of Logical Empiricism upon the Symbolic Paradigm

As support for the view that the ideas of logical empiricism have exerted an influence upon the symbolic paradigm, here first is Harder (1997: 52):

> The basic problem with the classical computational approach was that it smuggled a number of assumptions associated with logical positivism into the supposedly new mental framework, instead of facing the challenge of actual mental phenomenon.[2]

Harder goes on to say that this challenge is met by cognitive linguistics, an enterprise to which Chapter 6 of this book is devoted. Now consider the following from Gardner (1987: 64–5):

> a major ingredient in ongoing work in the cognitive sciences has been cast in the image of logical empiricism: that is, the vision of *syntax* – a set of symbols and the rules for their concatenation – that might underline the operations of the mind (and a correlative discomfort with issues of mental *content*). Thus, when Noam Chomsky (1965) posits the basic operations of a grammar, when Richard Montague (Thomason 1974) examines the logic of semantics, when Allen Newell and Herbert Simon (1972) simulate human reasoning on a computer, or when Jerome Bruner (1973) and George Miller (1956) seek to decipher the rules of classification, or 'chunking', they are trying to decipher a logic – perhaps *the* logic – of the mind. This vision comes through even more clearly in the writings of Jerry Fodor, who explicitly searches for a 'language of thought' and even appropriates certain of Carnap's methods. Thus, a model that proved inadequate for the scientific enterprise as a whole still motivates research in circumscribed cognitive domains.

Let me pick up on Gardner's point that logical empiricism is implicit within Fodor's 'language of thought' hypothesis. Fodor is a thinker firmly entrenched within the symbolic camp, who offers the view (1975) that mental representation occurs within a 'language of thought' (often referred to as *mentalese*) where mental representations encode propositional information via a language-like syntactic structure. The connection between Fodor's mentalese and logical empiricism should be apparent. This connection is also evident in a more recent articulation of Fodor's position in Fodor and Pylyshyn (1988), to which I drew attention in 3.2.1. I indicated that both Fodor and Pylyshyn (1988) stress the syntactic nature of thought and that human cognition is wired to assemble complex symbols from rudimentary ones. Similar to logical empiricism, they hold that thought is compositional. Their view that a thought's meaning is regarded as a function of the meaning of its parts, molecular representations being formed out of atomic constituents, is a logical empiricist echo of Russell's work where atomic propositions are more primitive than molecular ones.

In the next section, I outline the classical approach to categorisation, which can also be subsumed under symbolicism.[3] In Chapter 4, I will also indicate how the classical approach to categorisation informs some aspects of how CDA highlights mystifying text.

3.4 THE CLASSICAL THEORY OF CATEGORIES

3.4.1 Orientation

In 3.2 we saw that reason has been commonly understood by philosophers in terms of formal deductive logic; reason is the mechanical manipulation of symbols which acquire meaning through their capacity to refer to things in the world. This is a disembodied view of reason since it is not dependent on neural 'wetware'. As Lakoff (1987a: 8) writes:

> The view of reason as the *disembodied* manipulation of abstract symbols comes with an implicit theory of categorization. It is a version of the classical theory in which categories are represented by sets, which are in turn defined by the properties shared by their members.

The classical theory of classification is synonymous with Aristotle's ideas and it is from its roots in antiquity that this theory of categories derives its name (Taylor 1995: 22). In *Metaphysics,* Aristotle draws a distinction between the *essence* of a thing and its *accidents*. The *essence* is 'all parts immanent in things which define and indicate their individuality, and whose destruction causes the destruction of the whole' (*Metaphysics* 5.8.3); that is, the essence is what constitutes and thereby defines the thing. *Accidents* are, on the other hand, what may be called incidental properties and are not central to divining what a thing is: "Accident" means that which applies to something and is truly stated, but neither necessarily nor usually' (*Metaphysics* 5.30.1). As illustration, consider Aristotle's definition of 'a two-footed animal' for 'man'. For Aristotle, 'two-footed animal' is the essence of man. In contrast, since definition relates to essence not accidents, the properties of 'whiteness', 'being cultured' and so on do not determine whether a thing is a man since they are merely accidental. In more modern parlance, Aristotle regards 'two-footed' and 'animal' as *necessary* features of 'man', and jointly the two features are deemed to be *sufficient*.

The notion that categories can be defined in terms of discrete necessary features, which taken as a set are sufficient, is a key assumption of the classical approach. This assumption entails an absoluteness to the issue of category membership. Any entity which manifests the number of necessary features required for sufficiency is a member of the category. Vice versa, if any one of the necessary features for sufficiency is absent, then category membership is denied. As an illustration of this, consider the category of 'bachelor'. Katz and Postal (1964) represent the meaning of this word in terms of four semantic features, namely [human], [male], [adult] and [never married]. Together these are a sufficient set of features for capturing the essence of bachelor, and likewise, if any of these necessary features is absent, the category of bachelor cannot be ascribed.[4]

Other aspects of Aristotelian theory conjoin with the above assumption. These derive from the 'law of excluded middle' and the 'law of contradiction' *(Metaphysics* 4.4*)*. The law of contradiction states that a thing cannot be and not be, and the law of excluded middle states that a thing must either be or not be. What follows from these 'laws' are that features are binary, indicating presence [+] or absence [−], since categories have clear unambiguous boundaries. One other aspect that follows from these 'laws' is that all members of a category have equal status. In other words, if three necessary features are required for sufficiency in X, and only two of these are present in Y, then Y cannot be less of an exemplar instance than X.

3.4.2 The Classical Theory of Categories and the Symbolic Paradigm

The classical theory of categories links in with the symbolic paradigm. On this link, here is Lakoff (1987a: 8):

> There is a good reason why the view of reason as disembodied symbol-manipulation makes use of the classical theory of categories. If symbols in general can get their meaning only through their capacity to correspond to things, then *category* symbols can get their meaning only through a capacity to correspond to *categories* in the world (the real world or some possible world). Since the symbol-to-object category

correspondence that defines meaning in general must be independent of the peculiarities of the human mind and body, it follows that the symbol-to-category correspondence that defines meaning for category symbols must also be independent of the peculiarities of the human mind and body. To accomplish this, categories must be seen as existing in the world independent of people and defined only by the characteristics of their members and not in terms of any characteristics of the human.

So for Lakoff, the classical theory fits the needs of the symbolic paradigm because it defines categories via shared properties of its members rather than through characteristics of human understanding. That is, as in the symbolic paradigm, the classical theory of categories is not dependent on the contribution of the human understander.

Since I show in Chapter 4 that CDA notions of mental representation are essentially symbolic, partly at least because they were derived via adaptation of Chomskyan ideas, I need to manifest the essentially symbolic nature of Chomsky's work. This was already hinted at in the quote from Gardner (1987: 64–5). Since adaptations of Chomsky do not go beyond his work from the 1960s, the scope of this examination is restricted to Chomsky (1957) and (1965), works flagged as important for Critical Linguistics in Hodge and Kress (1993: 35–7).

3.5 CHOMSKY AND SYMBOLICISM

3.5.1 Synopsis of Chomsky's Early Position

I start with Chomsky's famous review of B. F. Skinner's *Verbal Behaviour*. In this review, Chomsky (1959) argued that the human capacity to learn a language could not be explained by Skinner's behaviouristic explanation: that all that was needed was linguistic input from the child's environment. In countering Skinner's argument, Chomsky highlighted (1) how any natural language has an infinite number of syntactically well-formed sentences, and (2) that speakers can understand and produce sentences that they had not previously encountered (Chomsky 1957). Chomsky maintained that the output of an infinite set of well-formed sentences could not be provided by an input of finite environmental stimuli (the 'poverty of stimulus' argument). Instead, Chomsky proposed that the potential for generating an infinite set of well-formed sentences exists because of an innate capacity in humans to do this. The approach that Chomsky offered to replace behaviourism became known as *generative grammar*.

In *Syntactic Structures* (1957), which has its roots in the work of his former tutor, Zellig Harris (1952), Chomsky laid the beginnings of a grammar which aimed in part to account for speaker intuitions regarding sentential relationships, for example, between the active and passive voice. In Chomsky's grammar, there is a set of algorithms that generates sentences in a language without utilising any information extraneous to the system. *Syntactic Structures* begins with phrase-structure rules that enable the generation of the core sentences, or kernel sentences. The kernel sentences are generated via a set of algorithms such as the following (which are not intended to be exhaustive):

1. Sentence → NP + VP
2. NP → (Det) + (A) + N
3. VP → V + NP
4. N → e.g. boy, girl, dog, cat, ice cream
5. V → e.g. eats, likes, bites
6. A → e.g. happy, lucky, tall
7. Det → e.g. a, the, one

[NP = noun phrase; VP = verb phrase; Det = determiner; A = adjective; N = noun; V = verb]

So taking the symbol S as the starting point, a kernel sentence such as 'The girl eats the ice cream' can be generated. From this platform, the other grammatical sentences of the language can be generated. This is not via the transformation of these kernel sentences, but via the transformation of a common underlying string. This is why Chomsky's grammar is also known as *transformational grammar*. Since transformations are algorithmic in nature and operate serially, conversion from one underlying string to another follows an established sequence. In consequence, intuitions, say, about actives and passives being related can be captured. In 1965, Chomsky tendered a new expression of transformational grammar in the form of the 'Standard Theory' in *Aspects of the Theory of Syntax*. The notion of kernel sentences was discarded. Instead, the concept of 'deep structure' was introduced where a transformational element mutates into other structures, the ultimate being the 'surface structure'.

3.5.2 Affinities Between Chomsky's Early Position and Symbolism

Clearly, there are affinities between Chomsky's approach to language and that of the logical empiricists: the concentration on syntax, the exhibition of underlying structure in natural language, kernel sentences as simples (akin to Russell's atomic propositions in their subject-predicate structure, declarative rather than interrogative or imperative, active rather than passive, and so on), and the application of formal mathematics to a natural language like English (although in Chomsky's case this was 'finite automata theory' and 'recursive function theory'). Indeed, Hacking (1975: 91) goes as far as to say that: 'Russell's idea of logical form as opposed to grammatical form is strikingly like Chomsky's idea of depth grammar as opposed to surface grammar.' Lakoff and Johnson (1999: 75–6) also locate (Chomskyan) generative linguistics in a traditional Anglo-American philosophical lineage (that is, Russell, logical empiricism, and so on):

> First-generation cognitive science evolved in the 1950s and 1960s, centering on ideas about symbolic computation. It accepted without question the prevailing view that reason was disembodied and literal – as in formal logic or the manipulation of a system of signs. In those years, Anglo-American philosophy fitted very well with certain dominant paradigms of that era: early artificial intelligence, information-processing psychology, formal logic, generative linguistics, and early cognitive anthropology, all of which played a role in first-generation cognitive science. This was no accident. Many of the practitioners in these paradigms had been trained using the assumptions of Anglo-American philosophy.

Ties between Chomsky and the symbolic paradigm of cognitive science include the algorithmic nature of transformations, the serial manner of their operation. As Gardner argues (1987: 188):[5]

> [Chomsky's] view of grammatical generation was based on the notion of an automaton – a machine in an abstract sense which simply generates linguistic strings on the basis of rules that have been built (programmed) into it . . . Clearly, Chomsky was a child of the new era of Wiener, von Neumann, Turing and Shannon . . .

The cognitive linguist Langacker (1987b: 6) concurs in regarding Chomsky as a progeny of the first generation of artificial intelligence:

> linguistic theory in the generative tradition presupposes the von Neumann architecture, accepting without question the need for discrete and explicit rules couched in some 'propositional' format, and which constitute an algorithm specifying the sequential manipulation of abstract strings of symbols.

The symbolic grounding of Chomskyan thought is also attested to by Brown (1991: 491):

> although in *Syntactic Structures* Chomsky was very concerned to explore the mathematical properties of PS [phrase-structure] rules, little attention was devoted to the mathematical power of transformations. Once the mathematical properties of this kind of rule were explored, *it became clear that a grammar with transformations has the formal properties of a **universal Turing machine**:* in other words, they are such a powerful tool that they can explain nothing except that language can be described in terms of some set of rules. [my italics; author's bold]

And what of the relationship between the classical theory of categories and Chomsky? The classical Aristotelian model of categorisation is apparent in the status of grammatical categories in Chomsky's transformational paradigm where there is the requirement that membership is a clear-cut matter. Transformational rules operate on noun phrases, independently of the semantics of the lexical items that fill the category slots. Because of this, grammatical categories are 'necessarily' clear-cut entities (Taylor 1995: 186–7). The 'obviousness' of Aristotelianism is also a basic assumption of Chomsky and Halle (1968: 297): 'In view of the fact that phonological features are classificatory devices, they are binary ... for the natural way of indicating whether or not an item belongs to a particular category is by means of binary features.' Phonemes are classified in terms of binary features which can be present or absent, for example [+high] or [−high]. These features cannot be decomposed and so are said to be *primitives*.

An examination of semantic categories along the lines of phonology has been studied within the transformational-generative paradigm by Katz (Katz and Fodor 1963; Katz and Postal 1964) and Bierwisch (1967, 1970). Chomsky has made claims for the universality of primitive semantic features. Just as the set of universal primitive phonological features defines the sound-producing capabilities of humans, so the set of universal primitive semantic features defines our cognitive capabilities:

> It is important to determine the universal, language-independent constraints on semantic features – in traditional terms, the system of possible concepts. The very notion 'lexical entry' presupposes some sort of fixed, universal vocabulary in terms of which these objects are characterized, just as the notion 'phonetic representation' presupposes some sort of universal phonetic

theory. It is surely our ignorance of the relevant psychological and physiological facts that makes possible the widely held belief that there is little or no a priori structure to the system of 'attainable concepts'.

(Chomsky 1965: 160)

The postulation of universal semantic primitives is not an innovation of generative linguists. The philosopher Leibniz, in the seventeenth century, set himself the task of discovering the 'alphabet of human thought', a set of basic conceptual building blocks not susceptible to further decomposition, whose combination might underlie all possible concepts (Eco 1995: 270).

I have established that Chomsky's perspective has been influenced by symbolic cognitive science, logical empiricism and the classical theory of categories – all highly interrelated areas. In Chapter 4, I show how many of the symbolic language processing assumptions of CDA which affect how it highlights mystifying text have been absorbed, in part, via CDA's adaptation of Chomsky. Chomsky only ever claimed to have produced a model of linguistic *competence* rather than linguistic *performance*. In other words, transformational grammar is a description of knowledge of language rather than an account of how we process syntax. Despite this, the relevance of transformational grammar for sentential production and comprehension was investigated in a series of fairly well-known experiments. In the next section, I outline an attempt to implement transformational grammar as a model of performance known as the *Derivational Theory of Complexity*. I then go on to outline other performance models which, while not 'Chomskyan', evoke the symbolic spirit in placing a large emphasis on syntactic considerations in processing. Again, as for previous sections, we shall see in Chapter 4 that much of what is outlined below is reflected in how CDA highlights mystifying text.

3.6 APPROACHES TO LANGUAGE PROCESSING THAT PLACE EMPHASIS ON SYNTAX

3.6.1 Derivational Theory of Complexity

The main assertion of the Derivational Theory of Complexity (DTC) was that the more involved the transformational history of a sentence, the more processing labour would be required. Initial evidence appeared to support the above hypotheses (Miller 1962; Miller and McKean 1964; Savin and Perchonock 1965). Miller reasoned that a passive sentence should take more effort to process than a simple, active, affirmative and declarative sentence. He tested this hypothesis by giving subjects two columns of shuffled sentences, and asking them to find consonant pairs. In one section of the experiment, actives and passives were shuffled so that a passive like, say, 'the rioters were shot by the police' had to be matched with its intended companion sentence 'the police shot the rioters'. In timing his subjects, Miller found that it took nearly twice as long to match sentences which differed by two transformations. On this experimental evidence, Miller concluded that transformations were psychologically real.

Belief in DTC did not last long after criticism by Fodor and Garrett (1966, 1967). Fodor and Garrett highlighted the fact that there could be other reasons for the difference in processing time other than processing histories. For example, with the passive, there is agent displacement away from the beginning of the sentence and so extra cognition time is necessary to locate and then link agent to process. Moreover, compared with active verb forms in present and past simple tenses which are also affirmative and declarative, parallel passives introduce auxiliaries. The latter lengthens the syntactic string and thus cognition time. In other words, the extra processing time needed for passives may be unconnected to the intricacy of a transformational history. They also found that there was no detectable time difference in comprehension between 'John phones up the girl' and 'John phones the girl up'. If DTC was correct, then the second should involve more processing labour since a 'particle separation' transformation is entailed. After the initial hope and excitement, the idea that transformational grammar was a model of language production and comprehension was abandoned. For Chomsky, it should be made clear, such refutation would be immaterial since his model was one of competence and not performance.

3.6.2 Canonical Sentence Structure (CSS)

I have indicated how Fodor and Garrett (1966, 1967) denied the possibility of there being psychologically real transformations. Fodor and Garrett nevertheless claimed that the end-product of syntactic processing was a syntactic representation equivalent to the deep structure as posited by Chomsky (1965). But if syntactic processing did not operate via transformations, how was it done? Fodor and Garrett (1967) argued that, instead, parsing was performed by perceptual heuristics or surface structure cues. They detailed a number of parsing strategies that used only 'surface syntax' as a cue. One strategy became known as *canonical sentence structure* (CSS). In English CSS is essentially subject-verb-object and so, given this, it is reasonable for a comprehender to initially assume that many sentences conform to this structure. On such a heuristics, comprehenders intuitively try a simple strategy like CSS first and, failing this, move on to other more complex ones. Perceptual heuristics as an approach to sentential parsing was further developed in Fodor, Bever and Garrett (1974). It is easy to trace echoes here of the symbolic emphasis on syntax and thus the symbolic separation of syntax from semantics.

3.6.3 Modularity Hypothesis

The general principle that when readers parse, they employ 'surface syntactic' cues has remained influential in certain psycholinguistic quarters and has gradually become more and more systematised. It tends to go hand in hand with an espousal of syntactic autonomy: that there exists an autonomous syntactic processor. This assertion is incarnate within the symbolic *modularity* hypothesis in Fodor (1983). For Fodor, modules are discrete centres of cognition dedicated to specific cognitive tasks. For example, Fodor posits that there are different modules in the visual system devoted to stereoscopic vision, colour vision, and so on. Language is also regarded as being modular, the syntactic processor being one module among others in the linguistic system. Input modules are separate from the central processor whose remit is to infer inductively from what the modules despatch. Modules are differentiated from the central processor in certain respects:

1. Domain specificity of modules – processing in the syntactic module transpires only in the language domain
2. Mandatory functioning of modules – processing not under conscious control
3. Modules have restricted access to the central processor – only the final yield of processing is open to higher-level (top-down) processors which cannot ingress the module and affect performance.
4. Processing in modules is encapsulated – only following an entire operation is processing yield made available to other systems.

For Fodor, it is the modularity of syntactic processing which sanctions its speed and involuntariness.

3.6.4 Late Closure and Minimal Attachment Strategies

The idea of reader-employment of surface-structure cues was cultivated in different directions by Kimball (1973), Frazier and Fodor (1978) and

Frazier (1987). In Frazier (1987), a somewhat strong version of the autonomy of syntactic parsing prior to semantic processing is postulated. Frazier puts forth two strategies for retrieving the underlying syntax:

1. *late closure strategy* – if grammatically feasible, each new item is hooked to the clause or phrase currently being processed.
2. *minimal attachment strategy* – the reader mentally constructs the phrase structure such that the number of attachments (for example to a verb phrase) are kept to a minimum.

Late Closure

Frazier appeals to the phenomenon of 'garden-pathing' in substantiating her claims. 'Garden-path' sentences are those where the smoothness of processing is interrupted midstream. The reader is forced to backtrack and use an alternative parsing strategy because they have been 'led up the garden-path'. Consider the sentence 'Since Jay always jogs a mile and a half seems like a short distance'. For Frazier, this sentence institutes a 'garden-path' effect because readers typically employ the strategy of 'late closure'. The reasoning is as follows. 'Jogs' is a constituent of a verb phrase and the next input is a noun phrase ('a mile and a half'). On the strategy of late closure, the new input would be fastened to the verb phrase currently being processed. The result is the erroneous interpretation where the noun phrase ('a mile and a half') is the object of the verb 'jogs'.

Minimal Attachment Principle

In another set of experiments and along with two colleagues, Frazier aimed to highlight how readers operate on a syntax-first strategy despite pragmatic implausibility. Rayner, Carlson and Frazier (1983) examined subjects' eye movements while reading sentences like 'The spy saw the cop with binoculars but the cop didn't see him' and 'The spy saw the cop with a revolver but the cop didn't see him'. The syntax-first strategy of minimal attachment should lead the parser to attach the prepositional phrases 'with a revolver' or 'with binoculars' to the verb phrase rather than to the noun phrase 'the cop' so as to keep the number of attachments overall to a minimum. This would lead to a plausible reading in the first sentence but an implausible one in the second. Let me explain what is meant by minimal attachments here. Consider 'The spy saw the cop with binoculars'. The verb phrase is 'saw the cop with binoculars'. If we take the reading that the spy was looking at a cop who was holding binoculars, within that verb phrase we have the following: the noun phrase 'the cop with binoculars' which in turn contains the noun phrase 'the cop', and the prepositional phrase 'with binoculars'. In contrast, if we take the reading where the spy is using the binoculars to see the cop then the verb phrase contains one less phrase. This is because it now only contains the noun phrase 'the cop', and the prepositional phrase 'with binoculars'. In other words, on the latter reading, there is one less attachment of phrases to the verb phrase. Hence, on the minimal attachment perspective, this is the predicted reading. To return to the results of Rayner et al. (1983), they found that subjects hesitated on 'revolver' in the second sentence but not on 'binoculars' in the first. For Rayner et al., this shows that syntactic parsing transpires independent of and prior to the construction of semantic representations. When the minimal attachment principle is consistent with plausibility, smooth comprehension ensues. Conversely, when the minimal attachment principle is incongruous with plausibility, comprehension is frustrated.

In the last section of this chapter, I want to briefly indicate how the emphasis on syntax in accounts of language processing, outlined above, has meant that inferential processes have been downgraded in emphasis. Again, in the next chapter, we shall see that this perspective underlies many of CDA's text commentaries.

3.6.5 A By-Product of Syntax-First Processing: Inference Last

One of the by-products of a syntax-first approach to processing in certain psycholinguistic quarters, and an emphasis on sentential form in general, is that inference generation is given much less prominence. This can be seen in the stipulation of Fodor's modularity hypothesis concerning higher-level (top-down) processing. In other words, the generation of inferences would be *separate* from and only *succeed* modular syntactic processes. The lack of emphasis upon inference generation as a mandatory process is encapsulated in the following from Fodor, Fodor and Garrett (1975: 526):

> the distinction between processes that are involved in understanding a sentence and processes that are involved in drawing inferences from it corresponds to a distinction between mandatory, on-line psychological processes and optional, long-term psychological processes. For, by hypothesis, the output of the sentence comprehension system is that representation of the sentence which must be recovered by anyone who understands it. But the application of principles of inference is presumably

largely context-determined. What inference we draw from what we hear must be a question of what we take to be relevant to the task at hand.

Thinkers such as Fodor are firmly entrenched in Chomskyan ideas, and so we might regard a perspective that regards inferences as being separate from the comprehension process proper as being a part of, or at least an implicit part of, the symbolic vision which awards primary status to syntactic representation.

NOTES

1. Truth values for the logical connector &:

A	B	$A \& B$
T	T	T
T	F	F
F	T	F
F	F	F

2. The expression *logical positivism* is commonly used to refer to logical empiricism. But logical positivism has also been used to refer to the work of Comte in the early nineteenth century. For Comte, knowledge progresses when each science attains *positive* knowledge. The logical empiricists of the Vienna Circle, in fact, preferred to avoid the term positivism since they regarded Comte's philosophy of history as non-scientific ('metaphysics') (see Outhwaite (1987)).
3. In 3.4, I have relied heavily on Taylor (1995).
4. Logical form translations of sense relations between predicates reflect this 'all or nothing' attitude to category membership. Take the sense relation of:

    Hyponymy: $\forall x [C(x) \rightarrow D(x)]$

    Paraphrased as: for all xs if x is a C then x is a D, for example, if x is a car then x is a vehicle.
5. Gardner (1987: 188) does indicate, all the same, that 'some of his [Chomsky's] specific ideas about how language works ran directly counter to information-theory notions'. By this he is referring to Chomsky's criticisms of finite-state grammar whose provenance lay within 'Information Theory' (for example, the work of Shannon, Weaver et al.).

CHAPTER 4

The Symbolicism of CDA

4.1 INTRODUCTION

Chapter 3 provided an outline of symbolicism; this chapter shows how symbolicism informs the way in which CDA isolates mystifying text. Symbolic assumptions have been carried through to CDA from the Critical Linguistics of Fowler et al. (1979) and Kress and Hodge (1979). Since there has been little subsequent development in mystification analysis in CDA, these assumptions continue to affect how CDA highlights mystifying text. In Section B we shall see that the symbolic assumptions that inform how CDA detects mystifying text are problematic, which has repercussions for how CDA does this. To begin with I highlight how the structure CDA uses as a basis for mystification analysis – agent-process-affected – is actually a 'simple' resting on symbolic assumptions. In different places in CDA this is explicitly acknowledged as a simple with privileged status and at other times only implicitly acknowledged as such. Below I give examples of both its implicit and explicit acknowledgement.

4.2 CDA'S SIMPLE

4.2.1 Implicit Acknowledgement of the Simple

What follows is from Clark (1992). It includes an extract from *The Sun* newspaper (11 November 1986) with her critical examination. I also include Simpson's (1993) supporting commentary and extension of Clark's (1992) analysis. The main thrust of Clark's critical examination below is to highlight how the agent of a rape was mystified through sentential configuration. I highlight this particular work here, and refer to it in other chapters of this book, since it has had a certain resonance in CDA. Like Trew (1979) it is one of the most referred-to CDA articles. Clark's analysis is not only reproduced (in part) and commented upon in Simpson (1993) but also appears in Montgomery (1995). Clark (1992) also has a certain resonance in feminist linguistics. It is cited favourably in West et al. (1997), a chapter synopsis on feminist discourse analysis in a volume edited by the critical discourse analyst Teun van Dijk, the volume consisting of chapter synopses of differing strands within discourse analysis. More significantly, the article is reproduced in Cameron (1998), a well-known anthology of feminist writings on language. Here is the excerpt from *The Sun's* text in Clark (1992: 215):

1) Two of Steed's rape victims – aged 20 and 19 – had a screwdriver held at their throats as they were forced to submit.
2) His third victim, a 39-year-old mother of three, was attacked at gunpoint after Steed forced her car off the M4.
3) Two days later, he gunned down call-girl, Jacqueline Murray, 23, after picking her up in London's Park Lane.

Clark (1992: 215) alleges that in (1) and (2) 'the perception of Steed as rapist is reduced by making the sentences passive and deleting him as Agent', that is, the semantico-syntactic encoding diminishes Steed's responsibility.

Here now is Simpson (1993: 170–1) (in what follows and elsewhere, the participant, 'goal', is equivalent to that of 'affected'):

GOAL	PROCESS	CIRCUMSTANCE
His third victim . . . mother of three	was attacked	at gunpoint

In fact, the agency involved in this process has to be inferred by implication from the process expressed by the second clause where Steed does now feature in the role of ACTOR/AGENT:

ACTOR/AGENT	PROCESS	GOAL	CIRCUMSTANCE
Steed	had forced	her car	off the M4

The message is constructed in such a way as to obscure the relationship between Steed and the attack. The only entity upon which Steed acts as AGENT is 'her car', whilst the victim of the attack, although prominent in the information structure of the report, is acted upon only by an implicit and unspecified agency. Indeed, so obscured is the relationship between attacker and victim that it allows a possible reading wherein someone else attacks the woman at gunpoint while Steed only forces her car off the road . . . We see a wilful refusal to 'tell it like it is'. What, for instance, is so difficult about presenting the details of the story in the following way, where the relationship between attacker and victim is not obfuscated:

(1) Steed held a screwdriver at the throats of two of his victims as he forced them to submit.
(2) Steed attacked at gunpoint his third victim, a 39-year-old mother of three, after he had forced her car off the M4.

Recall some of the premises of logical empiricism. The world is constituted by well-defined objects with well-defined inherent properties, the result being that objects can be ascribed discrete names. Since these objects have well-defined properties, each of these properties can be ascribed a predicate corresponding to each of those properties. And since the objects stand in fixed relations to one another, a series of predicates can be ascribed so as to correspond to each relation. As we saw in 3.3.5, the natural consequence of such a perspective is to regard semantics in a 'building-block' or *compositional* fashion. Moreover, since for meaningfulness to transpire, sentential structure must necessarily mirror the structure of the world, the syntax needs to be composed of simples. For Clark and Simpson, these simples are *agent-process-goal* (or *agent-process-affected*) structures although this is only implicitly acknowledged. On this reasoning then, if one of the 'necessary' building blocks required to construct a simple is absent – that is, the 'agent' – as Simpson and Clark highlight, then this would render the sentence less meaningful. But not only that. Because it is assumed in CDA that the sentence is both the vehicle of computation and the vehicle of mental content, then an absence of a 'necessary' semantic component is consonant with an absence of a necessary thought – hence mystification.

The assigning of truth values (a feature of logical empiricism) is also a covert issue in the above. Consider first the following from Ellis (1992: 74):

When considering entire texts and sequences of interaction, according to standard structural semantics, it is necessary for every sentence in a text to be true if the entire text is going to be true. Such a requirement leads to some logical inconsistencies that cannot be resolved because the structure of a text, and not only truth values, can determine whether or not a sentence is true.

In 'standard structural semantics' (which has similar foundations to logical empiricism), for a text to be true, each of the sentences should be true. The rather odd corollary of this is that sentences in a text should be logically independent of one another. Ellis is, of course, right to point out that the structure of a text has a bearing on 'whether or not a sentence is true'. But as in logical empiricism and 'standard structural semantics' where simples are logically independent of one another, so Simpson sees sentences in terms of logically independent simples – his simple implicitly being the agent-process-goal structure. He makes no allowance for how the local, co-textual meaning and, as Ellis implies, global co-text might close down on the meaning of a particular sentence. Indeed the fixation on the *structure* of this simple is evinced in the alternative sentences. Simpson neglects to include the category of 'rape' and so his alternatives might be said to be mystifying, to some extent, of the actual event.

The symbolic assumptions of Clark (1992) and Simpson (1993) are emblematic of widespread symbolic assumptions in CDA. In Chapters 5, 6, 7 and 9 I will return to the Clark/Simpson analysis to show, via the paradigms of connectionism, cognitive linguistics, psycholinguistics and relevance theory, how co-textual meaning affects reading of the individual sentences of the 'Steed' text fragment. This, in turn, will make Simpson's alternative reading of sentence 2 where '*someone else* attacks the woman at gunpoint while Steed only forces her car off the road' difficult to accept. Another reason for using the same text and CDA commentaries is to facilitate comparison of these cognitive paradigms in relation to how they can help prevent over-interpretation in CDA.

4.2.2 Explicit Acknowledgement of the Simple

As I have noted, Hodge and Kress (1979/1993) is one of the cornerstones for mystification analysis in CDA. They found much of their examination of texts upon a set of basic models. One model they refer to is known as *actionals* (Hodge and Kress 1993: 9). The category of actionals, as the name suggests, subsumes 'actions'. Actionals consist of two sub-models, *transactives* and *non-transactives*. Transactives are explicit about causal relations and non-transactives are not. Take 'The batsman struck the ball'. This is transactive because, in the event, action flows from agent to affected and so, for Hodge and Kress, this sentence is explicit about causality. 'The batsman runs' is non-transactive since the absence of an affected means the sentence is inexplicit about the causal process. While the transitive/intransitive distinction, as traditionally defined, is a syntactic one, transactivity is semantico-syntactic. For Hodge and Kress

(1993: 8), 'The parcel weighs ten pounds', 'John plays tennis' and 'Bill resembles his father' are all transitive but they are not transactive since action does not flow from an agent to an affected. A corollary of all this for Hodge and Kress (1993) is that since transactives are explicit about causality, they are the preferred sub-model for describing causal processes. In this respect, transactives are akin to a simple.

Hodge and Kress (1993: 60) highlight Chomsky's use of kernel sentences (simple, active, affirmative, declarative structures) as some sort of legitimacy for assigning primitiveness to transactives:[1]

> Most linguistic theories assume that there is a limited number of basic sentence patterns or sentence types in a language, and that the vast variety of actual utterances are constructed around this basic set. Chomsky's *Syntactic Structures* (1957) used the concept of 'kernel sentence' . . . which could not be analysed in more basic terms.

But this justification is circular, that is, *most linguistic theories are predicated on basic sentence patterns, so it is legitimate to ground in basic sentence patterns because most linguistic theories are predicated on basic sentence patterns*. One reason that there seems to be no need for 'outside' justification for the rudimentary status of transactives is because the concept of a simple, via the weighty heritage of logical empiricism, can appear so natural. Because of this circular reasoning, Hodge and Kress's simple – the transactive – is merely a variation on simples put forward as primitives over the years by logical empiricists.

In common with the logical empiricists, Hodge and Kress (1993: 35) see their version of a simple as having propositional structure:

> *The standard that acts as the measure of what has been suppressed or distorted is given by the underlying structures uncovered by reversing transformations.* The 'relevant truth' which acts as a standard then is given by full propositions *in the form of basic models.*

The above is again circular since from the offset it is presumed that the standard is the basic model (transactive or relational) without supplying any evidence to this effect. Reliance on the notion of a transactive (or something like it) as a primitive, as having completeness of a 'thought' and thus propositional structure, is seen in many other CDA works such as Kress (1989), Fairclough (1992) and to some extent in others more loosely associated with CDA such as Martin (1989). In Chapter 5, we shall see how connectionism represents a challenge to this mode of propositional knowledge representation and ultimately to the idea of a simple, be it a kernel sentence or a transactive.[2]

Hodge and Kress (1993) imply that scientific description should contain a high proportion of transactives. The corollary of this is that the description of scientific processes that proceeds through non-transactives is unsophisticated. As one example of this, they describe how the growth of the turnip, in a story for five-year-olds (Southgate, *The Enormous Turnip*: no date), is described in non-transactive terms, thus mystifying the causal process for the child reader (1993: 48–50). Here is a fragment which they focus upon: 'As time went by, the rain fell on the seeds and the sun shone down on them, and the turnips began to grow.' Hodge and Kress (1993: 50) then compare both transactive and non-transactive descriptions, arguing that the transactives are now de-mystifying of causality:

non-transactive:	The rain fell on the seeds.
transactive:	The rain (water) moistened the seeds.
non-transactive:	The sun shone down on them.
transactive:	The sun warmed the soil.

In 3.3.4, I mentioned the logical empiricist philosopher Rudolph Carnap. Despite the titles of Carnap's books, *Philosophy and Logical Syntax* (1935) and *The Logical Syntax of Language* (1937), the nature of semantic categories was also important to this logical empiricist in assigning primitiveness. Primitive statements consisted of 'physicalist' categories rather than experiential ones. In what follows, I highlight how Hodge and Kress (1993) is redolent of Carnap's 'physicalism'. First, here is Carnap on the thesis of physicalism (1935: 89–90):

> this physical language is the basic language of all science . . . it is a universal language comprehending the contents of all other scientific languages. In other words, every sentence of any branch of scientific language is equipollent[3] to some sentence of the physical language, and can therefore be translated into the physical language without changing its content . . .
>
> For purposes of elucidation, let us take the following psychological statement: 'At ten o'clock Mr A was angry'. The equipollent sentence of the physical language is: 'At ten o'clock Mr A was in a certain bodily condition which is characterized by the acceleration of breathing and pulsation, by the tension of certain muscles, by the tendency to certain violent behaviour, and so on.

This emphasis on physical categories rather than experiential ones is very much a logical empiricist one, since it tries to remove the contribution of the human understander as much as possible (see 3.3.6). When we compare the sentences that Hodge and Kress recommended as demystifying, 'The sun warmed the soil' and 'The water moistened the seeds', we see that they are of a less directly experiential nature than their non-transactive counterparts, but all the same they are not outrightly physicalist. So while Carnap's physicalist/experiential distinction is absolute, we might regard Hodge and Kress's prescription as only moving towards physicalist descriptions. Indeed, it could be argued that the clause 'The water moistened the seeds' is *not* demystifying of the causal process and could provide the wrong impression about the nature of the causal processes. That is, it is not so much that the water moistens the seeds but rather it is the osmotic potential of the seeds' sugars which sets up conditions for drawing water into the seed. So if we are to follow Hodge and Kress's quasi-Carnapian line, a more 'representational' sentence might be 'The seed draws water into itself'. But that sentence still does not tell us the precise chemical processes that occur within the seed, for example, water triggers off hydrolytic enzymes which begin to break down food stores in the seed; soluble, mobile food molecules are then free to take part in growth, and so on (see Cook 1994: 75–8 on infinite detail).

The logical empiricist 'Carnapian' assumptions above, upon which Hodge and Kress's approach rests, were criticised by the philosopher Quine (1953). Quine denied the feasibility of Carnap's project of translating experiential language into a physicalist language. For Quine, the sentences that report on our direct sensory experiences are also part of a web of other sentences, as part of general theory of the world. On a Quinian perspective, the sentence 'The water moistened the seeds' is not discrete in its correspondence to a part of reality. Rather it is 'webbed' with the sentences 'The water moistened the outer-covering of the seeds', 'The water hydrated the seeds' sugars', and so on. It follows that a sentence like 'The water moistened the seeds' only makes sense holistically within the reader's 'store of other sentences'. Since the young children for whom the story is intended will not have such a dense 'store' of sentences relating to germination, respiration and photosynthesis, Hodge and Kress's transactives will still be 'mystifying' for young children. Indeed, for descriptions of scientific phenomena generally, it is often irrelevant whether sentences are transactive or non-transactive if there is an absence of sufficient knowledge to draw upon, that is, an absence of 'a store of appropriate sentences'. This is well exemplified by the following folk-explanation: 'The ice cooled her forehead'. The transactive status of the sentence means that for Hodge and Kress, at least, the causal relation is explicit, satisfying their criterion that this is a scientific statement. But the causal relation of the folk-explanation is misleading: ice does not cool a forehead. Instead, heat from a forehead disrupts the bonds between water molecules in ice leading to melting. It is because heat is transferred to the ice, rather than the ice doing something to her forehead, that the temperature of her forehead reduces. For the conflict between folk and scientific understanding of causality, see Wolpert (1992).

Another corollary of Quine's position is that it leads one to see sentences not as discrete *representations* of reality but as *cues* of background knowledge (one's 'store' of sentences). Consider the following from Slobin (1982: 131–2):

> A sentence is not a verbal snapshot or movie of an event. In framing an utterance, you have to abstract away from everything you know, or can picture, about a situation, and present a schematic version which conveys the essentials. In terms of grammatical marking, there is not enough time in the speech situation for any language to allow for the marking of everything which could possibly be significant to the message. Probably there is not enough interest, either. **Language *evokes* ideas; it does not represent them**. Linguistic expression is thus *not* a natural map of consciousness or thought. It is a highly selective and conventionally schematic map. At the heart of language use is the tacit assumption that most of the message can be left unsaid, because of mutual understanding (and probably also mutual impatience). The subset of semantic notions which is formally marked in a particular language serves more to guide the listener to the appropriate segments and categories of analysis than to fully represent the underlying notions. [my bold]

Paraphrasing what I highlighted in bold in the extract above, sentences *evoke* background knowledge, they do not *represent* the world.[4] Since linguistic meaning transpires within an extant theory, it is patent that Hodge and Kress have neglected the cueing aspect of language, its function in evoking background knowledge. Or to put it another way, they are in tune with the logical empiricist notion that sentential structure can reflect or represent the situation in the world independent of the contribution of the human understander (3.3.6). So if the background knowledge is rich, as would presumably be the case with a reading of the story by a botanist, then Carnapian 'translation', even to the limited extent of Hodge and Kress, would be otiose. But if background knowledge is impoverished, as is the case with five-year-old children, then Carnapian 'translation' to the extent of Hodge and Kress's translation into transactives would not be enough, as we saw in the last section. This is all because mental representation is the output of what sentences cue. This mental representation necessarily goes beyond the sentential structure and so is not, as implied in Hodge and Kress (1993), a facsimile of sentential structure. The notion of 'language as cues' is elaborated upon in much more detail later in this book, for example, when I highlight connectionist approaches to language processing in Chapter 5 and relevance theory in Chapter 9. The importance of taking account of background knowledge (the contribution of the human understander) for the issue of language mystification is dealt with from a more psycholinguistic point of view in Chapter 7.

In Chapter 3, I showed that the work of Chomsky was inherently symbolic. Below I show how, in adapting the work of Chomsky, early work in CDA was informed by the same assumptions. For mystification analysis, these assumptions have been carried over into current CDA.

4.3 CDA AND CHOMSKY: MYSTIFICATION AND TRANSFORMATIONS

In Chapter 2, I flagged Hodge and Kress (1993)/Kress and Hodge (1979) and Fowler et al. (1979) as providing the basis for mystification analysis in the interpretation stage of CDA. These seminal works draw heavily upon early Chomsky (1957, 1965) and adapt his competence model to a performance perspective for the isolation of mystifying text. Hodge and Kress (1993) adapt Chomsky's theory of transformations. Similar adaptation occurs in Fowler et al. (1979), and a more formal discussion of this adaptation is located within Hodge and Kress (1974). In this section, I deal mainly with Hodge and Kress (1993). Here is Hodge and Kress (1993: 10):

> In our account, transformations are a set of operations on basic forms, deleting, substituting, combining, or reordering a syntagm or its elements. So *The car was wrecked* is transformed from (*someone or something*) *wrecked the car*, with the actor (someone or something) deleted and the elements of the syntagm reordered in the passive.

Hodge and Kress's signalling of 'actor' rather than 'subject' point to a semantic adaptation of transformations whereas Chomsky's emphasis was syntactic. In their adaptation, Hodge and Kress (1993: 35) also do not regard transformations as innocuous operations: 'The typical function of transformations is distortion and mystification.' Here we have an explicit shift from Chomsky's formalist perspective to a functional one. Consider now an example of how transformations are meant to mystify or distort. Recall from 2.4.2 the examination by Hodge and Kress (1993: 21) of part of a newspaper editorial on the miners' overtime ban during the winter of 1972–3. The passage is rich in tacit symbolicism. The notion that a 'surface form' conceals an 'underlying' form echoes a similar assumption in logical empiricism which we saw in the previous chapter. Symbolicism is further echoed since mental representation for Hodge and Kress is tacitly *sentence-like*, where the necessary mental exercise will transform the surface form of 'picketing' into 'strikers picket a power station'. However, this mental representation is not the same as *mentalese* (see 3.3.7). Rather than a 'language of thought' we have something like 'thought consisting of language', a notion popularly associated with Whorf. Indeed, Whorf (1956) is twined with Chomsky in Hodge and Kress (1993) and cited throughout as theoretical substantiation. The result is that the underlying view of mental representation in Hodge and Kress (1993) is an amalgam of 'Whorfianism' and symbolicism. So, rather than advocating mentalese, for Hodge and Kress, thought seems to consist of what might be called *linguese*.

Following Chomsky's 'surface' and 'deep' structures, Hodge and Kress seem to be advocating 'surface' linguese and 'deep' linguese. But Chomsky's distinction between 'surface' and 'deep' structure is itself a logical empiricist notion (redolent of Carnap, Russell and the early Wittgenstein) and so a logical empiricist notion has been absorbed into Hodge and Kress. However, Hodge and Kress's 'deep linguese' consists of language and is not the same as the Chomskyan deep and abstract underlying string. Here are Hodge and Kress again (1993: 28):

> deletion, simplification, collapsing of forms into single units, all act to alter the way in which a reader meets the material and tend to structure his interpretations in specific ways. He is continually coerced into taking the surface form as the real form; and that surface is a radically transformed version of the originally chosen linguistic form.

Hodge and Kress seem to imply that symbols are cognitively reiterated as 'surface' linguese. Like mentalese, the sentence for Hodge and Kress is both the vehicle of computation *and* the vehicle of mental content. Returning to the quote in the previous section, cognitive labour is involved in transforming 'surface' linguese into transactive 'deep' linguese. Transactives represent reality more 'fully' (they do not entail mystification of what really occurred), but for Hodge and Kress (1993), there is a paucity of transactives in the text. So, for a reader to have a 'fuller' appreciation of the events in question, considerable cognitive effort is necessary to transform the 'surface' linguese into 'deep' transactive linguese ('about a dozen times on every full line of newsprint' (Hodge and Kress 1993: 22)). Since such effort will not normally be invested (see also 2.4.2), the events being reported are mystified for the reader.

I have dealt specifically with how Chomskyan 'borrowings' in Hodge and Kress (1993) have absorbed symbolic postulates. We now move on to look at these assumptions more specifically in relation to language processing.

4.4 CDA AND SYMBOLIC APPROACHES TO LANGUAGE PROCESSING

4.4.1 Hodge and Kress (1993) and Psychological Realism

Hodge and Kress's (1993) assumptions of transformation processing are very much akin to the 'Derivational Theory of Complexity' (DTC) outlined in 3.6.1. In their formulation of transformations, Hodge and Kress (1993: 35) assert the following: 'We take a strongly realist position and regard all transformational analyses as hypothetical reconstructions of psychologically real processes.' But, as we saw in Chapter 3, the early promise for the psychological reality of transformations from the experiments of Miller (1962), Miller and McKean (1964) and Savin and Perchonock (1965) was dashed by the experimental evidence of Fodor and Garrett (1966, 1967). All this is fairly well-known. In the light of the psycholinguistic evidence against DTC, it is surely misplaced of Hodge and Kress (1993: 35) to claim that their position is explicitly 'strongly realist' regarding 'all transformational analyses as hypothetical reconstructions of psychologically real processes' (see Widdowson (1997) for a more detailed questioning of the psychological reality of Hodge and Kress's (1993) transformational model). In turn, this problematises Hodge and Kress's (1993) analysis of the text on the miners' overtime ban which we saw in 2.4.2.

In 3.6.1, I outlined Fodor and Garrett's (1966, 1967) rebuttal of the possibility of there being psychologically real transformations. Fodor and Garrett (1967) went on to argue that instead parsing was performed by perceptual heuristics or surface structure cues, claiming the end-product of syntactic processing was a syntactic representation equivalent to the deep structure as posited by Chomsky (1965). I indicate below how something like *symbolic* 'perceptual heuristics' also inform processing assumptions in CDA.

4.4.2 Perceptual Heuristics and CDA

In 3.6.2, we saw that Fodor and Garrett (1967) highlighted the strategy of perceptual heuristics known as *canonical sentence structure*. In English this is subject-verb-object, Fodor and Garrett positing that comprehenders initially assume that many sentences will conform to this structure. On such a heuristics, comprehenders supposedly try a simple strategy like canonical sentence structure first and, if this fails, move on to other more complex ones. We also saw that the strategies of late closure and minimal attachment and the phenomenon of garden-pathing are in accordance allegedly with an initial preference in comprehension for subject-verb-object structure.

While we have seen that some CDA authors base their analyses of news texts on something similar to the Derivational Theory of Complexity, at other times something akin to perceptual heuristics is drawn upon. Consider the following from Fowler and Kress (1979a: 42), an examination of a fragment from a set of university regulations (University of East Anglia, *Calendar* 1977–8, p. 128). The fragment is quoted first:

> 'All students matriculating in the University shall, so long as they remain in attendance, be bound by the following Regulations and by such other Regulations as the University may from time to time determine.'
> The deep structure is actually something like:
> The University (AGENT) binds (PROCESS) all students (OBJECT) by Regulations (INSTRUMENT).
> But in the passive surface structure, the nominal designating the object ('all students') has been placed in the position of theme, i.e. the left-most noun phrase in the sentence, and this is a position normally associated with the role of agent. **The syntax strongly encourages one to read the first part of this sentence with the expectation that it is going to describe some action carried out by 'all students'**; this illusion is heightened by the presence of an active verb of a subordinate clause ('matriculating') immediately following 'all students'; and by the extreme distance between the subject 'all students' and the main verb 'be bound', a distance which forces the reader to cling on to a hypothesis about the way the sentence is going to turn out. The easiest hypothesis is that we are waiting for a main verb

which will tell us what action 'all students' perform; but this hypothesis will prove incorrect, since it is actually the University which is doing something. **The reader has, however, made strong use of the hypothesis that 'all students' are the agent of the sentence, and is likely to retain some sense that the sentence does mean that.** [my bold]

Fowler and Kress (1979a: 42) conclude that, in making use of the above hypothesis, the reader processes 'all students', those actually affected by the process, as occupying a syntactic position 'which makes them appear responsible for their own fate'. Also, recall from 2.4.4, Kress's (1993: 181–2) analysis of the sentence 'His parents could not afford a uniform' and his argument that:

> many readers of the *Daily Express* may read across this clause in reading the text, and read it as fully semantically transitive, which I shall call, following Hodge and Kress (1993), a 'transactive'. In support of that reading, these readers might say: 'We scrimped and saved, and we afforded a uniform for our children, so why can't they?!'

What characterises these and many other CDA analyses is a syntax-first approach, in line with the symbolic separation between syntax and semantics, which we saw in the previous chapter. In other words, it is assumed readers initially follow syntactic cues as part of their perceptual heuristics, trying a simple strategy like canonical sentence structure first. The extra step here for these CDA practitioners is that having begun from subject-verb-object as a perceptual heuristic, readers could then 'read across' this syntactic form reading it in semantically transitive (transactive) terms whether the sentence has this semantic structure or not. So for Kress (1993) (and implied by Fowler and Kress (1979a)), this perceptual heuristic is capable of misleading – the syntactic form itself is so powerful that it suggests semantic (transactive) meaning. In short, Kress details a type of shallow processing since the processing of the actual semantics of the clauses outlined is shallower than the processing of the syntax. The theme of shallow processing is something I return to later in this book.

The previous two sections have been concerned with how symbolic notions of syntax have imbued CDA. In the next section, I focus on how the symbolic notion of *compositionality* informs CDA's assumptions of processing.

4.5 CDA AND COMPOSITIONAL PROCESSING

In 3.2.1 and 3.3.5, I highlighted the symbolic notion of compositionality: that the meaning of a sentence is regarded as the meaning of its parts and that these parts are discrete, enduring symbols such that 'a word makes approximately the same semantic contribution to the meaning of every sentence in which it occurs' (Fodor and Pylyshyn 1988). In semantic analysis, compositionality seems a reasonable assumption. In order to make a discussion of semantic meaning manageable, it seems acceptable to 'atomise' meanings by removing environmental constraints. Standard semantics is largely unconcerned with the actualities of cognition. As Langacker (1987b: 1) submits: 'the whole point of truth-conditional, semantics is to avoid any postulation of mental constructs in the characterization of semantic structure'. However, mystification analysis in CDA is implicitly or explicitly concerned with the actualities of cognition, that is, the effects of texts on readers. And since CDA is bound up with symbolicism, compositionality, rather than being an analytical procedure, has often been tacitly treated as being a psychologically real facet of cognition in CDA. As an example, I consider an extract from Fairclough (1995a: 110–3) who presents an analysis of how 'the poor' in the 'Third World' are represented in a television documentary ('A New Green Revolution?' in the science documentary series *Horizon*, broadcast in January 1984 on BBC2).

Fairclough (1995a: 112) highlights how the documentary represents the poor as passive, merely the outcome of a set of circumstances beyond their control, 'as patients – as people who are affected by the actions of others'. First, here is an excerpt from the narration, taken from the 'third extract' that Fairclough offers for examination: 'Everywhere in the Third World life in rural areas gets harder – and poor people flock to the city. The urban poor get poorer.' Here now is Fairclough (1995a: 113) who, having commented that the text backgrounds 'the poor' as agents of their circumstances, mentions what seems to be an exception to this analysis at first glance:

> there are only two Actors in the third extract, the New People's Army and, exceptionally, the poor, in *the poor people flock to the city*. Interestingly, the Action here is one more usually associated with sheep – notoriously passive – than people, so the exception does not really contradict what I have said so far.

Intuitively, both the immediate lexical environment of 'flock' and the previous co-text effects closure on the possibility that 'flock' refers to a collection of sheep and thus that 'the poor people' are acting passively (in

Chapter 5, I examine the connectionist approach to processing which corroborates this intuition). 'The poor people flock to the city' is read while making the inference that 'the poor people' make the *active* decision to escape something negative: rural hardship. Such an inference surely inflects upon the meaning of 'flock', reducing its capacity to signal passivity. To make this point clearer, let me give some examples:

1. The band gave such a bad performance that the audience started flocking to the exit halfway through the set.
2. Elvis Presley had such charisma that women flocked wherever he went.
3. The guru had such control of our minds when we were at his talk that we flocked to join his commune.

In the first example, it would be difficult to argue that 'flock' referred to a passive bunch of people. As in the documentary extract above, people (audience members) make an individual decision to escape something they perceive as negative. In the second example, people ('women') do not want to escape something negative but are drawn to what they perceive as being positive. Because Elvis Presley's charisma draws in women, one might argue that they are not behaving with 'full' agency. To some extent in 2, then, 'flock' signals passivity. In the third example, 'flock' would seem to signal total passivity, at least in the evaluation of the speaker. The overall point I want to make is that whether the meaning of 'flock' is seen as involving passivity depends on the previous co-text and the inferential relations between the previous co-text and the clause with 'flock' in it. This inferential meaning will inflect upon the meaning of 'flock'. We cannot just assume that 'flock' means passive collective movement in every example.

In assuming that the meaning of 'flock' in the documentary extract is that of a *collective of sheep*, what assumption about cognition and language might enable Fairclough to postulate this? One supposition would be that compositionality is an actual feature of cognition, symbols being discrete and enduring. Fairclough's neglect of how the semantico-syntactic environment might close down on the possible meaning of 'flock' is consonant with such a supposition. Moreover, compositionality facilitates his choice of the ovine sense of 'flock' so as to suit his line of interpretation.

As another example of compositionality being drawn into notions of mental representation in CDA, consider the following from Fowler (1986: 20):

> consider phrases like 'my wife', 'my son', 'my assistant'. Being any of these people involves activity, relationship. But the syntax

which is conventional in English – Possessive + Noun – has the unfortunate effect of encoding a human relationship as an *object*, a possession of another person, so that 'my wife' seems to be as totally owned by me as my hand or my books or my car. Obviously, this syntactic structure, apparently so 'natural', embodies a theory of personal relationship as ownership with dominance, with the dominated partner reduced to the status of an object. Once recognized, such processes are seen as ideological and objectionable. It is claimed that they encourage habits of mind and behaviour which are prejudicial to the dignity and the economic progress of the people presented as 'possessed'.

Notice how the compositional arrangement of the grammar has become conflated with how the 'human relationship' is understood. The notion of possession is equated to a discrete symbol. Indeed, the symbolic assumption of *compositionality* – that the symbol 'my' is discrete and enduring – is so strong that it goes unnoticed that 'my' is actually a deictic determiner whose meaning is reliant on context. Taking Fowler's compositional building-block approach to meaning to its conclusion, the meaning of 'my' in 'my boss', for example, would also have to be regarded as possessive.

One of the origins of this assigning of meaning to syntactic categories derives from an amalgamation of compositionality with 'Whorfianism' (see 4.3 and also Hodge and Kress (1993)). In 'Whorfianism', language is equated with thought: we think in language or 'linguese'. This is a common notion in CDA as well as in related disciplines such as stylistics. So even in circumspect discussion of 'Whorfianism', the authors of a book on stylistics, Leech and Short (1981: 146–7), still assert the following:

> The classical statement of the view that languages determine the way in which their speakers interpret and categorize experience is that of B. L. Whorf (1956). Recent thinking has suggested that there is a great deal more in common between languages in this respect than Whorf acknowledges; but whatever stand one takes on the issue, the fact remains that *we conceptualize in terms of the categories our language provides for us*. [my italics]

However, if we actually think in the categories of our language, that is, if the compositionality of a sentence on a page is replicated in thought, then it is not a huge step to believing that the syntactic nature of a category is intact in our compositional thought. In other words, our thinking will be guided by the syntactic nature of the category. This point has particular relevance for 4.6.1 below.

In 3.4, I outlined the classical theory of categories. In the next section, I highlight how some postulates of language processing in CDA are also bound up with the classical theory of categories.

4.6 CDA AND THE CLASSICAL THEORY OF CATEGORIES

4.6.1 Nominal Form, Objectifying Effects and Mystification

There is a tendency in CDA to regard all nouns as things, to see 'thingness' as a necessary and sufficient condition for nounhood. As an example, consider the following from Hodge and Kress's (1993: 23–4) commentary on fragments from an editorial from *The Guardian* (20 December 1973):

> In discussing the next two examples, *the miners lift their overtime ban*, and *the ban cuts production*, we begin to deal with words whose status as stable nouns is unquestionable . . . Both ['ban' and 'production'] are descriptions of actions which involve participants, both in fact are descriptions of transactive actions:
>
> someone bans something → ban
> someone produces something → production
>
> . . . we might assume that speakers use these words, and hearers understand them, as though they were like *apple* or *bench*, but referring to things which happen to be abstract, not concrete physical things. For this kind of speaker or hearer, the linguistic form creates a world of thinglike abstract beings or objects, which are capable of acting or being acted on. Here language determines perception in two ways, by creating an alternative world which can only be 'seen' in language and by imposing this alternative world, with its apparent solid reality, on the material world, so that we no longer see or believe in the world of physical events.

By nature of the fact that 'ban' and 'production' function as nouns in the editorial, it is assumed that they must share the same properties of nounhood as 'apple' and 'bench', that is, 'thingness'. As we saw in 2.4.3, for CDA, an excess of nominalisations 'objectifies' events being described. This mystifies the nature of the events since, for these authors, events are better 'captured' with material action processes. Clearly, the classical theory of categories is in the background here, that is, the all-or-nothing criterion that all nominals are 'thingy'. In Chapter 6, I will outline the enterprise of cognitive linguistics and highlight problems with this all-or-nothing criterion for category membership and in turn for which aspects of language CDA regards as being mystifying.

Ascribing meaning to grammatical form, as Hodge and Kress (1993) do, assumes that syntactic information and semantic information are discretely processed. This is consonant with symbolism since in symbolicism:

> the rule-governed processes that operate on representations are syntactic; that is, they are applied with respect to form, not meaning, and can apply at any level of the constituent structure that satisfies a specified structural description.'
> (Bechtel and Abrahamsen 2002: 157)

An accompanying feature of isolating syntax from the semantics of the sentence and then attributing meaning to the syntax is that the notion of compositionality becomes reinforced. This is because while we can imagine such a phenomenon as the global semantic meaning of a sentence, it is difficult to imagine the 'global syntactic meaning' of a sentence. Thus, in focusing on syntax separate from semantics, individual syntactic categories inevitably become associated with a discrete meaning.

4.6.2 Nominals and 'Scientific Language'

Consider the following from Ogborn et al. (1996: 51), one of whose authors is the CD analyst Gunther Kress:

> Scientific texts are well known for their high concentration of events and processes presented as if they were things. Simple examples include evaporation, crystallization, ionization, speciation, oscillation. Any scientific textbook or journal will yield a multitude of them, as transparent as 'magnification' or as opaque as 'commensurability oscillations in the resistivity' (culled from a relatively non-specialized journal). Their presence is not due to the barbarous linguistic habits of scientists. They exist in texts and talk as entities because they exist in the thinking of scientists as entities. They are . . . things with which to think.

This has parallels with section 4.6.1 where nominal expressions necessarily correspond to 'nominal' thoughts. It also has parallels with 4.2.2 since, in the over-emphasis on the form of scientific expressions and their capacity to influence thinking, there is a neglect of the scientist's own 'scientific knowledge'. There is no notion that 'crystallization', 'ionization' and so on are linguistic cues of scientific knowledge associated with these terms rather than mere 'thinking entities'.

4.7 CDA AND THE DEMOTION OF INFERENCES IN SYMBOLICISM

In 2.4.1, I outlined how different CDA authors regarded the issue of inference generation in mystification analysis. Trew's (1979) view of inference generation is endorsed by Toolan (2001), Lee (1992) and Montgomery (1995) as well as by Simpson (1993). They all contend implicitly that sentential structure should reflect reality and thus that an inference that has to be generated across sentences or clauses can be treated as a weak representation ('has to be inferred by implication' (Simpson 1993: 170)). If we return to 2.4.1 and the extract from Trew (1979: 98–9), we can see that the sentential focus is quite pronounced. (While for Trew the agency of the police 'is identified only weakly by implication' in the first sentence of the text body, this ignores the fact that agency was given in the headline.) Clearly in both Trew and Simpson there is an echo of logical empiricism where the structure of meaningful sentences must mirror the structure of the event independent of the contribution to processing of the human understander (see 3.3.6). We also saw in 4.2.2 that Hodge and Kress (1993), in emphasising the importance of semantico-syntactic structure, implicitly downplay the importance of background knowledge in processing and thus inferences generated on the basis of background knowledge. The alliance between CDA and something akin to the derivational theory of complexity also accounts for the emphasis on propositional form and deeper structure. In turn, this also means that non-propositional factors such as background knowledge and inferences generated on the basis of this knowledge are downplayed.

As another example of the symbolic demotion of inferences in CDA, consider the following excerpt from a booklet (Morris, *The Baby Book* (1986)) issued to 'expectant parents' by hospitals (Fairclough 1992: 170–1), and then some of Fairclough's (1992: 182–3) commentary upon it:

> A complete physical examination will then be carried out which will include checking *your breasts, heart, lungs, blood pressure, abdomen and pelvis*. The purpose of this is to identify any *abnormalities* which might be present, but which so far have not caused you any problems. [my italics]

Nominalization turns processes and activities into states and objects, and concretes into abstracts. For example, it is one thing to refer to concrete processes in pregnancy which may not be developing normally; it is another to refer to identifying 'any abnormalities which may be present', which creates a new category of abstract entities. The creation of new entities is a feature of nominalization which is of considerable cultural and ideological importance. For instance, an advertisement for cosmetic surgery has the headline 'Good looks can last you a lifetime!'; 'good looks' is a nominalization (from concrete relational processes such as 'you look good!') which entifies a local and temporary condition into an inherent state or property, which can then itself become the focus of cultural attention and manipulation (good looks, can, for example, be cultivated, enhanced, looked after; they can be said to bring people good fortune, make them happy, give them trouble). Accordingly, one finds nominalizations themselves taking on the roles of goals and even agents of processes. (For further discussion of the properties of nominalization, see Kress and Hodge 1979, Chapter 2.)

In the text, 'abnormalities' is patently cohesive with 'checking your breasts, heart, lungs, blood pressure, abdomen and pelvis'. Intuitively, one readily makes the inference that 'abnormalities' refers to possible problems with 'breasts', 'heart' and so on. In other words, the more general and abstract 'abnormalities' is 'filled in' intuitively in processing and made more concrete via the information 'your breasts' and so on.[5] So while 'abnormalities' may be a distinct lexical item as input, this is not the same as saying that it is, in processing output terms, 'a new category of abstract entities'. Why does Fairclough suppose that 'abnormalities' is 'a new category of abstract entities'? One probable explanation is that Fairclough is operating on the symbolic assumption that symbols are discrete and enduring in cognition. Another assumption may be the logical empiricist postulate that symbols derive their meaning from referring to the world. On this perspective, the use of a category presupposes a referent. For Fairclough, it seems, the use of a 'new' category presupposes a 'new' referent.

Return also for a moment to the analysis from Clark (1992) from 4.2.1. Consider again the first two sentences from *The Sun* newspaper (11 November 1986) on which she focuses:

1) Two of Steed's rape victims – aged 20 and 19 – had a screwdriver held at their throats as they were forced to submit.

2) His third victim, a 39 year old mother of three, was attacked at gunpoint after Steed forced her car off the M4.

as well as the following from Clark (1992: 215):

In both descriptions of the rapes (1) and (2), the perception of Steed as rapist is reduced by making the sentences passive and deleting him as Agent. This perception is further reduced by using the euphemism 'attacked' to mask the terrible details of abduction, repeated rape, and death threats (not mentioned at all in this newspaper).

Once more, like Fairclough, the more general category 'attack' is not seen as being 'filled in' by the more specific category 'rape' even though it is in the previous sentence. And again, what would account for this is the symbolic assumption that symbols are discrete and enduring in cognition.

In 2.6 I drew attention to a number of tensions between the mystification analyses and the socio-cognitive analyses I included as examples. One tension was that the mystification analyses were bottom-up and the socio-cognitive analyses were top-down. What follows will indicate why this is the case. As illustration I refer to a mystification analysis and socio-cognitive analysis from the same book, Fairclough (2001). Consider first the following text and Fairclough's (2001: 42–3) mystification analysis:

QUARRY LOAD-SHEDDING PROBLEM
Unsheeted lorries from Middlebarrow Quarry were still causing problems by shedding stones on their journey through Warton village, members of the parish council heard at their September meeting.
The council's observations have been sent to the quarry management and members are hoping to see an improvement.
Lancaster Guardian, 12 September 1986

Causality is attributed to *unsheeted lorries from Middlebarrow Quarry*. This itself contains unspecified causality again, for *unsheeted* implies the failure of a process to happen – someone did not put sheets over the loads, when (one assumes) they ought to have done. It is difficult to take literally the notion that the *lorries* are the cause of the problem, and it is evident that in a different representation it could be this 'someone' – presumably the *quarry management* or people under their control. Yet the quarry management figure only in the second paragraph in this representation as in receipt of the council's *observations*, a term which again avoids attributing any responsibility (it might have been *complaints*).

That Fairclough contends it is hard to take seriously that the lorry is the cause of the problem suggests that for Fairclough the 'surface' structure prevails over more top-down inferences as to causal responsibility. That the 'surface structure' mystifies as to causal responsibility is again in line with the syntax-first/inference-last symbolic assumption: that is, by implication an inference as to causal antecedence is a weaker representation than if causal antecedence had been *directly* specified in the sentential structure. However, the downplaying of inference generation in this analysis is in tension with Fairclough's (2001: 44–5) socio-cognitive analysis of the 'Jenny Keeble' text (see 2.5.1) where inferences were *strong* representations since they could lead to the reproduction of sexists.

If it is clear that logical empiricist/symbolic assumptions govern why inference generation is so downplayed in Fairclough's mystification analysis above, why should inference generation be given prominence in Fairclough's socio-cognitive analysis of the Jenny Keeble text? This is because what informed Fairclough's socio-cognitive analysis of the Jenny Keeble text was the *script* theory of Schank and Abelson (1977). Consider Fairclough's follow-up (2001: 133) to the Jenny Keeble text analysis:

> the text implicitly conveys the meanings that Jenny Keeble is a 'good wife' and admirable person, through the expressive values of attributes attached to her.
> ... the meaning that Jenny Keeble is a 'good wife' is not explicitly expressed in the text, and it is only because interpreters have in their heads a mental representation of what a 'good wife' is stereotypically supposed to be that they are able to recognize attributes thereof which occur in the text and **so infer the meaning**. In the terms of the preceding section, interpreters make use of a *script* for 'the good wife'. In fact, schemata and frames as well as **scripts** can be regarded as playing a role in the interpretation of point: they act as stereotypical patterns against which we can match endlessly diverse texts, and once we identify a text as an instance of a pattern, we happily dispense with the mass of its detail and reduce it to the skeletal shape of the familiar pattern for purposes of longer-term memory and recall. [my bold]

Schank and Abelson (1977) regard the background-knowledge component in a processor as supplying the bulk of processing requirements.

This background knowledge component embodies a series of well-delineated knowledge scripts. Scripts delineate information associated with particular events or situations such as eating in a restaurant. They are something akin to a complex semantic network that forms the parameters of a stereotypical set of events. So, a restaurant script might house information about menu selection, the order of courses, paying the bill, leaving a tip, and so on. Schank and Abelson's (1977) assumption is that a cue such as 'menu' evokes the entire script, the reader making default assumptions that stereotypical events transpire. So such a restaurant script enables a reader to infer stereotypical information when confronted with a text that alludes to a restaurant. With such an emphasis, Schank and Abelson thus regard higher-level processes as influencing parsing, their model exhibiting strong interaction between semantic and syntactic processing.

It should now be clear why there exists a conceptual tension towards inference generation in Fairclough (2001) as well as between the mystification analyses and socio-cognitive analyses in 2.6. That is, script theory is drawn upon in socio-cognitive analysis and so there is a top-down approach to processing where syntax and semantics are treated interactively. However, the cognitive assumptions in Fairclough's analysis of the 'Quarry load-shedding problem', and the mystification analyses of 2.6, are not top-down based, but in line with logical empiricism and Chomsky where syntax is treated as a separate phenomenon from semantics. Indeed, this conceptual tension is all the more marked since Schank (1980: 36) was hostile to Chomskyan modularity, promoting the view that semantics and pragmatics are central in language and downplaying the role of syntax: 'It is impossible to produce a model of language alone . . . apart from beliefs, goals, points of view and world knowledge' (1980: 36).

4.8 CDA, HALLIDAY AND SYMBOLICISM

At various points in Chapter 2 and this chapter, we have seen how detection of mystification in CDA has been done via use of Hallidayan metalanguage. I mentioned at the end of 2.3 that an implicit cognitive assumption in Halliday's work has lent support to how CDA goes about detecting mystifying text. But before I get on to what this is, consider the following from Widdowson (2000: 16–17):

> Halliday . . . apparently makes no distinction between
> grammatical and textual units of meaning. The functions which
> are formally encoded in grammar simply get reanimated when

used in texts. So the grammar 'is at once both a grammar of the system and a grammar of the text' (Halliday 1994: xxii). It is not then surprising that critical discourse analysts should find Halliday's grammar so well suited to their purposes. It is tailor made for them: 'the aim has been to construct a grammar for the purposes of text analysis' (Halliday 1994: xv). This would seem to suggest that if you can identify part of a text as manifesting a grammatical feature of whatever kind, all you need to do is to read off the meaning it encodes. There would in this case be no difference between semantic signification and textual significance. The text is thus taken to be a static patchwork. The dynamic inter-relationships which grammatical features contract with each other are disregarded as irrelevant.

By 'dynamic inter-relationships', Widdowson refers to how co-textual factors alter meaning. One example of this would be how Fairclough's (1995a) compositional analysis of the process 'flock' (see 4.5) does not take into account such 'dynamic inter-relationships' in the co-text, which include the generation of inferences.

On the basis of Widdowson's argument, Halliday's work would seem to give warrant to an analytical procedure which assumes clauses are mentally facsimiled in cognition, thus substantiating the *consumption* metaphor of CDA. That Halliday's thinking indeed does give warrant to such a perspective becomes very clear when we consider the following:

> In the first place, language serves for the expression of content: it has a representational, or, as I would prefer to call it, an ideational function . . . it is through this function that the speaker or writer embodies in language his experience of the phenomena of the real world; and this includes his experience of the internal world of his own consciousness: his reactions, cognitions, and perceptions, and also his linguistic acts of speaking and understanding.
> (Halliday 1996/1971: 58)

> [The ideational function] is the component through which the language encodes the cultural experience, and the speaker encodes his own individual experience as a member of the culture.
> (Halliday 1978: 112)

I include these quotes rather than extracts from later work because the key critical linguistic texts, which still influence mystification analysis in

CDA, were both published in 1979. I include the first quote especially since it comes from an article that is referred to in the Critical Linguistics of both Fowler et al. (1979) and Hodge and Kress (1993)/Kress and Hodge (1979), indeed extolled as 'brilliant' in the latter (Hodge and Kress 1993: 40). Another key work in Critical Linguistics, Fowler (1996b) includes the first quote in a chapter on 'language and the representation of experience' and signals that it draws on Halliday (1978) for the 'linguistic position' taken in that chapter (Fowler 1996b: 31).

For Halliday, we can see from the quotes that language 'embodies' or 'encodes' a person's cognition. But this is quite a peculiar thing to say the more one realises how much humans rely on *non-linguistic* cognition (such as visual cognition, spatial estimation). Since mental representation of language goes beyond the linguistic input, the latter evoking background knowledge and so on, language can be *cues* of non-linguistic cognition (see 4.2.2 and Section B). The converse of this is that language is a *trace* of a person's cognition of the world, cognition which would naturally include non-linguistic cognition as well as linguistic cognition. Or put more simply, when a text is written, text is the trace of the discourse (1) of the writer. These quotes from Halliday, then, are the converse of the symbolic assumption that mental representation of a sentence is primarily a reflex of that sentence. And so on the basis of Halliday's outlook (at least the outlook indicated in his work in the 1970s) it would be natural to regard reading as 'consumption' of text, that clauses on a page are mentally facsimiled in cognition, particularly for the unsuspecting reader, thus helping to warrant the CDA interpretative practice that we have seen in this chapter. Interestingly, while Halliday and Chomsky are usually regarded as being polar opposites in linguistics – Halliday a functionalist, Chomsky a formalist – they are not so different as regards symbolicism, given Halliday's position above.

I mentioned in 4.7 that Schank and Abelson's (1977) model treats semantics and syntax interactively. In the next chapter, I outline the enterprise of connectionism which also favours interaction between syntactic and semantic information. I show how connectionism problematises many of the precepts of symbolicism, in turn problematising the language processing assumptions of CDA and thus what CDA highlights as being mystifying text.

NOTES

1. In fact, Chomsky had jettisoned the idea of kernel sentences by the time he wrote *Aspects of a Theory of Syntax* (1965).

2. Widdowson (1998: 140) highlights a contradiction in CDA in relation to the notion of the transactive:

    In the Hodge and Kress conception, they convert one kind of sentence into another. This would seem to imply the existence of neutral non-transformed sentences which are, by definition, innocent of any representational significance . . . even if we were able to identify the neutral sentences, their very existence means that it is in principle possible, by a judicious avoidance of transformation, to produce language which is entirely free of representational subjectivity. But this contradicts the critical linguistic tenet that there is no neutral language: *all* of it is loaded, 'ideologically saturated' as Kress puts it (Kress 1993: 174).

3. 'Equipollent' is a term used in logic to refer to two propositions that are logically deducible from one another.
4. Widening the perspective with Peircian categories, while *iconic* signs can be taken to 'represent' the world to varying degrees, *symbolic* (linguistic) signs do not usually do so unless they are configured iconically.
5. This type of 'filling-in' inference, where a general category is made more concrete in context, is known as an *instantiation*. For example, in 'The fish attacked the swimmer', fish is instantiated readily by the reader as 'piranha' or 'shark' etc. Instantiation, along with other types of inference, is dealt with in Chapter 7.

SECTION B

Newer Approaches to Language Cognition: Implications for CDA

Section B comprises three chapters which outline three newer approaches to language cognition. In Chapter 5, I outline connectionism; in Chapter 6 I give an outline of cognitive linguistics; and in Chapter 7 I outline recent psycholinguistic evidence on inference generation. What I include is with a view to: (1) indicating how symbolicism is problematised by these three paradigms; and (2) highlighting elements of these three paradigms which the reader will later see feeding into the idealised reader framework in Section C. In Section B, I also flag the implications of problematising symbolicism for CDA's assumptions of language cognition and thus for how it highlights mystifying language and manipulative language generally.

CHAPTER 5

Connectionism

5.1 INTRODUCTION

In this chapter, I provide a general portrait of an approach to cognitive modelling known as *connectionism*. In the last chapter, I highlighted the symbolic assumptions at work in many CDA analyses of mystifying text. Symbolicism and connectionism in cognitive science are the two dominant approaches to cognitive modelling. But on many, if not most, of the central issues in cognitive science they are diametrically opposed to one another. The function of this chapter is to problematise the symbolic cognitive assumptions of CDA from the most established oppositional paradigm. In turn, I will show that what CDA regards as mystifying language is also problematised. I will do the same, where appropriate, for manipulative language more generally. Another function of this chapter is to set out elements of connectionism which will find their way into the idealised reader framework of Section C.

I should stress from the outset that, in showing how connectionism problematises symbolicism, I do not offer connectionism as some kind of universal explanation of all issues of language comprehension. As MacDonald and MacDonald (1995: xvi) acknowledge, 'connectionist architectures promise to provide novel and important insights into human behaviour and cognition, but the development of the theory of such architectures is still in its infancy'. Similarly, as Schopman and Shawky (1996: 70) remark, 'the connectionist point of view does not mean that no problems are left, perhaps even new ones have been introduced'. Rather my aim in Chapter 5 and Section B generally is to produce a timely exploration of the paucity of appreciation of mental representation in CDA. Because of the constraints of this book my use of connectionist modelling is selective. Consequently my use of the term 'connectionist' is short-hand for a selected group of connectionist authors. Significantly, however, this group includes one of the 'fathers' of connectionism, James McClelland.

5.2 CONNECTIONISM: THE GENERAL PICTURE

5.2.1 Orientation

In the previous chapter, we saw that CDA's approach to identifying mystifying text places a great deal of emphasis upon syntax and that this was in line with the syntax-first approach to processing based on modularity. One of the significant features of connectionism is that it regards syntactic and semantic processing as being simultaneous and interactive and so does not operate on a syntax-first basis. Pre-connectionist research into this kind of interactive processing, and thus the non-autonomy of syntax, can be found in Just and Carpenter (1980), Marslen-Wilson and Tyler (1980), Crain and Steedman (1985), Altmann and Steedman (1988), and Taraban and McClelland (1988). Moreover, as highlighted in 4.7, Schank and Abelson (1977) regard semantics and syntax as interactive in processing. Taraban and McClelland are two authors associated with connectionism but the following outline of experimental evidence from their paper of 1988, for the interaction of semantics and syntax in comprehension, does not have an explicit connectionist emphasis.

5.2.2 Taraban and McClelland (1988)

The evidence from Taraban and McClelland's (1988) experiments is offered as refutation of the syntax-first/minimal attachment perspective (see 3.6.4). The following consists of what subjects had to read in one of the experiments in Taraban and McClelland (1988):

The janitor cleaned the storage area with the
a) broom
b) solvent
c) manager
d) odour
because of many complaints.

For Taraban and McClelland (1988), the above sentence contains a verb which leads to the expectation that an instrument will be mentioned in the prepositional phrase; that is, the prepositional phrase will attach to the verb phrase and inadvertently in accordance with the minimal attachment principle. This is shown in (a). A less expected instrument is shown in (b) and a less expected role is shown in (c). The sentence with either (a), (b) and (c) is in line with the minimal attachment principle but with (d) it is not. From the perspective of the minimal attachment principle, a less expected syntactic attachment is shown in (d), attaching to the noun phrase 'storage area' rather than the verb phrase 'cleaned . . .'.

The results indicated a significant increment in reading times for the word ('because') following the focal noun when the focal noun was either an unexpected role (c) *or* an unexpected attachment (d). As a result, McClelland and Taraban induced that it is *semantic content* and not syntax which determines interpretation. That is, the slow reading times in (c) and (d) were due to the presence of unexpected roles irrespective of whether interpretation is consonant with the minimal attachment principle as in (c) or not as in (d). In conclusion, Taraban and McClelland argue that a system of parallel constraint satisfaction (that is, a basis of connectionism), where syntactic and semantic information are processed coterminously, is a more valid explanation for the process of sentence comprehension.

The papers of McClelland and Kawamoto (1986), McClelland, St John and Taraban (1989), St John and McClelland (1992) and St John (1992), which are drawn upon in this book, also deal with interactive processing. Where they differ from Taraban and McClelland (1988) is that these authors attempt some simulation of neural activity. This modelling of neural processing is known as *connectionism* or *parallel distributed processing (PDP)*. In the sections below, I outline the basis of connectionist models and then go on to discuss connectionist approaches to multiple constraint satisfaction in sentence processing. Throughout, I explore the repercussions for the symbolic cognitive postulates of CDA and thus how connectionism problematises its approach to highlighting mystifying text. First, let me outline some common arguments that processing models should attempt to simulate neural activity.

5.2.3 Arguments for Neural Modelling

We saw in 3.2, briefly, reasons why the mind has been treated separately from the brain in symbolism. In symbolism, change in mental states is achievable through the rule-governed manipulation of sequences of mentalese-sentence strings. Language cognition on the symbolic perspective is, then, essentially mentalese sentence-crunching. Since mentalese sentence-crunching is algorithmic, it need not be implemented in neural matter, thereby reducing the importance of locating mental states with brain states. A large number of thinkers regard this perspective, however, as suffering from a series of difficulties: for example, Anderson and Hinton (1981); Churchland (1986); McClelland, Rumelhart and the PDP Research Group (1986); and Edelman (1992). Below is a synopsis of these difficulties.

1. Tasks that pose no problems for von Neumann machines (for example, mathematical calculations, logical reasoning) are usually either poorly performed by humans or require substantial effort. By the same token, tasks that humans take for granted (such as facial recognition) are poorly simulated on von Neumann architectures.
2. The brain is an extremely dense interconnected neural network. Purkinje cell neurons can have more than 80,000 input connections, and neurons in the cerebral cortex can have in excess of 10,000 output connections. The brain's *parallel* nature conflicts, then, with the serial architecture of von Neumann machines. Further evidence for the parallel status of the brain comes in the following. Many tasks such as facial recognition and simple responses to questions take about 0.5 seconds. On the basis of what is known about neural firing rates, conduction velocities and synaptic delays in neurons, this allows approximately five milliseconds per stage in the cognitive process. This would allow only about 100 stages, which for a serial programme supported on a von Neumann architecture would be far too slow. Feldman and Ballard (1982) have coined this the *hundred-step rule*.
3. Neural networks degrade gracefully and, like brains, are relatively tolerant of localised deterioration. Von Neumann architectures, however, cannot tolerate localised deterioration since this will lead to either total breakdown or significant handicap.
4. The existence of extensive individual variation in cognitive systems negates the fundamental postulate of symbolicism that representations have meaning independent of their physical instantiation. Human experience is not based on so simple an abstraction as a Turing machine; our experience of creating and understanding meaning goes hand in hand with our personal development as social interactants. In contrast to computers, the patterns of nervous system response depend on the individual history of each system, because it is only through interactions with the world that appropriate response patterns are selected.

5. Basing cognition on mentalese-sentences proves problematic for non-verbal animals. Either non-verbal animals do employ mentalese sentence-crunching as a basis for cognition or their cognitions are distinct from human cognitions. Neither alternative seems plausible. The first one is lacking in evidence and the second entails a disruption of evolutionary processes. The additional entailment is that evolutionary biology is somehow erroneous. Indeed, as Churchland (1986: 388) argues:

> Sentence-crunching is certain to have been a cognitive latecomer in the evolutionary scheme of things, and it must have knit itself into the preexisting nonsentential cognitive organization or ... evolved out of preadaptive nonsentential structures. To be sentence-crunching 'all the way down' implies either that cognition must have been sentence-crunching 'all the way back', which is implausible, or that sentence-crunchers have no cognitive heritage from earlier species, which is also implausible given the evolution of the brain.

The symbolic emphasis on 'sentence-crunching' or the syntax-first approach, as inadvertently employed by CDA, does not, then, sit so easily with an evolutionary perspective.

5.2.4 Modelling Neural Activity

In this section I outline some fundamentals with regard to connectionist modelling of neural activity. To see in which ways connectionist networks attempt modelling of actual neural networks, let me start with the nature of real neural networks. Actual neurons are simple processing elements which gather electrochemical pulses on their input side. Connections between neurons are known as synapses. If the combined total of incoming pulses reaches a particular *threshold of activation*, a neuron will generate an *action potential*. An action potential is a pulse that is conducted along the axon, a long, thin fibre on the neuron's output side. The rate of the action potential is consonant with the strength of the signal. Since neurons are massively interconnected in a parallel network, the firing or non-firing of particular maps of neurons can either excite or inhibit the activity of other neural circuits.

Artificial neurons in connectionist networks are much simpler than the variation in neural structure. A connectionist model consists of a multitude of simple processing elements. Each element is known as a *unit* or a

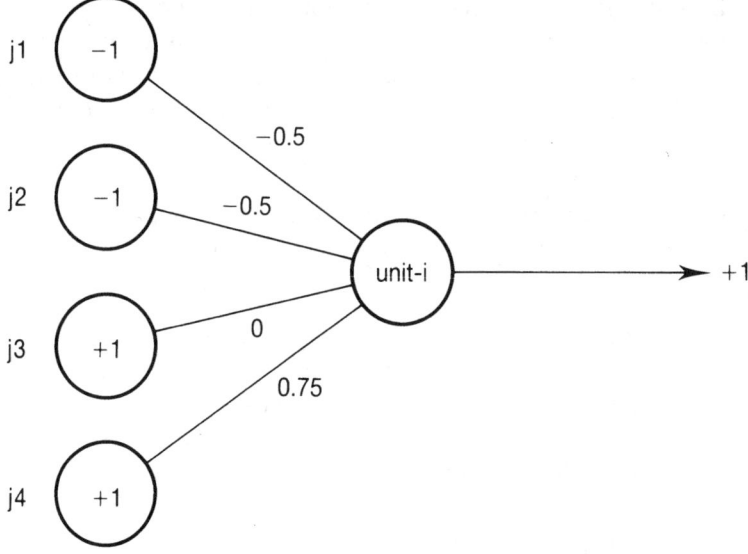

Figure 5.1 Diagram showing how the inputs from a number of units are combined to determine the overall input to unit-i. Unit-i has a threshold of 1; so if its net input exceeds 1, then it will respond with +1, but if the net input is less than 1, then it will respond with −1. (Source: Eysenck and Keane (1995: 11), reproduced by permission of Psychology Press)

node and each unit has many connections with other units (see Figure 5.1). The unit is analogous to a synapse and the connection to a neuron. Units affect other units by either exciting or inhibiting them. Units have *activation levels*, analogous to the *threshold of activation* in neural pathways, a number usually between the (arbitrary) limits 0 and 1, or −1 and +1, which fluctuate along with the activity around a unit. The strengths of connection between units are known as *weights* (w in Figure 5.1) and these carry a numerical description according to the strength of firing. The weight may be either positive or negative. With two active units A and B, A will tend to excite B if the weight of the A/B connection is positive. When the weight of the A/B connection is negative, A will tend to inhibit B. Because connectionist networks are usually densely interconnected, usually any unit will be simultaneously excited and inhibited by a host of other units, the activation of each unit calculated as the weighted sum of its inputs (see Figure 5.1). Connectionist processing ends when the system reaches a *stable state*; in other words, where activation through

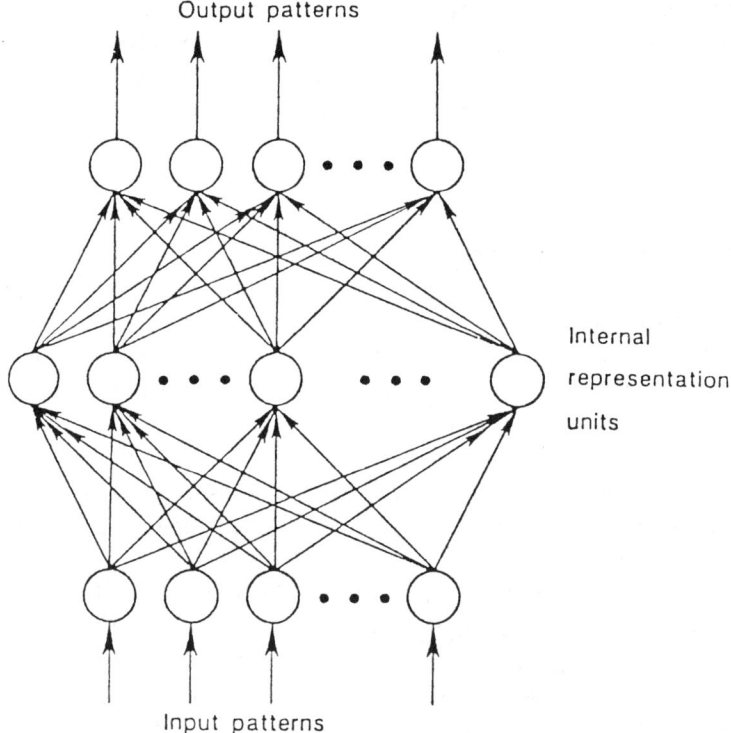

Figure 5.2 A multi-layered connectionist network with a layer of input units, a layer of internal representation units or hidden units, and a layer of output units. Input patterns can be encoded, if there are enough hidden units, in a form that allows the appropriate output pattern to be generated from a given input pattern. (Source: Rumelhart, McClelland and the PDP Research Group (1986: 320), reproduced by permission of The MIT Press)

the network does not lead to activation strengths in the units being changed.

I have indicated something of how a connectionist network bears some analogy to a neural network. This attempt to model neural behaviour distinguishes connectionist networks from symbolic computer modelling. But there are other differences. Understanding these differences we need to know something of two stages associated with connectionist networks: *training* and *testing*. Training involves setting up the networks so that a set of outputs concur with a set of inputs (see Figure 5.2). Let us say in response to a number of graphemes as input, we want the connectionist network to produce as output phonemes which correspond to these graphemes. To begin with, the network is trained with appropriate phoneme and grapheme data. Connections and weights are established so that for this data-set the connectionist network can accurately associate corresponding graphemes as output with phonemes as input. In order to achieve the appropriate connections, excitations and inhibitions, networks not only need a layer of input units and a layer of output units but also intermediate layers, or 'internal representation units' (see Figure 5.2). Because of the complexity of jigging connections and weights, the training process inevitably involves trial and error before the network has 'learned' the association between different inputs and outputs. To achieve such 'learning associations', *learning rules* are used to systematically calibrate the connection strengths between particular units. A widely known learning rule is the *backward propagation of errors rule (BACKPROP)*. Initially, the weight values within the network are randomised. In the early learning phase, following introduction of the input pattern, the output units often spawn responses that are not the desired outputs. To remedy this, BACKPROP compares the undesired output with the desired output, registering the errors. What it then does is to backpropagate activation though the network modifying the connection strengths until the desired output pattern is produced.

In order to see whether it can go beyond its training and deal with new instances, following training the connectionist network is then *tested* with new data. In other words, the connectionist network is tested to see whether it has 'learned' a particular behaviour. There is an analogy here with neural structure and learning. If we think of our own learning, say as children finding the right shaped hole for particular objects, a certain amount of trial and error is involved in training ourselves to accomplish such tasks. This is because a certain amount of time is necessary before appropriate neural connections can be established so that a particular behaviour can be reproduced successfully on subsequent occasions. What is interesting about 'learning associations' between input and output in connectionist networks is that cognitive processes are portrayed without appealing to the kind of explicit rules characteristic of symbolic models (despite the infelicitous phrase, learning *rules*). All the same, when the network works with new input subsequent to training (that is, once the network has 'learned' to create a particular response at the output layer), it may appear that a rule of the form 'If X then Y' is being followed. Connectionist networks have been employed in a variety of ways. For example, in Sejnowski and Rosenberg's (1987) network, NETtalk, following a BACKPROP learning rule, the network was given graphemic inputs and informed of the correctness of the phonemic outputs (I was alluding to this network above). On each training, the automatic learning procedure modified the connection strengths, bringing the system closer to the desired output. After this training, when further English graphemic input was introduced in testing, the network was able to produce a 90 per cent accurate phonemic output. NETtalk appeared then to have 'learned' 'English pronunciation rules' although of course it was not programmed with explicit rules.

In general, two kinds of network have been employed: *localised* and *distributed* networks. In *localised* networks each unit stands for an object or property. So in a localised network model for word recognition, each unit would represent an aspect about a feature, letter or word (see, for example, Feldman and Ballard 1982; Rumelhart and Norman 1982; Cottrell and Small 1983). In *distributed* networks, on the other hand, representation of a particular phenomenon is over a set of units. In other words, representation is consonant with distributed patterns of activation (Rumelhart, McClelland and the PDP Research Group 1986).

5.2.5 Sub-symbols/Microfeatures

One important characteristic of distributed representations is their *sub-symbolic* nature. In contrast to those operating within symbolism, connectionists do not regard cognition as the computation of structured symbolic strings. Instead, they hold that a lexical item such as 'ball' will be construed differently in a distributed representation in accordance with the particular semantico-syntactic environment. This is because in a distributed representation concepts are profiled in terms of sub-features. 'Ball', for example, could be profiled with the following sub-features for 'sphericalness'/'non-sphericalness', 'hollowness'/ 'non-hollowness', 'hardness'/'softness', and so on. These sub-features are termed *sub-symbols* or *microfeatures*. Consider the following:

1. The toddler kicked the ball.
2. The batsman struck the ball and it smashed the window.

Looking at 'ball' in terms of microfeatures, the likely meaning of 'ball' in the above depends on the environmental constraints. That is, from a connectionist perspective, the environment of 1. might be said to inhibit the microfeatures 'non-hollow' and 'hardness' and excite instead 'hollowness' and 'softness'. The opposite would be the case for sentence 2. (I show in the next section that the probabilities of microfeature inhibition and excitation are one of the fundamentals of a connectionist network.) The 'concepts' of ball in sentences 1 and 2 in connectionist network processing can be activated over a distributed representation. I flag 'concepts' with inverted commas since for Smolensky (1995/1988) our conscious, verbal notion of a stable, well-defined 'ball' is merely an approximation. Instead 'concept' is a convenient fiction that stands for the convergence of situationally specific aspects of a ball which are *emergent* in cognition. For Smolensky (1995/1988: 68) the differences between the symbolic and connectionist paradigms can be seen in their approaches to context:

> in the symbolic paradigm, the context of a symbol is manifest *around* it and consists of *other* symbols; in the sub-symbolic paradigm, the context of a symbol is manifest *inside* it and consists of sub-symbols. [my italics]

Smolensky's emphasis on the microfeatural level is also endorsed by other cognitive scientists:

> In our view, the most interesting relation between subsymbolic emergence and symbolic computation is one of *inclusion,* in which we see symbols as a higher-level description of properties that are ultimately embedded in an underlying distributed system . . . symbols are not taken at face value; they are seen as approximate macrolevel descriptions of operations whose governing principles reside at a subsymbolic level.
> (Varela, Thompson and Rosch 1991: 101–2)

However, while Smolensky argues that symbols are approximators of sub-symbols, the actual relationship between symbols and sub-symbols in cognition still needs to be accounted for in much greater detail.

Let me now consider a connectionist approach to the modelling of *sentence* processing. The connectionist approach to modelling that I want to consider is that of McClelland and Kawamoto (1986). The reason I outline McClelland and Kawamoto (1986) is principally to problematise symbolic assumptions of mental representation in CDA and thus what is highlighted in CDA as mystifying text. Why is McClelland and Kawamoto (1986) a suitable choice to accomplish this? First, it is one of the foundational papers in connectionism, deriving from the connectionist 'bible', McClelland, Rumelhart and the PDP Research Group (1986). Its ideas and principles continue to be used in present-day connectionism and accordingly it is one of the most cited papers in connectionism. Indeed, given the significance of McClelland and Kawamoto (1986), and the influence it has exerted, I will refer in other parts of this chapter to connectionist models of sentence processing and text processing which build on it, that is McClelland, St John and Taraban (1989) and St John and McClelland (1992). The latter are also well-known and well-cited articles in connectionism.

5.3 AN OUTLINE OF MCCLELLAND AND KAWAMOTO'S CONNECTIONIST MODEL OF SENTENCE PROCESSING

5.3.1 Outline of McClelland and Kawamoto

McClelland and Kawamoto (1986) display in a simplified way how the capacity of connectionist models for simultaneous interactive processing of syntax and semantics might be utilised in sentence comprehension and in the assigning of semantic roles (for example, agent) to parts of a sentence. McClelland and Kawamoto (1986) refer to semantic roles as *case roles*. They were interested to see whether a network could generalise its learning by providing accurate case-role assignment for sentences different from those in training. The model is a distributed one and comprises two sets of units: one for representing the syntactic structure of the sentence and one for representing the case (semantic) role structure. The model is trained so as to 'learn' the association between sentential input and the desired output of correct case-role assignment. In testing (that is, subsequent to training), the model is presented with new surface-structure sentential input and the output the model produced is examined to see if the model has successfully matched case structure to surface structure. The sentences processed in the model comprise a verb and from one to three noun phrases, of which one is always a subject. If an object noun phrase is present, there may also be another noun phrase as a sub-constituent of a prepositional phrase. An example sentence is 'The boy broke the window with the hammer'.

Words from the input sentences in training are represented as groups of microfeatures. For both nouns and verbs, the features are assembled into dimensions, and for each dimension there is a set of microfeatures. I detail the dimensions and microfeatures in Figure 5.3. The noun dimensions in Figure 5.3 are fairly self-explanatory. The verb dimensions in Figure 5.3 are regarded as capturing aspects of a scenario designated by the verb. The following unpacks the verb dimensions:

>   DOER – whether agent initiates an event.
>   CAUSE – whether verb is causal. If not, this dimension indicates whether this is due to an absence of a specified cause, 'The window broke', or because there is no change, 'The boy touched the girl'.
>   TOUCH – whether the Agent, Instrument, both, or neither touches the Patient.

NOUNS

DIMENSION	MICROFEATURES			
HUMAN	human	nonhuman		
SOFTNESS	soft	hard		
GENDER	male	female	neuter	
VOLUME	small	medium	large	
FORM	compact	1-D	2-D	3-D
POINTINESS	pointed	rounded		
BREAKABILITY	fragile	unbreakable		
OBJ-TYPE	food	toy	tool	utensil
	furniture	animate	natural-inanimate	

VERBS

DIMENSION	MICROFEATURES				
DOER	yes	no			
CAUSE	yes	no-cause	no-change		
TOUCH	agent	instrument	both	none	AisP
NAT_CHNG	pieces	shreds	chemical	none	unused
AGT_MVMT	trans	part	none	NA	
PT_MVMT	trans	part	none	NA	
INTENSITY	low	high			

[AisP = Agent is Patient; NA = not applicable]

Figure 5.3 Microfeatures for Noun and Verb Dimensions

> AisP – coincidence of Agent and Patient as in ergatives, for example, 'The cat moved'.
> NAT_CHNG – nature of change in the Patient.
> AGT_MVMT – movement of the Agent.
> PT_MVMT – movement of the Patient.
> INTENSITY – forcefulness of action.
> Note that 'Patient' is a case (semantic) role equivalent to 'affected' or 'goal'.

The dimensions and values in Figure 5.3 are chosen on the basis that they are often salient ones, particularly in the case of verbs, in case-role assignment. However, the authors are explicit about the fact that these dimensions and microfeatures should not be regarded as comprehensive (McClelland and Kawamoto 1986: 278).

5.3.2 How the Model Shades Meaning

In the model, a word is represented by a *vector* (an ordered pattern of distributed representation) in which one microfeature of a dimension is ON and the other is OFF. Microfeatures that are ON are represented in the vectors as 1s. OFF values are represented as dots ('.'). In the training inputs, the noun 'ball' was assigned the microfeature SOFT (SO). Going back to the noun dimension table in Figure 5.3, the microfeatures for the dimension, SOFTNESS, are SOFT and HARD in that order. So the training inputted microfeature value of SOFTNESS for 'ball' was (1.) (see below and refer to the noun dimension table in Figure 5.3 for the significance of HU, GND and so on):

```
        HU    SO   GND  VOL   FORM   PO   BR   OBJ_TYP
ball    .1    1.   ..1   1..   1...   .1   .1   .1 .....
```

However, following training, when the model was tested with the sentence 'The ball broke the vase', the output for the SOFTNESS dimension of 'ball' was (.1); the microfeature HARD was activated instead of SOFT. In a sense, this could be treated as an 'error' since the model had been trained with the information that 'balls' were SOFT. However, the adjustment that the model made was perfectly reasonable since all of the other instruments of BREAKING (for example, 'rock', 'baseball-bat', 'hammer' and so on) were HARD. The model responded to this and shaded its interpretation of the meaning of 'ball' in 'The ball broke the vase' accordingly. For the model, while 'balls' may be SOFT, 'balls-used-for-breaking' are HARD. This property of the model to shade meaning according to lexical environment is impressive to connectionist commentators such as Clark (1989: 109):

> this property, which comes for free with parallel distributed storage and retrieval (at least with all genuinely *distributed* approaches), allows PDP models to provide a mechanism well suited to supporting a variety of important semantic phenomena. Of all the interesting properties of such models, this one, I believe, most firmly fixes any conceptual or qualitative advantages that PDP might have over other approaches. And indeed, McClelland and Kawamoto themselves describe the capacity to represent 'a huge palette of shades of meaning' as being 'perhaps . . . the paramount reason why the distributed approach appeals to us'.
> (1986: 314)

This shading of meaning in the model concurs with the flexibility and holistic grasp that humans enjoy and so in a sense the connectionist network's ability to shade meaning can be treated as some kind of illumination of what takes place in human neural networks (Clark 1989: 108). A further point to make is that microfeatural shading of meaning is *automatic* in connectionist networks. Shading of meaning in humans intuitively appears to be an automatic process. Again, since connectionist networks attempt brain network simulation, then this lends support to the idea that shading of meaning in the brain actually is an automatic process. To put this another way, since non-compositional processing of words in a sentence is automatic in a connectionist network, this lends support to the notion that non-compositional processing of words is automatic in humans too. All this conflicts with the symbolic notion of compositionality in mental representations that we saw in the previous chapter.

Section 4.5 explained how compositionality, rather than being an analytical procedure, has been tacitly treated as being a psychologically real facet of cognition in CDA. So, for example, I commented on how Fairclough isolates the process 'flock' from its semantico-syntactic environment as though it functioned compositionally in mental representation as a discrete symbol. However, the capacity for semantic closure and multiple constraint satisfaction of McClelland and Kawamoto's connectionist model, that is, non-compositional/sub-symbolic processing, problematises this symbolic assumption of mental compositionality.

5.3.3 How the Model Assigns Case (Semantic) Roles

As I have stated, McClelland and Kawamoto (1986) were interested to see if their model could correctly assign case (semantic) roles to sentential input. As an example, let me focus on the verb 'break'. The network was given the training input for 'break' as follows:

	DO	CAU	TOUCH	N_CHG	A_MV	P_MV	IN
broke	1.	1..	.1...	1....	.1..	..1.	.1

(See the verb dimensions in Figure 5.3 for full versions of abbreviations.)

After completion of all other training, the network was tested to see if it could successfully assign the correct output case (semantic) roles (see Table 5.1, right-hand column) to the sentential input (Table 5.1, left-hand column).

Table 5.1

SENTENTIAL INPUT	CORRECT CASE ROLES
The boy broke the window with the hammer	(brokeAVPI)
The dog broke the plate	(brokeAVP)
The hammer broke the vase	(brokeIVP)
The plate broke	(brokePV)

[A = agent; P = patient (equivalent to 'goal' or 'affected'); I = instrument; V = verb]

In order to see if the model could provide contextually correct case-role readings of the verb 'break', the model was required to assign to each of the sentences in the left-hand column in Table 5.1 the appropriate microfeature pattern set from the patterns shown in Table 5.2. In testing, the model was able to do this successfully.

Table 5.2

	DO	CAU	TOUCH	N_CHG	A_MV	P_MV	IN
broke AVPI	1 .	1 ..	. 1 ...	1	. 1 ..	.. 1 .	. 1
broke AVP	1 .	1 ..	1	1	. 1 ..	.. 1 .	. 1
broke IVP	1 .	. 1 .	. 1 ...	1	... 1	.. 1 .	. 1
broke PV	1 .	. 1 .	... 1 .	1	. 1 ..	.. 1 .	. 1

Let me proceed now to consider what McClelland and Kawamoto (1986: 288) say about the success of the model to provide case-role representations (what they refer to as case-frame representations or slots) for the sentences in Table 5.1:

> Several things should be said about case-frame representations. **The first thing is that the slots should not be seen as containing lexical items**. Rather, they should be seen as containing patterns that specify some of the semantic properties assigned by the model to the *entities* designated by the words in the sentences. Thus, the pattern of feature values for the verb *break* specifies that in this instance (*the boy broke the window with the hammer*) there is contact between the Instrument and the Patient. This would also be the case in a sentence like *The hammer broke the window*. However, in a sentence like *The boy broke the window*, with no Instrument specified, the pattern of feature values specifies contact between the Agent and the Patient. Thus, the verb features provide a partial description of the scenario described by the sentence. The noun features, likewise, provide a partial description of the players in the scenario, and these descriptions . . . may actually be modulated by the model to take on attributes appropriate for the scenario in question. [my bold]

For McClelland and Kawamoto (1986: 316) features in the input representation are not necessarily preserved in the output representation of the connectionist network:

***all* the words work together to provide clues to the case frame representation of the sentence**, and *none* of the words uniquely or completely determine the representation that is assigned to any of the constituents of the underlying scenario. [my bold]

In the previous chapter I discussed how CDA authors associated semantic meaning with the nature of a syntactic category. This is particularly the case with nominals. In CDA, if an event is described with nominalisations, the event is commonly regarded as being objectified, thus mystifying the dynamics of the event. For McClelland and Kawamoto (1986), both verb and noun features provide only *partial* excitations and inhibitions of activation patterns, and the individual 'verbs' and 'nouns' of the input are not even present in the output pattern of activation. McClelland and Kawamoto's (1986) connectionist perspective on language processing output thus problematises the symbolic CDA focus upon the syntactic nature of the units in an expression and in turn the ascribing of meaning to the syntactic nature of a constituent, that is, that a nominal expression will be mentally reflexed as a 'thing'. In turn, their connectionist model thus problematises the CDA notion that when nominals are used to describe events, their syntactic nature necessarily mystifies the dynamics of the event. Indeed, from a connectionist perspective, syntactic and semantic information are always integrated (see also Churchland and Churchland 1996: 238), further ruling out a compositional isolation of a syntactic category and ascribing meaning to it. Finally, the integration of semantic and syntactic information in connectionism also conflicts with the processing assumption of Fowler and Kress (1979a) and Kress (1993) (see 4.4.2 and 2.4.4) that people begin with a perceptual heuristic of subject-verb-object but may read across this structure and confuse semantic transitivity (transactivity) with syntactic transitives.

McClelland and Kawamoto (1986: 312–13) highlight how there are problems with treating case roles as being *unitary* since:

> some but not all of the Patient properties generally hold for the role nominally identified as Patient. Similarly, some but not all of the Agent properties generally hold for the role nominally identified as Agent. In certain cases, as with sentences like *The boy moved*, enough of these properties hold that we were led to assign *the boy* to both roles at once.

Trying to solve this problem by creating more roles leads to a proliferation which is 'ungainly . . . and detracts considerably from the utility of the idea of roles as useful descriptive constructs'. However, on a distributed representation made up of microfeatures:

> If each role is represented by a conjunction of role properties, then far more distinct roles can be represented on the same set of role units. Furthermore, what the Agent roles of two verbs have in common is captured by the overlap of the role features in the representation of their roles, and how they differ is captured by their differences. The notion of a role that represents a combined Agent/Patient as in *The boy moved* is no longer a special case, and we get out of assigning the same argument to two different slots.

McClelland and Kawamoto's (1986) idea of a distributed representation of case-roles (that is, without unitary status) has also been applied by Touretzky and Geva (1987) and is highlighted in McClelland, St John and Taraban (1989).

McClelland and Kawamoto's (1986) fine-grained approach to case (semantic) roles throws into relief the reductionism of coarse-grained semantic roles in Hallidayan metalanguage. Of course, the sharpness required of a tool depends on its purpose. If the purpose of Hallidayan meta-language is to highlight the broad semantic structure of a sentence, then this is acceptable. However, what can happen in CDA is that meaning is ascribed to the metalinguistic description of a sentence and used to bolster a particular interpretation. Often this meaning is 'in excess' of the actual meaning of the sentence, leading to over-interpretation. To indicate what I mean, consider the following leader (from *The Times*, 2 June 1975) and Trew's (1979: 102–3) analysis:

> THE RIOTS IN SALISBURY
> The rioting and sad loss of life in Salisbury are a warning that tension in that country is rising as decisive moves about its future seem to be in the offing. The leaders of the African National Council have ritually blamed the police, but deplore the factionalism that is really responsible.
>
> Trew: No mention is made of the 'police' except as those 'ritually blamed' – and note how even in this one reference the syntax has 'Africans' as agents and 'police' as affected participants (the victims of blaming!).

If we were to assign a fine-grained microfeatural profile to 'blame' in the above, we would designate *no-contact* (TOUCH) between Agent and Patient. There is also no *movement of the agent* (AGT_MVMT) nor *movement of the patient* (PT_MVMT). It is not, then, an instance of prototypical material transitivity. Since there is no PT_MVMT, the police are hardly candidates for being assigned the prototypical semantic role of 'affected'. Because of this, it is dubious to equate the semantic meaning of 'affected' with 'victims'. The coarse-grained analysis can be seen as projecting an extra meaning which suits Trew's line. We can see, then, that while grammatical metalanguage describes a clause, a certain type of use of the coarse-grained nature of Halliday's semantico-grammatical metalanguage not only describes the clause but can distort the nature of the scenario.

5.4 CONNECTIONISM AND INFERENCE GENERATION

5.4.1 Orientation

In this section, I refer to the connectionist models of St John and McClelland (1992) and of McClelland, St John and Taraban (1989), both of which build upon McClelland and Kawamoto (1986). Both sets of authors deal with connectionist processing of sentences but St John and McClelland (1992) also deal with short text ('story') processing. Like McClelland and Kawamoto (1986), both models are successful at 'extracting' information from a training input consisting of syntactically structured representations without being programmed as to syntactic rules. The issue I want to highlight in the connectionist networks of these authors is how these deal with *inference* generation. Given the constraints of the book and the fact that I have already outlined in some detail a connectionist sentential processing model, I confine myself to the broad principles and results of connectionist models in St John and McClelland (1992) and McClelland, St John and Taraban (1989). Another reason is that in Chapter 8, I provide a more detailed description of connectionist simulation of inference generation in short text processing.

5.4.2 Connectionism and Inference Generation

Both St John and McClelland (1992: 100) and McClelland, St John and Taraban (1989: 293) highlight the human ability to readily infer other constituents such as instruments when the context is sufficiently constraining. So, for example, in:

1. The boy spread the jelly on the bread
2. The knife was covered with poison

coherence between sentence 1 and sentence 2 is smooth for the above authors since 'knife' will be readily inferred in 1). Now, in the connectionist models of McClelland, St John and Taraban (1989) and St John and McClelland (1992), handling implied constituents is not a problem since inferences are an inherent part of sentence processing rather than an extra process. McClelland, St John and Taraban (1989: 316) explain why it was 'natural' for their connectionist network to 'learn' that eating steak always involved a knife as an instrument:

> There is no special 'inference step' required to fill in the knife. This is in part a direct result of the fact that there is no prior stipulation that a particular part of the representation of the sentence corresponds to the internal reflex of each particular constituent of the sentence. It's just that events described by sentences with 'ate' as the verb and 'steak' as the object always involve knives as instruments.

The prior stipulation that McClelland et al. (1989) refer to is Fodor and Pylyshyn's classical principle of compositionality (see 3.2.1). In contrast, the connectionist models in St John and McClelland (1992) and McClelland et al. (1989) do not construct a classical, compositional representation with combinatorial syntax and semantics. Given that connectionist models attempt some simulation of neural mechanisms, the above models raise the following prospects:

1. that humans can also understand sentences without representing them in a syntactically structured internal 'language' (mentalese).
2. in human processing, inference generation is not a special extra step but simultaneously integrative with the integrative processing of semantics and syntax.

Nevertheless, as Bechtel (1996a: 72) points out, some circumspection is necessary:

> St John and McClelland's network can only process a small fragment of English, and it remains a question whether networks of this kind could eventually handle the full range of complexity found in human natural languages. The answer to the question will only come from further empirical investigation.

Crucially, however, Bechtel does add that human ability should not be exaggerated, mistakes being common in the comprehension of complex sentences. Given this, networks should not be expected to perform better than humans when inputted with, for example, sentences with many clausal embeddings. Indeed Elman's (1990) connectionist network made exactly these kind of human errors. His network shows a discrepancy in the type of productivity it manifests and the kind of open-ended generative productivity in Chomskyan models. In a long sentence with more than three relative defining clauses, the network is prone to errors. Symbolic algorithms do not show such a failure pattern. This lack of open-ended productivity is not only in marked contrast with Chomsky's model, but also strengthens the case for connectionism over the symbolic paradigm as a better simulation of human language processing, given that limitation on open-ended productivity is a characteristic of human cognition as well. For an overview of Elman's (1990) network, see Bechtel and Abrahamsen (2002).

The connectionist principle that inferences are inherent to sentence processing and not an extra stage conflicts with the downgrading of importance of inference generation in symbolicism as well as its emphasis on syntactic processing, for example, Fodor, Fodor and Garrett (1975). It also conflicts with the neglect of inference generation in symbolic CDA in its focus on surface structure in its mystification analysis, for example, Fairclough's (2001) analysis of the 'Quarry load-shedding problem' text (see 4.7).

5.4.3 Strength of Interpretation in Short Text Processing

McClelland and St John (1992: 97) point out how 'traditional story processing algorithms have viewed comprehension as the sequential building and connecting of text-based propositions' (for example, Charniak 1983; Schank and Abelson 1977; van Dijk and Kintsch 1983; Wilensky 1983) as if each sentence were a context-free proposition. And indeed we have seen how some of CDA is along these lines, for example, Clark (1992) and Simpson (1993). However, St John and McClelland's (1992) model does not process sentences in this way. This is because the network exhibits 'parallel constraint satisfaction' where interpretation of a sentence is predicated on the strength with which other sentences constrain support for that interpretation. Here are St John and McClelland (1992: 122):

> The combined set of constraints from the text are used as evidence to support an interpretation that best satisfies the strongest and the most constraints from the text. Each part of the text supports many aspects of the interpretation. A specific

proposition, therefore, will constrain the interpretation to represent the information it contains explicitly, and also constrain it, to varying degrees, to represent correlated information. All of this correlated information constitutes inferences.

It is because the results of computation are not just based on context-free propositions that *extra* computational results (that is, inferences) are present as a natural consequence. As St John and McClelland (1992: 122) state: 'in parallel constraint satisfaction ... as in sentence comprehension, inference-making is inherent to processing the explicit text'.

Consider again the *Sun* text extract from Clark (1992: 215) that I quoted in 4.2.1 and Simpson's (1993: 170) commentary. From the basic principle of parallel constraint satisfaction – that of *global constraints* where all of the evidence from the text is involved – the 'weights' for Simpson's alternative scenario that 'someone else might have attacked' would be low. Simpson's view that it is a possible interpretation is emblematic of the *local* fixation CDA has on individual sentences, as if they were context-free propositions.

5.4.4 Summing-Up

In this section, I have highlighted how connectionism conflicts with symbolic accounts where inference generation is downplayed and syntactic processing made prominent. Inference generation is not a special, extra or subsequent process to syntactic processing but, by nature of connectionist models, intrinsic to linguistic processing. A corollary then for mystification analysis in CDA, and especially if connectionist networks are seen to provide some kind of simulation of human processing, is that connectionism problematises its concentration on surface structure to the detriment of inferential processes. The assumption of Trew (1979), subsequently endorsed in mystification analysis in CDA, that inference generation is an extra, separate step in sentence processing, and is then a weak representation, is also problematised. Furthermore, St John and McClelland's (1992) model takes into account how co-text affects interpretation of a sentence. This problematises CDA's often de-cotextualised focus on sentences. Indeed, if connectionist networks can be taken as some kind of simulation of human processing, then they would lend support for my analysis of 'flock' in 4.5. That is, the meaning of 'flock' will depend both on the co-text of 'flock' as well as on the nature of inferential processes resulting from that co-text. St John and McClelland's model would also problematise what we saw in 4.7: that Clark's (1992) compositional isolation of the verb 'attack' leads her to treat it as a euphemism, and thus mystifying, irrespective of how the general verb 'attack' could be 'filled in' by the reader with the aid of co-text.

Having detailed a model of sentence processing in 5.3, and having highlighted the centrality of inference generation to connectionist networks in 5.4, let me now widen the discussion to the issue of mental representation in connectionism and how this differs from the symbolic attitudes to mental representation in CDA.

5.5 CONNECTIONISM AND MENTAL REPRESENTATION

5.5.1 Gross Descriptivism versus Gross Internalism

In Clark (1996: 1–2), the following positions are listed in a discussion of whether there are mental analogues to folk psychological vocabulary such as 'concept':

i) *Gross Descriptivism*: The common-sense constructs (concepts, beliefs, propositionally identified contents etc.) are *nothing but* descriptions of large-scale behavioural dispositions of whole agents. According to this view, no neat inner analogues to the folk constructs are to be found.

ii) *Modest Internalism*: The common-sense constructs serve to pick out transient and/or large-scale features of internal (e.g. neural or computational organization). Examples might include the identification of concepts with distributed, context-dependent patterns of neural activity (see Clark, A., 1993) or the identification of mental images with temporarily time-locked activity in multiple neural regions (see Damasio, 1994). In such cases the folk items (images, concepts) do not have neat, highly manipulable and/or spatially localizable inner analogues. But there remain fairly robust patterns of widespread neural/computational activity which the folk discourse at times succeeds in tracking.

iii) *Gross Internalism*: The common-sense constructs (or, in this case, some favoured subset such as concepts or (most) lexical items) have matching, highly manipulable, object-like inner analogues, e.g. a complex thought, folk-psychologically described might thus appear as a complex inner state with independently manipulable parts which match the independently recombinable concepts we deploy in its common-sense characterization.

We can see that Hodge and Kress (1993), in highlighting 'transactives' as a privileged representation, chimes with 'gross internalism'. I indicated in 4.8 that Hallidayan functional grammar has had a strong influence on CDA interpretative practice. By returning to the quotes from Halliday's work in the 1970s in 4.8, work which was influential for Critical Linguistics, it should be apparent that his perspective that language 'embodies' thought chimes with *gross internalism*. Now, for McClelland and Kawamoto (1986: 316), 'words themselves are no longer present in the scenario'; for McClelland, St John and Taraban (1989: 316), 'there is no prior stipulation that a particular part of the representation of the sentence corresponds to the internal reflex of each particular constituent of the sentence'. That is, in their connectionist networks, linguistic input is not the same as output. In contrast to Halliday's gross internalism, this position chimes with *gross descriptivism*. So, if connectionist networks in some way simulate brain networks, then mental reality is less likely to be equivalent to linguistic symbols, *pace* the Hallidayan position; rather, linguistic symbols are input cues for mental activity which thus goes beyond the input.

Now, consider the following:

The propositional attitude statement provides a gloss on the system's state, but not a description of its internal structure.
(Bechtel and Abrahamsen 1991: 290)

The currency of our systems is not symbols, but excitation and inhibition.
(Rumelhart and McClelland 1986: 132)

Connectionist networks dispense with internalist propositionally based representation consisting of symbols. So from the vantage point of a connectionist network, CDA's simple – the transactive – would lose its privileged status. This is not only because propositions in connectionism are merely glosses of the system. Symbolic representations are discrete, highly grammatical and concatenatively compositional. These are all features of transactives. Connectionist distributed representations, on the contrary, are continuous, non-grammatical and non-concatenative (Miikkulainen 1993: 21), that is, all features which do not characterise transactives.

5.5.2 Representation versus Enactment

In Chapter 3, I outlined the philosophical position known as logical empiricism. The simple in logical empiricism is connected with the notion of epistemological foundation (foundation of knowledge). Indeed, the desire for providing epistemological foundations is actually prevalent throughout the history of philosophy, common to both empiricist and rationalist traditions:

> [philosophy] understands the foundations of knowledge, and it finds these foundations in a study of man-as-knower, of the 'mental processes' or the 'activity of representation' which make knowledge possible. To know is to represent accurately what is outside the mind; so to understand the possibility and nature of knowledge is to understand the way in which the mind is able to construct such representations. Philosophy's central concern is to be a general theory of representation . . .
>
> (Rorty 1980: 3)

But in connectionist philosophy, inspired by a desire to ape brain behaviour in some way, there has been a shift away from concerns of representation. The principal activity of networks is their *self-modification* rather than representing the external world.

As an outline of such a perspective, consider the following from Schopman and Shawky (1996: 69–70):

> during the course of learning the neural structure reorganizes itself, so that the result is a changed internal structure. This structural change cannot be called a representation of the original input, because the restructuring is the outcome of an interactive process between the state of the organism and the input. That means that the changed structure does not represent the external world, but it represents – if one wants to stick to the term – the interactive process: input-organism's or environment-organism's interaction. Thus, one can say that it has a relation with the input, the external world . . . one can say that the learned structure-change has its own intrinsic semantics; nothing has to be ascribed to it and it requires no external interpretation. The important consequence for our story is that the problem of how to find the semantic relation has evaporated.

Let me just dwell a moment on 'the problem of how to find the semantic relation has evaporated'. In 3.3, I outlined how logical empiricism strove to mirror a pre-given world that is constituted by well-defined objects with well-defined properties, with the objects standing in fixed relations. This desire, from the connectionist perspective outlined by Schopman and Shawky, is no longer a concern. There is a shift away from the idea of a world being independent to the idea that understanding of the world is inseparable from the patterns of self-modification. As for Schopman and Shawky, for Varela et al. (1991: 140) such systems do not work on the basis of representation. Crucially, 'instead of *representing* an independent world, they *enact* a world as a domain of distinctions that is inseparable from the structure embodied by the cognitive system'. Viewing cognition in terms of *enactment*, the realism–idealism dichotomy is circumvented. That is, we no longer have to see linguistic description as 'mirroring' the world [realism]; nor do we see our linguistic representations of the world as mediating between the world and what we can know of it [idealism]. Instead, sentences are cues or *enactors* of understanding of the world, not representations [whether realist or idealist] of the world or of cognitive processes. The circumvention of the realist–idealist dichotomy is attractive for another reason. It avoids the realist emphasis on 'exact match'. Since 'connections between actions and the facts of the world can be represented as statistical correlations' and 'connectionist reasoning is evidential rather than logical' (Waltz 1989: 58), instead of *exact match* we have something like *best fit*. A connectionist perspective on mental representation does not require the assumption that the world was contrived to be recognised by humans nor that humans are bestowed with a ready-made key to it all. Sentences are not direct reflections of structures in the external world, *pace* a Carnapian logical empiricist perspective and *pace* the inadvertent use of this perspective in CDA (see Chapter 4).

5.5.3 Connectionism and the 'Representational' Language of Science

For the connectionist philosopher, Bechtel (1996b), rather than being something innate, 'our knowledge of grammar, for example, may consist in knowledge of *procedures* for comprehending and producing sentences in spoken or written speech' (Bechtel 1996b: 127). On the basis of such a perspective, then 'written documents are not transcriptions of our mental representations, but specifically constructed representations with which we have learned to interact' (1996b: 128). That is, natural language text provides an externalist rather than internalist system of 'representations'. Bechtel develops this point by asserting (1996b: 141) that although scientific theories may take a sentential form:

> these representations are not translations of what is in the heads of the scientists; rather, they are devices used by scientists. Scientific theories may take a sentential form even if, in using

these theories, scientists rely on weights on connections within their heads. Consequently, we should not seek to localize the story of scientific development in representations and processes occurring in the head. Instead, we need to take seriously the fact that scientists are situated cognizers whose cognitive processes involve interactions with external representations as well as physical devices.

All this problematises the analysis of scientific language in Hodge and Kress (1993) (see 4.2.2). This is because their analysis of scientific language is predicated upon the notion that discrete 'scientific' transactive sentences can reflect reality, and in turn become a mental representation which is directly reflective of that reality. Bechtel (1996b) would also conflict with the notion in Ogborn et al. (1996: 51), outlined in 4.6.2, that nominal descriptions of scientific phenomena (for example, evaporation, crystallisation, ionisation, speciation, oscillation) mean they are treated mentally as 'things'. As a final point, Bechtel's view of text as not being a transcription of mental representation but rather an external device for interaction with a human cogniser is on a par with the notion of language as a set of cues rather than a representational medium (see 4.2.2 and 5.5.2). In turn, all of this conflicts with the internalism in CDA, internalism which is warranted on a Hallidayan outlook (4.8).

5.6 ENDPOINTS

In this chapter, I have shown how connectionist principles problematise those of symbolicism. By extension, I have shown how these principles problematise language processing assumptions in symbolic CDA and in turn how CDA highlights mystifying language and manipulative language generally. While connectionism is still in its 'infancy', the ability of connectionist networks to shade meaning non-compositionally and to include inference generation as an integrative part of language processing are features which capture the automatic flexibility and holistic grasp of meaning in human language processing more readily than approaches we saw in Chapter 3. This is especially pertinent given that one of the aims of connectionist networks is to provide some simulation of human neural network activity. In Chapter 7, we shall see that the capacity of connectionist networks to tie in with the above aspects of human language processing is in fact supported by psycholinguistic evidence.

CHAPTER 6

Cognitive Linguistics

6.1 INTRODUCTION

In this chapter, I outline the enterprise of *cognitive linguistics*, an enterprise with many similarities to connectionism. I do this so as to indicate how cognitive linguistics problematises symbolism and in turn assumptions of language cognition in CDA, as well as how CDA highlights mystifying text. Another function of this chapter is to set out elements of cognitive linguistics which will find their way into the idealised reader framework of Section C. In 3.4, I mapped out the classical theory of categories which, as we saw, is bound up with symbolicism. A salient assumption in the classical theory is that categories are defined in terms of a set of necessary and sufficient conditions. In the postwar period, a number of philosophers and linguists, gathering momentum under the banner of cognitive linguistics, began to challenge this classical postulate. Notable among these challenges is Lakoff's (1987a) *Women, Fire and Dangerous Things*, as well as the experimental work of Rosch. Lakoff terms the classical theory of categories – 'objectivism'. In objectivism, (1) no members are better examples of a category than other members, and (2) categories are independent of human neurophysiology.

Cognitive linguistics is founded on the rebuttal of the absoluteness of (1) and (2). In 6.2 and 6.3, I discuss the cognitive linguistic dissension from (1) and (2) respectively. In this chapter, I draw much on the seminal work of Lakoff (1987a), given its continuing significance in the field of cognitive linguistics. I also draw much on Ungerer and Schmid (1996), one of the best-known overviews of work in cognitive linguistics.

6.2 CATEGORIES AND PROTOTYPICALITY

6.2.1 Prototype Effects

Early Rosch

In the early to mid-1970s, the results of a series of experiments conducted by Eleanor Rosch cast doubt on the notion that category membership was along the lines of Aristotelian absoluteness (see 3.4.1). In Rosch (1975b), for example, students were asked to assess the 'typicality' of members of certain categories. Subjects tended to define categories (for example, 'bird') by identifying certain prototypical members of the category (for example, 'robin'), where there exists the greatest density of attributes for the category (for example, 'can fly'); they recognised other non-prototypical members (for example, 'ostrich') that differ in various ways from the prototypical ones. Rosch's experimental results, then, conflict with the assumption inherent within the classical theory that no members should be better examples of the categories than any other members. This is not to say that all of the objectivist or classical theory is challenged by Rosch's results (Lakoff 1987a: 586). Certain geometrical shapes such as squares and spheres can be described by a complete set of necessary and sufficient conditions, although what constitutes the expected size, for example, of such shapes may be grounded in prototypicality (Armstrong et al. 1983).

Referring to Rosch's results, Lakoff (1987b: 63) highlights how prototype effects were interpreted in two ways as indicating something *direct* about the nature of categorisation:

i) *The Effects = Structure Interpretation*: Goodness-of-example ratings are a direct reflection of degree of category membership.
ii) *The Prototype = Representation Interpretation*: Categories are represented in the mind in terms of prototypes (that is, best examples). Degrees of category membership for other entities are determined by their degree of similarity to the prototype.

Later Rosch's More Tentative Position

In the early part of her career, Rosch accepted the above as valid interpretations of her experimental results. Later, she (1978: 40–1) was to form a more tentative position:

> The pervasiveness of prototypes in real-world categories and of prototypicality as a variable indicates that prototypes must have

some place in psychological theories of representation, processing, and learning. However, prototypes themselves do not constitute any particular model of processes, representations, or learning. This point is so often misunderstood that it requires discussion:

1. To speak of a *prototype* is simply a convenient grammatical fiction; what is really referred to are judgments of degree of prototypicality . . .
2. Prototypes do not constitute any particular processing model for categories . . .
3. Prototypes do not constitute a theory of representation for categories . . . As with processing models, the facts about prototypes can only constrain, but do not determine, models of representation . . .
4. Although prototypes must be learned, they do not constitute any particular theory of category learning.

Lakoff (1987a: 44–5) elaborates upon this position. In the early to mid-1970s, empirical goodness-of-example ratings were taken as supporting the notion that a penguin is less a member of the category 'bird' than a robin. But this was later regarded as a mistaken interpretation of the data because the responses by subjects as to the goodness-of-example are just *ratings*. And indeed, as Lakoff (1987a: 45) states, the ratings fit in with the interpretation that the category *bird* has tight parameters and that robins, owls and penguins are all full members of this category. Lakoff, then, tallies with Rosch's circumspection. He goes on to state that prototype effects are really 'superficial' in the sense that they are *by-products* of 'internal structure'. In Lakoff (1987a: 45), 'prototype effects result from the nature of cognitive models, which can be viewed as "theories" of some subject matter'. He gives the example of the pope as a non-prototypical bachelor.[1] A prototype effect arises here because of a lack of 'fit' between two cognitive models: one for bachelor and one for the pope.[2]

Barsalou

For Lakoff (1987a: 45–6), the work of Barsalou (1983) confirms that prototype effects arise from the nature of cognitive models. Barsalou focuses on *ad hoc categories*: non-conventional categories which are created 'on the fly' for some particular goal in a particular context, for example, 'things to take from one's home during a fire'. Certain things (such as one's children) can be regarded as prototypical and others (such as a box of paper clips) as non-prototypical. However, despite the fact that the category is non-conventional, it can be said to have a prototype structure. For Barsalou, such a non-conventional category is determined by goals, and goals are part of a speaker's cognitive models. From a Lakoffian perspective then, prototype effects arise when a cognitive model for one thing (such as paper clips), which includes understanding of habitual purposes, fails to fit with the 'on-the-fly' created cognitive model. The importance also of goals in the type of prototype effects created becomes clear when we see that in Rosch's early experiments the respondents' goal was to deliver ratings of typicality of particular categories.

Co-Text Dependency of Prototype Effects

What Barsalou's non-conventional examples also indicate is that prototype effects are context-dependent. Context can also include *co-text*, the surrounding text. Co-textual influence on prototype generation is appreciable in the following, taken from Ungerer and Schmid (1996: 43–4) (see also Roth and Shoben 1983):

  i) The hunter took his gun, left the lodge and called his dog
  ii) She took her dog to the salon to have its curls reset

The first dog prototypically would be a retriever while the prototype for the second sentence might be a pekinese. Outside the above co-texts, a retriever could be construed as a prototypical dog but a pekinese is unlikely to be. What these examples indicate is that Rosch was right to adopt a more tentative position, since the influence of context (including co-text), engagement of cognitive models and specific goals indicate that prototypes are created 'on the fly' rather than being stored representations; see also Rosch (1978: 42–3) for a discussion of the role of context in prototype effects. All this is not to deny the reality or salience in human reasoning of prototype effects:

> In many cases, prototypes act as *cognitive reference points* of various sorts and form the basis for inferences (Rosch 1975a, 1981). The study of human inference is part of the study of human reasoning and conceptual structure; hence, those prototypes used in making inferences must be part of conceptual structure.
> (Lakoff 1987a: 45)

The importance of prototypes to inference generation will become apparent in Section C of this book.

Having introduced the phenomenon of prototypicality, I now outline the relationship between prototypicality and syntactic categories, going on to highlight implications for CDA.

6.2.2 Prototypicality and Syntactic Categories

For Lakoff (1987a: 57) it is important to see that prototype effects arise not only in non-linguistic conceptual structure, but in linguistic structure also. Indeed, the work of Hopper and Thompson (1985) has indicated that the status of a word within its respective grammatical category is by no means a fixed property. The extent to which (1) a noun refers to an identifiable, enduring entity and (2) whether the verb refers to a specific dynamic event can vary. Moreover, in line with what I have indicated about the co-textual influence on prototype generation, the variation in typicality of verbs and nouns is also dependent on co-text. As illumination of all this, consider the following sentences:

1. The lorry shed its load on the building site
2. Load-shedding is frequent on the building site

The verb, 'shed', is marked for tense, polarity, mood and voice. The noun, 'load', could also appear as singular or plural, and be preceded by a determiner, adjective(s) and so on. A whole range of typical verb and noun properties are possible because in sentence 1 'load' refers prototypically to a discrete, identifiable entity and 'shed' refers prototypically to a single, identifiable event. In sentence 2, however, 'load' does not refer to a discrete identifiable entity, and 'shed' does not refer to a single identifiable event. The generality of sentence 2 also leads to a loss of nounhood status for 'load-shedding' and thus a reduction of the prospects for plural inflection and determiner modification. '*The* load-shedding is frequent on the building site'; *Five* load-sheddings *are* frequent on the building site' and so on would have a restricted usage at best. It follows that 'load-shedding' is a non-prototypical noun in sentence 2.

Now, recall, in 4.7, Fairclough's (2001: 43) analysis of the news text with the headline 'Quarry load-shedding problem'. Here is part of Fairclough's analysis of this headline: 'The grammatical form in which the headline is cast is that of *nominalization*: a process is expressed as a *noun*, as if it were an entity.' An assumption here is that mystification can occur because the reader is prevented from seeing reality in active terms. Understanding of the dynamism of the reality (that is, the nature of the causal relationship and agent responsibility) is prevented by the 'objectifying' effects of the nominalisation. But we have seen that it is possible that a gerund such as 'load-shedding' can suffer decategorisation, particularly if it is used generally rather than referring to a single identifiable entity. 'Load-shedding' is not connected to a single identifiable entity in 'Quarry load-shedding problem' and so cannot be considered to be a prototypical noun. Besides, here 'load-shedding' functions as a modifier. And so the morphological and distributional attributes of the noun class are even more reduced, making 'load-shedding' in this context even more of a non-prototypical noun. In Chapters 4 and 5, we saw that much of CDA's approach to mental representation was predicated upon an *internalist* view of mind. Since 'load-shedding' in the headline is a non-prototypical noun, on an internalist view the reader's mental representation of 'load-shedding' would not be so 'entity-like'.

The oddness of seeing all nouns as entities can be seen by considering the lexical items 'verb' and 'nominalisation', the latter being a central facet of Hodge and Kress's (1993) conceptual apparatus. Does the nounhood status of 'verb' impede understanding that a great number of verbs are processes? Does the nounhood status of 'nominalisation' prevent understanding that this term refers to a process, that is, the process of making verbs into nouns? On Hodge and Kress's reasoning the answer would have to be in the affirmative, but this paradoxically would problematise their use of the concept 'nominalisation' since its grammatical form would mystify understanding of how such processes are supposed to mystify. All the above problematising can also be applied to Fowler's (1986: 20) treatment of 'my wife' (see 4.5). In other words, Fowler ignores the fact that there are prototypical uses of 'my' to indicate possession ('my wallet') as well as non-prototypical uses ('my round of drinks') where possession diminishes as a feature of the situation. Similar points can be made against how Hodge and Kress (1993: 23–4) regard nouns such as 'ban' and 'production' (see 4.6.1). In the light of all this, and as I argued in Chapter 5, it is unwise to simply 'read off' meaning from metalinguistic descriptions of syntax.

In 6.1 I covered how, in objectivism, 'categories are independent of human neurophysiology'. I now move to a discussion of the basic level of categorisation, a type of category salient in cognitive linguistic explanations, which is linked to human neurophysiology and is thus in tension with the above precept of objectivism.

6.3 BASIC-LEVEL CATEGORIES

6.3.1 Orientation

To begin this section, let me outline the findings of Berlin et al. (1974). The aim of their project was to scrutinise the 'folk taxonomy' used by the

Tzeltal (a community in southern Mexico) for classifying and naming the plants in their environment, as well as to compare this taxonomy with Western scientific classifications. It was found that Tzeltal plant categories were most numerous on the *generic* level with 471 genera, for example, corn, bean, pine, willow. In contrast, the number of superordinate categories was exceedingly low, with no more than four plant names – tree, vine, grass, broad-leafed plant. 'Species' was well represented but membership was more restricted than on the generic level, there being 273 species, for example, genuine pine, red pine, white bean, common bean. The level below species was minimal, consisting of five plant names, such as red common bean and black common bean. Generic categories were not only more numerous than categories on other levels but were the ones that were most commonly chosen by Tzeltal speakers. Moreover, in Tzeltal, culturally salient categories are much more likely to be generic categories than superordinate ones. For example, 'corn' and 'beans' form two basic ingredients of the Tzeltal diet (see also Ungerer and Schmid (1996) for a precis of Berlin et al. (1974)).

What is interesting about the folk taxonomy in Tzeltal compared to folk taxonomies used by English speakers is that the latter's cognitively basic level is also the generic level. Generic category names such as 'car' and 'dog' are first learned by children. We use them frequently, something which is reflected by their simplicity (that is, they are often undecomposable morphemes) (Brown 1958, 1965). This applies to Tzeltal generic categories too. Speakers also tend to prefer category names such as 'car' and 'dog' in neutral contexts or when introducing new categories into conversation (Cruse 1977). Brown's observations about the use and acquisition of cognitive categories, together with Berlin et al.'s investigation of the Tzeltal, seems to indicate that the generic or intermediate level of categorisation is more important. This is partly due to the fact that categories at this level not only have cultural salience but biological salience. For example, such categories are used to refer to objects and actions which are bound up with motor interaction (Lakoff and Johnson 1999: 28). This will become apparent in the next section. Following Lakoff (1987a), I shall refer to the biologically salient generic-level of categorisation as the *basic level*.

6.3.2 Direct Understanding of the Basic Level

Consider the difference in direct understanding between 'The pig ate the carrot' (which uses basic-level categories) and 'The organism ingested the food' (which uses superordinate categories). Why is 'The pig ate the carrot' more directly meaningful? For Lakoff (1987a), it is because basic-level categories are bound up with our neurophysiological capacities for motor interaction and mental imagery. Because we can hold a carrot, chop a carrot, pull a carrot out of the ground etc. – that is, we can can motor-interact with a carrot – we find it relatively easy to generate 'carrot' as an image. It is harder, however, to generate the image of motor-interacting with food. The image is much vaguer because we do not motor-interact with food but with types of food. We also find the basic level easy to understand because we understand objects on this level of categorisation (for example, pig) in terms of an overall shape, that is holistically via a *gestalt* (Lakoff 1987a: 33) (a gestalt is a perceptual pattern which possesses qualities as a whole which cannot be described merely as a sum of its parts). It is because of the capacity of basic-level categories to give rise to direct meaningful sentences that basic-level *metaphors* are comprehensible (Lakoff 1987a: 303). Basic-level metaphors may not only communicate conceptual content but *interactional* properties also. As an example of a basic-level metaphor, consider the mouse pad on a laptop computer. A mouse pad bears no relationship to the external mouse, that is, it does not have the inherent properties: it is usually made of hard plastic, may have a ball mechanism underneath, and so on. But referring to this laptop item with the *basic-level* category 'mouse' enables the hearer to realise the particular motor-interactionality and purposive properties associated with a laptop mouse pad. That is, in context, when one is told this aspect of the laptop is a mouse pad, perceptual properties (it looks like a mouse) are inhibited and purposive properties (it serves the purpose of an external mouse) and motor-interactional properties (with some adjustment, you handle it like an external mouse) are activated.[3]

6.3.3 Cognitive Economy of the Basic Level

The basic level is where perception of obvious differences amongst organisms and objects is most salient, consonant with 'the most obvious discontinuities in nature' (Kay 1971: 878). Experimental evidence suggests that there are more attributes associated with the basic level than with the superordinate level (Rosch et al. 1976). In other words, the basic level is informationally rich. Compare, for example, the basic-level category 'dog' with the superordinate category 'mammal'. In contrast to the basic level, it should be apparent that the superordinate covers such a disparate array of items that any similarities are only apparent from a general perspective, that is, there is no common shape for the category which could be applied to dogs, elephants, giraffes and so on. Like basic-level categories, *subordinate* categories (for example, 'retrievers') do possess a common defining shape. However, the differentiating power of subordinates does not match that of basic-level categories. Differentiation between 'retrievers' and 'poodles' is much less than between 'dogs' and 'giraffes', for example (Ungerer and Schmid 1996: 69). While it is on the basic level that objects and organisms can be distinguished by the differences in how humans interact with them (for example, cats versus dogs), for the *subordinate* level, however, 'it is difficult to imagine that different kinds of cats are stroked in different ways' (Ungerer and Schmid 1996: 69). Conversely, it is more difficult to distinguish between superordinate categories (for example, 'furniture' and 'mammals') in terms of one's motor-interaction.

To sum up, compared to the superordinate and subordinate levels, (1) we readily understand basic-level objects in terms of their overall shape, holistically via a gestalt, and (2) we readily make distinctions between basic-level objects in terms of the differences in our motor-interactions with these objects. So the basic level is not only informationally rich but also more readily yields information compared with the superordinate and subordinate levels. In other words, the basic level is the category level where the largest amount of information about an item is understood with the least cognitive labour. This characteristic of the basic level has been termed *cognitive economy* (Rosch 1978) and, as Ungerer and Schmid (1996: 68) assert, this phenomenon 'probably explains best why the basic level is particularly well suited to meet our cognitive needs'.

6.3.4 Challenging Objectivism

Let me now indicate how what I have detailed in 6.3 challenges the objectivist ('classical') approach to categories that was outlined in 3.4. Lakoff and Johnson (1980: 119–21) provide a good example of how objectivist views of categories omit any treatment of interactional properties by referring to the concept of a 'fake' gun. On an objectivist entailment: this is a black gun *entails* this is a gun; this is a fake gun *entails* this is not a gun. Fakeness is taken to be an inherent part of the gun, that is, it will not fire real bullets. But the gun's fakeness is not so simple. This is because while 'fake' negates a gun's inherent properties, it still preserves interactive properties. I elaborate upon Lakoff and Johnson (1980: 121) in Table 6.1. Lakoff and Johnson suggest that we conceptualise a gun in terms of a multidimensional gestalt of properties where the dimensions are perceptual, motor-active, purposive, functional, mechanical and so on. What is interesting is that a number of these properties are not an inherent part of the gun but interactional properties. This causes a problem for the objectivist Aristotelian view of 'essence' (see discussion in 3.4.1) and thus for deciding on set membership of a category according to attributes of

Table 6.1

FAKE preserves: *INTERACTIVE PROPERTIES*	perceptual properties (a fake gun looks like a gun) motor-interactional properties (you handle it like a gun) purposive properties (it serves some purpose of a gun – to threaten or scare)
FAKE negates: *INHERENT PROPERTIES*	mechanical properties (a fake gun does not shoot bullets)

an object. Objectivism discounts the mind of the observer since, from an ontological viewpoint (that is, what exists), it only deals with what Searle (1995) calls *ontologically objective* properties. The interactional properties of an object are what Searle terms *ontologically subjective* properties [although *ontologically interactional* would be more felicitous].

The relatively new perspective on categorisation, which takes into account the ontological subjectivity associated with basic-level categories, is termed *experientialism* by Lakoff (1987a). In experientialism, meaningful thought is embodied, conceptual systems growing out of bodily experience and the interactions of the body with the environment. Since in experientialism, language is bound up with other aspects of cognition, it conflicts with the modular hypothesis associated with Chomsky that syntax is a separate system independent of the rest of cognition (Langacker 1987a; Lakoff 1987a: 225–7). On these grounds, then, cognitive linguistics problematises the attribution of meaning in CDA to the nature of a syntactic category separate from its actual semantic meaning. That is, the symbolic assumptions that were problematised on these grounds by connectionism in Chapter 5 are also problematised by cognitive linguistics, for example, the assumption of Kress (1993) (see 2.4.4) that people may operate on a syntax-first basis, reading across the syntactic structure 'subject-verb-object' and, in doing so, inadvertently bestowing the *semantic* structure of 'agent-process-affected' regardless of whether this is the clause's actual semantic structure. In Chapter 8, I draw out more explicitly the similarities between connectionism and cognitive linguistics in the construction of the idealised reader framework.

6.3.5 The Role of Context and the Basic Level

As a coda to this section on basic-level categorisation, it should be stressed that the degree of expertise of a particular domain and context-specific goals will affect what is regarded as the basic level. As Harley (2001: 290) points out:

Birdwatchers, for example, know nearly as much about the subordinate members such as blackbirds, jays, and olivaceous warblers, as they do about the basic level. Nevertheless, although expertise increases the knowledge available at other levels, the original basic level retains a privileged status (Johnson and Mervis 1997).

Similarly, Rosch (1978: 42) indicates that a man in a furniture store surrounded by an array of chairs will obviously be speaking and thinking at a level subordinate to the basic level.

In the next section, I demonstrate the link between the basic level and prototypes.

6.4 THE SYMBIOSIS OF THE BASIC LEVEL AND PROTOTYPES

6.4.1 Orientation

I mentioned in 6.2 that prototype effects are superficial, based on internal structure. I now want to look at one provenance for these effects: our neurophysiological capacity for motor-interaction, gestalt perception and image generation. It is because these give rise to basic-level effects that prototype effects are associated with the basic level. Here are Ungerer and Schmid (1996: 72):

> The basic level provides the largest amount of relevant and digestible information about the objects and organisms of the world (e.g. information about bird-like animals) or, to put it more technically, it offers the largest bundles of correlated attributes. These attributes are accumulated in their most complete form in the prototype (ROBIN in the case of BIRD) and expressed by the category name (e.g. *bird*).

Another reason is because 'the basic level is where the overlap of shapes is so great that it permits reliable gestalt perception, which is particularly easy for prototypical examples (like the ROBIN)'. The symbiosis between prototypicality and basic-level categorisation can be seen clearly if a basic-level expression is used to refer to a non-prototypical instance. Here is Lakoff (1987a: 452–3):

> if a sparrow lands on the front porch, it is not misleading to report this by *There's a bird on the porch*. But it would be quite misleading

to use such a sentence to report that an eagle had landed on the porch or that a penguin had waddled up the front steps. Similarly, if John hit a baseball with a bat in the usual way by swinging the bat at the ball, we could straightforwardly report that *John hit a ball*. But if he hit a beachball with a pizza platter, or if he hit a ball by throwing a rock at it, it would be misleading to describe such an event to someone who didn't see it as *John hit a ball*, even though such a description, strictly speaking, would be true. *Hit a ball* has an associated conventional image that characterizes the normal case, and with no further modification we assume that the normal case holds. Thus, conventional images are used to understand even the simplest, most straightforward sentences with no idioms in them.

A corollary of all this is that prototypes are more likely to be generated from basic-level categories than non-basic-level categories. To understand the readiness of generation of prototypes from the basic level compared to the superordinate level, again compare 'The pig ate the carrot' with 'The organism ingested the food'.

6.4.2 Causality as Interaction

I now come to making explicit the relationship between prototypes and the basic level of categorisation with regard to *causality*. For Lakoff (1987a: 54–5) prototypical causality is understood in terms of a cluster of 'interactional properties' since prototypical causality 'appears to be direct manipulation'. The cluster acts as a gestalt which is psychologically simpler than its parts. I list the properties of prototypical causality below:
  1. There is an agent that does something.
  2. There is a patient that undergoes a change to a new state.
  3. Properties 1 and 2 constitute a single event; they overlap in time and space; the agent comes in contact with the patient.
  4. Part of what the agent does (either the motion or the exercise of will) precedes the change in the patient.
  5. The agent is the energy source; the patient is the energy goal; there is a transfer of energy from agent to patient.
  6. There is a single definite agent and a single definite patient.
  7. The agent is human.
  8. a. The agent wills his action.
     b. The agent is in control of his action
     c. The agent bears primary responsibility for both his action and the change.

9. **The agent uses his hands, body or some instrument.**
10. The agent is looking at the patient, the change in the patient is perceptible, and the agent perceives the change. [my bold]

[Note that 'patient' is equivalent to 'goal' or 'affected'.]

Lakoff (1987a: 55) continues by highlighting how the most representative examples of 'humanly relevant causation' possess all of the above properties, citing the examples 'Max broke the window' and 'Brutus killed Caesar'. I have put property 9 – that the agent uses their hands, body or some instrument – in bold to highlight the link between the basic level of categorisation, prototype theory and causality. Prototype effects, with regard to causality, are by-products of our internal neurophysiological capacity for motor-interaction, which in turn is associated with the basic level.

Recall Hodge and Kress's (1993) stipulation (see 4.2.2) that transactives are a privileged mode of representation of causal processes ('action going from an actor to an affected'). We saw in Chapter 4 how their focus assumes that written language structure is cognitively reiterated intact into linguese mental representation. However, from a cognitive linguistic perspective, the rationale for highlighting transactives in Hodge and Kress (1993) does not include what prototypical causality involves: an experientially simple gestalt, basic-level categories, and 'direct manipulation' via hands, body, an instrument and so on. Their focus ignores the broader cognitive (interactional) perspective of processing in which syntactic structure is only *one* aspect.

As a more concrete example, recall the following extract from *The Times* and the analysis in Trew (1979: 98–9), which I highlighted in 2.4.1 and referred to in 4.7 in order to indicate symbolic assumptions of processing in CDA: 'Eleven Africans were shot dead and 15 wounded when Rhodesian police opened fire on a rioting crowd of about 2,000 . . .' We saw that Trew assumes (and it is endorsed generally in CDA) that because of the agent deletion in the first clause, the 'police' as 'agents' of the shooting need to be inferred from the second clause; however, this is a weak inference, and thus a weak mental representation for Trew, and so agency is mystified. On the basis of CDA's internalist postulates of mental representation, a better version for Trew would presumably be, 'Rhodesian police shot dead 11 Africans and wounded 15 when they opened fire on a rioting crowd of about 2,000 . . .'

Recall the quote from Lakoff (1987a: 452–3) at the end of 6.4.1. For Lakoff, 'John hit a ball' could be understood prototypically in the United States with a conventional image involving a baseball bat being swung at the ball. That is, the understanding of 'John hit the ball' involves the generation of a gestalt, a motor-active image and so on, which *go beyond* the linguistic representation. Similarly, 'opened fire' is prototypically associated with phenomena which go beyond an understanding of the linguistic representation: motor-interaction around rifles, trigger-pulling and a gestalt of causal interaction where agents shoot guns at affecteds, that is, where the agents use their hands, body and instruments. Since this prototypical causal interactive gestalt is likely to be generated from 'shot' in 'Eleven Africans were shot dead', readers are likely to automatically assume the involvement of an agent. Given that in *The Times* 'Rhodesian police' is the subject of 'opened fire', itself part of the gestalt of 'shoot', readers are unlikely to have difficulty in linking 'Rhodesian police' with the action of 'shooting dead'. So from a cognitive linguistic point of view, mental representations of each sentence are likely to include similar gestalts, similar 'neurophysiological understandings' regardless of the different semantico-syntactic structures. Trew's perspective does not, then, take into account ontologically subjective properties and so in this respect acts inadvertently in an objectivist/symbolic manner. Moreover, these extra neurophysiologically related phenomena in mental representation, similar for both sentences, are in tension with the significance that CDA attaches to sentential structure.

Having shown the symbiosis of the basic level of categorisation with prototypes, I now go on to consider another type of symbiosis: the cognitive interdependence of basic-level nouns and basic-level action categories.

6.5 COGNITIVE INTERDEPENDENCE OF BASIC-LEVEL NOUNS AND BASIC-LEVEL ACTION CATEGORIES

6.5.1 Basic-Level Action Categories

Aside from basic-level categories which are associated with physical objects, Lakoff (1987a: 270–1) also argues that actions and properties can be basic-level:

> We have basic-level concepts not only for objects but for actions and properties as well. Actions like *running, walking, eating, drinking*, etc. are basic-level, whereas *moving* and *ingesting* are superordinate, while kinds of walking and drinking, say, *ambling* and *slurping*, are subordinate. Similarly, *tall, short, hard, soft, heavy, light, hot, cold*, etc. are basic-level properties, as are the

basic neurophysiologically determined colors: black, white, red, green, blue, and yellow.

Now, when attribute lists compiled by respondents for basic-level action categories like 'eat' or 'drink' are compared with those for related object categories such as 'bread' and 'soup', there is considerable overlap between the two. As Ungerer and Schmid (1996: 104) state:

> The names of some basic level food categories will be found in the attribute list of EAT, and conversely, the names of basic level action categories like EAT will certainly rank among the more important of the attributes of the basic level food categories.

The conclusion that Ungerer and Schmid (1996: 104) draw from this is that there is a strong *cognitive interdependence* between action and object basic-level categories. And, indeed, there is psycholinguistic support for such a conclusion. Gumenik (1979), cited in Garnham (1985: 164), investigated the cueing process for sentence recall. He was able to show, for example, how 'architect' is as good a cue for 'planned the house' as the sentence 'The man planned the house'. This demonstrates that there is cognitive interdependence between the *noun* 'architect' and the *verb* phrase 'planned the house'. Gumenik also showed that 'arctic' is a better cue than 'group' for 'The group built their houses out of ice', which indicates that adjectives can be cognitively interdependent with nouns and verbs also.

Finally, a few words of caution on the prospect of basic-level actions. To be directly meaningful, to produce a sharply defined gestalt, 'drinking' is more likely to be treated as being basic-level in the presence of basic-level objects such as 'cat', for example, in 'The cat drinks'.

6.5.2 Basic-Level Event Categories

The cognitive interdependence of basic-level action and basic-level object categories can also be seen in basic-level *event* categories, for example, the category of breakfast where there is a fusing of objects and activities (Ungerer and Schmid 1996: 104). Breakfast is a complex basic-level category since it comprises basic-level object categories (spoon, cup, table and so on) and basic-level action categories (eat, drink, cut and so on). Ungerer and Schmid (1996: 105) cite the experiments of Rifkin (1985) as supporting the view that event categories such as 'breakfast' are basic-level. Using an attribute-listing test, Rifkin (1985) demonstrated that subjects could supply large numbers of attributes for basic-level event categories such as 'breakfast', 'lunch', 'dinner', 'seeing a movie', 'taking a shower', 'murder', 'rape', and that such attributes did not just include object categories but action categories. For instance, for the (basic-level event) category of 'murder', subjects included both 'gun' and 'kill'. When subjects were asked to supply attributes for related superordinates ('meal', 'entertainment', 'hygienic activity', and 'crime'), their number was much smaller. For subordinates such as 'quick breakfast', subjects did not provide significantly more attributes than for basic-level categories. Here are Ungerer and Schmid (1996: 105) on basic-level events:

> Checking our examples of basic level events against the other two criteria of basic level categories, prototype structure and gestalt perception, we have no difficulty in imagining more or less typical instances of breakfasts or murders, and in categorizing these events as holistic gestalts.

The cognitive interdependence of basic-level noun and verb categories has consequences for CDA's emphasis on actions being described by verbs only – for instance, Martin's (1989: 43) claim (referred to approvingly in Goatly 2001; and see 2.4.3) that 'seal hunt' is mystifying because its nominal form is incongruent with action. 'Seal hunt' would constitute a basic-level event category where action ('hunt') and object ('seal') categories are fused and so, from a cognitive linguistic perspective, its nominal compound status is not likely to be mystifying of the action that transpires. In not taking into account the contribution of human understanding, Martin's analysis is implicitly symbolic.

In Chapter 5, I problematised the symbolic postulates operating in Simpson (1993: 170–1) (see 4.2.1) from a connectionist point of view. I will now do the same from a cognitive linguistic point of view. Simpson takes issue with the fact that 'the only entity upon which Steed acts as AGENT is "her car" . . . we see a wilful refusal to "tell it like it is"'. For Simpson, non-mystifying reporting of the event would involve agent-process-affected structures as evinced in the symbolically inspired alternative sentences he offers. Let me now focus on the fragment 'two of Steed's rape victims'. 'Rape' can be considered a *basic-level event* category (Rifkin 1985) and so consists of a fusion of basic-level action and object categories. Cognition of 'rape' in 'two of Steed's rape victims' is likely to yield sufficient information to understand the *event*. That is, it is likely from this fragment that readers will understand actual agency even if linguistic agency is not part of an agent-process-affected structure (see van Leeuwen 1996 on the lack of near fit between linguistic agency and actual agency).

Having examined the basic level of categorisation in some detail, let me now give some attention to the *superordinate* level of categorisation.

6.6 SUPERORDINATE CATEGORIES

6.6.1 Superordinate Noun Categories

How do superordinate categories compare to basic-level ones? As I stated in 6.3.3, there is no common shape and, correspondingly, no shared gestalt which underpins hyponyms of the superordinate. Rather, as Ungerer and Schmid (1996: 74) state, the gestalt properties of the superordinate are 'borrowed' from basic-level hyponyms. They refer to this 'borrowing' as *parasitic categorisation*. What this 'borrowing' also does is to highlight salient attributes of the basic-level hyponyms. So, for example, in calling a car a vehicle, what is automatically stressed is the function of 'moving persons or things around' (Ungerer and Schmid 1996: 78).[4] This 'borrowing' of attributes from the basic level means, again, that the basic level is the conceptually prominent level. Because of the phenomenon of parasitic categorisation, a crucial difference emerges between basic-level categories and superordinates. Parasitic categorisation and the lack of a common gestalt means that hyponyms of the superordinate are only related via what Wittgenstein (1953: 32) referred to as *family resemblances*. Wittgenstein's example was 'game' (Ungerer and Schmid 1996: 98), and he meant by this that '"games" form a family' but that there is no necessary feature for all games. Rather, different games are related through criss-crossing similarities between their different aspects.

In contrast to superordinates, because basic-level categories have a common gestalt, hyponyms of the basic-level category 'chair' (wooden-hard-backed chair', 'beanbag', 'bench', 'arm-chair', 'dentist's chair', 'electric chair' and so on) can be linked together via prototype structuring (likely to be something similar to 'wooden-hard-backed chair'). But the superordinate 'furniture' (or Wittgenstein's 'game') with no common gestalt resists the formation of a prototype, there being one or a few category-wide attributes which are salient. That basic-level categories manifest prototypicality and non-basic-level categories may not is often unnoticed. Hampton (1981) usefully points out that abstract concepts resist the formation of prototypes, for example, it being difficult to talk meaningfully of a prototypical 'truth' (cited in Harley (2001: 290) under the headline 'Problems with the prototype model').

6.6.2 Superordinate Action Categories

For Lakoff (1987a: 270–1) and for Ungerer and Schmid (1996: 102), nouns are not the only type of superordinate category. Verbs such as 'cause' can be seen as superordinates because:

> their main function is to highlight one very general attribute which is part of a whole range of basic level action categories ... Other candidates for superordinate action categories with a salient general attribute are HAPPEN, BECOME, BEGIN and STOP.
> (Ungerer and Schmid 1996: 102)

However, it is often the case that the superordinate status of a verb is less stable than that of a superordinate noun. If regarding a verb as superordinate, the following admonitions of Ungerer and Schmid (1996: 104) are worth bearing in mind:

> Of course, it is possible to assemble a hierarchy of actions, by arranging categories like STRIDE, WALK, MOVE, or MUNCH, EAT, CONSUME on the subordinate, basic, and superordinate levels respectively, but these hierarchies will more likely than not be scientific constructs and will not necessarily reflect the cognitive framework of the ordinary language user. In addition, these action hierarchies seem to be even more patchy than their counterparts in the domain of objects and organisms.
>   So we leave action categories with a feeling that they include a number of basic activities which are probably perceived in terms of prototype categories, but that the analysis becomes less conclusive as we turn to superordinates and subordinates and, more generally, to lexical hierarchies of action categories.

In 2.4.3, I explained that Martin (1989: 43) regarded 'killing techniques' and 'killing methods' as being mystifying of the 'unsavoury part of the seal hunt'. For Martin this is because 'killing', as the modifier of an abstract noun, is incongruent with action. 'Killing' is referred to indirectly as a result. Martin is correct to draw attention to 'killing techniques' and 'killing methods' since both can be mystifying of the 'unsavoury part of the seal hunt'. But this is not because the syntactic position of 'killing' diminishes the significance of the action. Rather it is because 'kill' is a superordinate action category and thus 'killing techniques/methods' are superordinate phrases. 'Clubbing techniques' as an example of a basic-level phrase is more likely to institute motor-actionality, gestalt and image formation and so would bring the reader closer to the event. However, the capacity of 'killing techniques' to shield readers from the unpleasantness of seal-culling would depend on an absence of information in the co-text which would 'fill in' 'killing' into something more concrete (see 7.2.5).

6.6.3 Translating Superordinates into the Basic Level

Read the following text from Bransford and Johnson (1973: 400) and see if you understand what is being referred to:

> The procedure is actually quite simple. First you arrange things into two different groups. Of course, one pile may be sufficient depending on how much there is to do. If you have to go somewhere else due to lack of facilities, that is the next step; otherwise you are pretty well set. It is important not to overdo things. That is, it is better to do fewer things at once than too many. In the short run this might not seem important, but complications can easily arise. A mistake can be expensive as well. At first the whole procedure will seem complicated. Soon, however, it will become just another facet of life. It is difficult to foresee any end to the necessity for this task in the immediate future, but then one can never tell. After the procedure is completed, one arranges the material into different groups again. Then they can be put into their appropriate places. Eventually they will be used once more, and the whole cycle will then have to be repeated. However, that is part of life.

The text is initially difficult for many to understand. It could be said to be mystifying of what is being described. Comprehension difficulty arises because of the excess of superordinate/abstract categories, such as 'things', 'groups', 'complications'. In referring to the above text, Rosch (1978: 45) makes the point that:

> what Bransford and Johnson call context cues are actually names of basic-level events (e.g., washing clothes) and that one function of hearing the event name is to enable the reader to translate the superordinate terms into basic-level objects and actions. Such a translation appears to be a necessary aspect of our ability to match linguistic descriptions to world knowledge in a way that produces the 'click of comprehension'.

Understanding of the above text can take place with the cue 'washing clothes' (what is being referred to in the text) because it is a basic-level event category. It consists of a fusion of basic-level object categories and basic-level action categories which are cognitively interdependent. Given this cognitive interdependence, 'washing clothes' can lead to a rich gestalt. So when the basic-level category 'washing clothes' is introduced, the superordinates can be 'translated', making the text easier to understand (see 8.4.1 for commentary on the above text as to how cognitive linguistic explanation relates to inference generation and shallow processing).

What are the repercussions for CDA? In the light of the above, consider the following from Fairclough (1995a: 112): 'A lot of nominalizations in a text... make it very abstract and distant from concrete events and situations (Kress and Hodge 1979).' Let us look again at the Bransford and Johnson text from this perspective. So, for example, 'The procedure is actually quite simple' contains the 'nominalisation' 'procedure' and indeed this 'nominalisation' appears on two other occasions. 'Denominalising' 'procedure' to its verb form, we might arrive at the *second person* 'how you proceed is quite simple...', and something similar can be done for the other two instances. But is this any easier to understand just because a participant has been included and the verb 'proceed' is employed? Even though there is less *interpersonal distance* signalled between author and reader, *ideational distance* still exists between cognition and what is described because 'proceed' is a superordinate category. (Ideational distance is the extent of separation between the actual event and the reader's understanding of what happened in that event; interpersonal distance refers to the level of formality or intimacy that a text sets up between author and reader.) Likewise, 'procedure' is mystifying not because it is a nominalisation but because it is a superordinate category. The fact that 'proceed' is a verb and 'procedure' is a noun is irrelevant. Since superordinates are not cognitively interdependent with one another, a rich gestalt is not forthcoming, which explains why the topic of the text is difficult to ascertain. Again, a corollary of this is that it is easy to see how narrowly oriented CDA is in its syntactic focus away from larger cognitive concerns.

Having discussed the phenomena of basic-level and superordinate categorisation, let me now consider how cognitive linguists treat compound nouns together with the implications for CDA.

6.7 COGNITIVE LINGUISTICS AND COMPOUNDS

Consider the following from Lakoff (1987a: 147):

> It is often the case that meanings of compounds are not compositional; that is, the meaning of the whole cannot be

predicted from the meanings of the parts and the way they are put together. The parts do play a role in the meaning of the whole expression – they *motivate* that meaning . . .

Lakoff (1987a: 144) gives a series of examples, of which 'red hair' exemplifies the point perfectly. Because 'red hair' is not focal red, we cannot treat 'red hair' compositionally in terms of the intersection of a set of red things and the set of hairs. If we cannot always treat compounds compositionally, that is, treating components of the compound atomically, then we are unlikely to always see compounds strictly speaking in terms of modifier and head. This is endorsed in Ungerer and Schmid (1996: 95).[5]

Now, recall from 2.4.3 Martin's (1989: 43) analysis of a text that details the killing of seals. For Martin, it is incongruous, in descriptions of action, to put 'the action into the modifier of an abstract noun', for example, 'sealing operation, killing techniques, slaughtering operation, killing methods'. The assumption here is that, because 'killing' and 'slaughtering' are modifiers – that is, they are subservient to the head in a noun phrase – somehow this mystifies the 'unsavoury part of the seal hunt'. Patently, from what we have seen of the cognitive linguistic perspective on compounds, this is not necessarily the case. Again, my analysis here supports my analysis of Martin (1989) in 6.5.2 and 6.6.2, and thus problematises the imparting of semantic meaning to a grammatical metalanguage and the making of tacit internalist claims of a relationship between syntactic structure and mental representation.

6.8 ENDPOINTS

It is apparent that the basic level is a privileged level of categorisation since (1) we derive meaning from basic-level categories directly, and (2) basic-level categories are characterised by *cognitive economy*. For Lakoff (1987a: 271) and Lakoff and Johnson (1999: 28–30), the basic level is epistemologically privileged not because it provides a mirror of nature in the sense that logical empiricist simples were thought to be epistemologically privileged but because of the basic level's association with motor-interaction, image generation, gestalt perception and so on, which assists the reader's or listener's understanding. So while in Chapter 4 we saw CDA's logical empiricist fixation on having sentential structure 'reflect' the 'structure of the event', in this chapter we have seen how this does not take into account the larger cognitive issue of how basic-level categories assist understanding by leading to the generation of information which *goes beyond* linguistic representation. That is, we have seen how this capacity of basic-level categories can be in tension with the emphasis given in CDA that certain phrase, clause and sentential structure can lead to mystification.

In 5.5.1, I included Clark's (1996) outline of three positions on mental representation: gross descriptivism, modest internalism and gross internalism. The two polarised positions are 'gross descriptivism' (characterising connectionism) and 'gross internalism' (characterising symbolicism). We saw that CDA, in its highlighting of 'transactives' as a privileged representation, chimes with 'gross internalism'. Clark (1996) locates 'modest internalism' as the mid-way position. The emphasis in cognitive linguistics on the basic level of categorisation would seem to place it in the modest internalism camp in terms of its place within Clark's mental representation scheme. In cognitive linguistics there is a rejection of gross internalism. But at the same time, representation in cognitive linguistics cannot be regarded as simply gross descriptivism since there is a strong connection between one type of category – the basic level – and neural activity, for example, the capacity for image generation, motor-interaction and so on.

NOTES

1. But from the perspective of *discourse*, it would be strange to regard 'the pope' as a non-prototypical bachelor in the same way that a penguin is a non-prototypical bird. Indeed, Lakoff's semantic analysis neglects the potential discourse meaning of 'bachelor' which often indicates much about the speaker's or writer's attitude.
2. Let me provide another situation where prototype effects are generated (this time a 'mind-reading trick') with an explanation in terms of cognitive models. You may derive a fuller appreciation of this from actually doing the following. Choose a number between one and ten. Multiply this number by nine. If you have a one-digit number, leave it alone. If you have a two-digit number, then add together the individual digits. From this sum, subtract five. On the series, if $A=1$, $B=2$, and so on, the number you have corresponds to a letter of the alphabet. Now, quickly, think of a country beginning with that letter. Locate the next letter along in the alphabet. Quickly, think of an animal beginning with that letter. Now think of a colour you would associate with that animal. Abracadabra . . . you have *Denmark*, *Elephant* and *Grey*.

   On Lakoff's scheme, all the countries beginning with 'D' can be defined in a classical way via a condition which is both necessary and sufficient. However, if you are a European dweller, you will likely possess a cognitive model where certain countries are more prominent. For this reason, Denmark will be more salient than Diego Garcia, for instance. It is because of this particular cognitive model that prototype effects can emerge, even though the category satisfies classical criteria, that is, Denmark belongs to the set of all countries beginning with the letter 'D'. The corollary of all this is that the prototype model is not as simplistic as it is often deemed. Some categories such as colour categories *are* scalar, where degrees of membership vary. Other categories such as countries beginning with the letter 'D'

have clear parameters, but within these parameters, graded prototype effects can arise.
3. In the same way that a mouse can be a pad on a laptop, a tricycle can also be a bicycle. Of course neither of these 'equivalences' can transpire on the basis of a necessary and sufficient set of conditions describing ontologically objective properties. It is, for example, a necessarily ontologically objective or inherent property that a bicycle has two wheels. However, since ontologically subjective properties are habitually taken into account in everyday classification, a tricycle may qualify as a non-prototypical bicycle owing to similar motor-interactions, and so on. Consider also the following lateral thinking puzzle:

A man has wood. On Monday, he shapes it into a cube. On Tuesday he shapes it into a sphere and on Wednesday into a pyramid. He does not touch it nor uses an instrument of cutting etc. How does he do it?

The man is able to do the above because the wood is actually *sawdust* which he pours in to moulds in the shapes of a cube, a sphere and a pyramid. The problem is difficult to solve because sawdust is non-prototypical wood from the point of view of motor-interaction and to many will be seen as having little function.
4. The capacity of superordinates to highlight a function and thus downplay others may also serve a pragmatic deictic role in the same way that use of distal demonstrative pronouns can express emotional displacement, for example 'Get *that* dog out of here' (see Wales 2001: 99). On being stopped by the police while driving, I was directed as follows: 'Could you step out of the vehicle'. The use of 'vehicle' is marked since under normal circumstances the basic-level category of 'car' is the more likely. In this situation, the superordinate 'vehicle' highlights the function of transport but also necessarily *downplays* the motor-interactional properties associated with the basic-level 'car'. The effect, immediately, was one of 'dislocation' from the car. Since the police were implicitly not recognising how I interacted with the car, more formal relations were instituted.
5. That ultimately the syntactic structure of a compound depends on its discourse meaning rather than the other way round is often exemplified in quips, for example, a mother taking her problem boy to the 'child psychologist' only to find out the psychologist is the same age as her son.

CHAPTER 7

Psycholinguistic Evidence for Inference Generation

7.1 INTRODUCTION

The notion of inference generation is present in the analysis of text by certain practitioners of CDA, as we saw in 2.4 and 2.5. However, in CDA, there is little appreciation of the complexities and the typology of inferences generated in reading, or of recent psycholinguistic experimental data which illuminate the nature of *on-line* inference generation. On-line inferences are those that would be produced habitually in reading. There is also little appreciation in CDA of how certain inferences are more likely to be generated for particular readers than others. While as yet, the understanding of inference generation in CDA is either neglected or superficially treated, an understanding of inference generation is crucial to any account of reading. As Sanford (1990: 515) asserts, 'The ubiquity of inferences in text comprehension makes the study of text comprehension look like a subset of the study of inference making.'

One purpose of this chapter is to raise more awareness of inference generation. I focus on recent psycholinguistic evidence for shallow processing (sometimes also called weak processing) with particular regard to inference generation in reading. The chapter is confined principally to four types of inference – causal antecedence, causal consequence, instrument and instantiation – that are significant for the idealised reader framework in Section C. I will deal, in Chapter 9, with other inferences used in the reader framework. Another purpose of this chapter is to show how psycholinguistic research on inference generation conflicts with assumptions of inference generation in CDA. Moreover, I will show how psycholinguistic evidence for inference generation, as well as other evidence of text processing, conflicts with the symbolically underpinned strategies in CDA for highlighting mystifying text. Finally, I will use the evidence of this chapter to demonstrate how certain CD socio-cognitive analyses over-interpret texts from the standpoint of a non-analyst.

The experimental evidence I will outline here is, of course, experimental and suffers from the standard problems of all psycholinguistic data generated under 'laboratory conditions'. For example, artificially constructed texts may be lacking an interpersonal function found in many everyday texts; the texts are often of limited size and may even consist of single sentences. Reading, of course, is a vastly complicated phenomenon and psycholinguistic experiments are limited to dealing with a selection of variables. However, the evidence I marshal below possesses validity in that it is largely evidence for which a consensus exists in current psycholinguistics. It is also readily available in standard psycholinguistic and cognitive psychology reference books (Gernsbacher 1994; Eysenck and Keane 2000; Harley 2001). Because it is evidence for which there is consensus, it has a consistency that compares favourably with some inconsistent psycholinguistic assumptions of processing in CDA which were outlined in Chapter 2. Moreover, because CDA draws upon sociocultural theory to the neglect of psychological theory, my use of psycholinguistic evidence provides some sort of balance, facilitating articulation of problems with CD analyses, which are felt intuitively. This has already been demonstrated in one respect when I indicated in 3.6.1 how the derivational theory of complexity, a model of processing analogous to that used implicitly in CDA, is countered by experimental evidence.

A final point. Unlike in Chapters 5 and 6, I will leave the implications of this psycholinguistic evidence for CDA until the end of this chapter, since this should make an understanding of the implications for CDA much clearer. In the first section, I detail types of inference, generated in the understanding of text, that have received much attention in psycholinguistics.

7.2 INFERENCES IN TEXT COMPREHENSION AND LIKELIHOOD OF THEIR GENERATION

7.2.1 Coherence versus Elaborative

A key distinction drawn in psycholinguistics is one between *coherence* inferences and *elaborative* inferences. Consider the following from Potts et al. (1988: 405) (see also Sanford 1990: 516–17):

(i) No longer able to control his anger, the husband threw the delicate porcelain vase against the wall. It cost him well over one hundred dollars to replace.

The inference that the vase broke is needed to make *coherence*. Hence it is known as a coherence inference. It is also known as a *backward* inference since the reader works backwards to make coherence. Now consider a variant on the above:

(ii) No longer able to control his anger, the husband threw the delicate porcelain vase against the wall. He had been feeling angry for weeks, but had refused to seek help.

Here, the inference that the vase broke is known as an *elaborative* inference. It is not necessary for coherence – it merely elaborates upon the text. The elaborative inference that the vase broke from ii) is essentially predictive and cannot be tied backwards to any supporting textual material. Thus, it is also known as a *forward* inference. But as we shall see in 7.2.3 elaborative inferences can be backward ones also.

7.2.2 Elaborative Inferences and the Likelihood of their Generation

Orientation

Psycholinguists have reached a firm consensus about certain inferences which are habitually generated in reading (see Eysenck and Keane 2000: 350–1). These inferences include the following: (1) referential inferences (to what previous words does this word apply?),[1] (2) role assignment inferences (for example, what is the agent, object and so on in the clause?), and (3) causal antecedent inferences (what caused this?) (see 7.2.3). These are all inferences necessary for coherence and so their habitual generation is not surprising. Indeed, in the experimental investigations of Potts et al. (1988), the coherence inference in text (i) of the previous section was habitually generated. But as we also saw in 7.2.1, the elaborative inference that the vase broke in text (ii) is not necessary for the coherence of the text because it is a forward inference. Below, I outline positions which aim to predict when such non-necessary or forward elaborative inferences might be produced.

The Early Constructionist Position

The *constructionist* position is derived from the work of Bransford (for example, Bransford, Barclay and Franks 1972) and later developed by others (Johnson-Laird 1980). Bransford argued that the comprehension process requires that the reader be actively involved so that information not explicitly textually rendered can be 'filled in'. A crucial aspect of the constructionist position is that there will be a rich set of elaborative inferences accompanying the generation of coherence inferences. Much of the early research that was marshalled in support of the constructionist position involved the use of memory testing for inference generation. For example, Bransford et al. (1972) gave their subjects sentences such as 'Three turtles rested on a floating log, and a fish swam beneath them', contending that the inference generated would be that the fish swam under the log. To test this they used a recognition memory test and provided subjects with the sentence 'Three turtles rested on a floating log, and a fish swam beneath it'. Most subjects replied they were confident that this inference was the original sentence. Bransford et al. (1972) judged that text inferences were stored in memory in the same way as text information. But subsequent findings (see Singer 1980) suggested that many inferences associated with recognition memory tests are, in fact, made during prompting for recall rather than on-line. Memory measures can then be only indirect measures of comprehension and may lead to over-estimation of the role of inference construction in comprehension. As a consequence, recognition memory tests are not used so often in inference research (Eysenck and Keane 2000: 347).

The Minimalist Hypothesis

Because of the problem with cue-recall experiments, certain theorists have argued that the constructionist position lacks compelling evidence. Principal among its detractors are McKoon and Ratcliff (1992: 440) who offer an alternative viewpoint: the *minimalist hypothesis*:

> In the absence of specific, goal-directed strategic processes, inferences of only two kinds are constructed: those that establish locally coherent representations of the parts of a text that are processed concurrently and those that rely on information that is quickly and easily available.

The minimalist hypothesis and the constructionist position both agree that coherence inferences are readily generated. Where they differ most starkly is in the conditions under which elaborative inferences can be considered to be *automatically* generated. For constructionists, automatic elaborative inferencing in reading is rife whereas under the minimalist hypothesis, automatic elaborative inferencing is much more restricted.

In a series of experiments, McKoon and Ratcliff (1986, 1989a) demonstrated that elaborative inferences were only partially realised because information was not quickly and easily available for subjects. They had subjects read short texts containing the following 'The director and cameraman were ready to shoot close-ups when suddenly the actress fell from the 14th storey'. This was followed by a *lexical decision task* where target words had to be ascertained very quickly as being present or not. Each test word was succeeded by a signal, and subjects were told to provide a response immediately after registering the signal. Target words such as 'dead' were consistent with the predicted elaborative inference, namely *that the actress had died*. McKoon and Ratcliff (1986, 1989a) found that target words that were consistent with a predicted elaborative inference were only weakly identified as being present in the text. This was in line with the predictions of the minimalist hypothesis:

> the inference about death is not necessary for local coherence if the text ends with the sentence about the fall. The event of falling from a 14-storey building is not familiar enough to make the inference easily available. So the minimalist hypothesis predicts that the inference about death will not be included automatically in the mental representation.
> (McKoon and Ratcliff 1992: 457–8)

The advantage of such a lexical decision task, where only *one* word cue is employed, is that it reduces the chances of an inference being constructed at the time of the test. This is in contrast to the memory-recognition test of Bransford et al. (1972) where subjects were presented with a *whole* sentence. While, in essence, the above experiment is a kind of memory recognition test, for McKoon and Ratcliff (1992: 458) 'the delay between test word and signal was short enough that slow, strategic processes (that might construct inferences at the time of the test) were eliminated'. Hence for McKoon and Ratcliff (1992: 458), this '*speeded* recognition memory test' avoids the problems of inferences constructed at the time of the test. The experiments of McKoon and Ratcliff (1986, 1989a) demonstrate that elaborative inferences are not inferable (or are weakly so, at best) when they rely on information that is not very familiar. As a final point, some of the experiments in McKoon and Ratcliff (1986) were followed up in Potts et al. (1988) (see 7.2.1). The experimental evidence of Potts et al. goes even further than that of McKoon and Ratcliff. This is because they indicate that the elaborative inference – the vase broke in text (ii) in 7.2.1 – was not generated by subjects, not even weakly.

To sum up, the minimalist hypothesis holds that coherence inferences are normally automatically generated and that elaborative inferences are only likely to be automatic, for a reader with no specific reading goals, if they rely on information that is quickly and easily available. Of course, if a reader *is* specifically goal-oriented, and willing to invest more cognitive effort in reading, then some elaborative inferences generated may not be automatic. McKoon and Ratcliff term these non-automatic inferences *strategic* inferences.

Vonk and Noordman (1990)

I now want to profile reasons why even certain kinds of coherence inferences may not necessarily be constructed, reasons which are all the same in line with the minimalist hypothesis. The experimental work of Vonk and Noordman (1990) presupposes that generation of coherence inferences is to a large extent dependent on the reader's familiarity with the material (that is, it is the same as with elaborative inferences), regardless of whether explicit cohesive markers are present. Vonk and Noordman (1990) examined the processing of sentences containing the conjunctions *because* and *but*, and they considered sentences such as 'Chlorine compounds are frequently used as propellants because they do not react with other substances'. In order to establish coherence for this sentence, the inference that needs to be generated is that good propellants do not react with other substances. Vonk and Noordman wanted to know whether this inference would be produced on-line. Using another sentence, 'John is a linguist, but he knows a lot about statistics', Vonk and Noordman were interested in knowing whether the inference necessary for coherence – that linguists do not know much about statistics – would also be generated. They used a combination of on-line reading time and question-answering time analyses. Inferences were presented as statements to be verified *after* reading sentences like the ones above. In some cases, inferences were already explicitly stated in the material to be read by subjects, and in other cases not. It was found that subjects answered more quickly in the verification stage when the inferences had been explicitly present in the reading material. The significance of all this? Vonk and Noordman concluded that when textual material is unfamiliar, even coherence inferences are not always constructed. With unfamiliar material, readers have a 'tendency to satisfy themselves with rather shallow processing' (Vonk and Noordman 1990: 462), especially if the reader 'does not have a vested interest in the material' as Sanford and Garrod (1994: 705) put it in their summary of Vonk and Noordman (1990). The reasoning behind this is that readers may satisfy themselves that the text is to some extent *coherent* because *cohesive* markers are present (as in the above examples).[2] In more detail, here are Vonk and Noordman (1990: 462–3):

> The control of inferences depends to a considerable extent on the reader's purpose and the reader's knowledge. Inferences are made on-line if they are related to information that is relevant to the reader's purpose, and inferences are more likely to be made if they deal with familiar topics.
>
> These results suggest that reading is a process in which a balance between costs and benefits is achieved. The benefits consist of the information extracted from the text; the costs are related to the extra mental processes that this requires. **The reader seems to be rather parsimonious in processing** ... Readers engage in inference processes because the costs are relatively low when the inferences are related to available knowledge. [my bold]

It would seem that coherence inferences that rely on specialised knowledge are not always generated. But this is still in line with the minimalist hypothesis since it indicates that inferences will only be generated if they rely on familiar and readily available information.

I have dealt very generally with the likelihood of elaborative inferences being produced, and I have also examined coherence inferences. When I introduced both types of inference in 7.2.1, I was dealing with a specific kind of coherence inference and a specific kind of elaborative inference, respectively *causal antecedence* and *causal consequence*. In the next two sections, I refer in more detail to the nature of these causal inferences particularly in relation to the likelihood of their generation.

7.2.3 Causal Antecedent Inferences and the Likelihood of Their Generation

I follow van den Broek (1994: 561–73) (in Gernsbacher 1994), breaking down causal antecedent inferences into three types:

(i) *connecting inference* – the reader establishes a link between the current focal event and prior information thus instituting a causal antecedent for the new event.
(ii) *reinstatement* – information from prior text which is currently not activated can be reactivated by the reader in order to establish a causal antecedent.
(iii) *elaborative* – the reader utilises background knowledge to establish a likely but unmentioned causal antecedent.

Notice (iii). Although causal antecedent inferences are necessary for coherence, and so are also *backward* inferences, they may also be *elaborative*. In other words, elaborative and forward inferences are not necessarily equivalent descriptions.

Keenan et al. (1984) put forward the hypothesis that if readers do institute causal antecedent inferences (that is, identifying causal relations which bridge adjacent clauses or sentences), then the stronger a causal relation in memory, the easier it would be for the reader to recognise it (see also Myers et al. 1987). In Keenan et al. (1984), subjects were shown sentence pairs that the authors regarded as differing according to the strength of the causal relation in memory. For Keenan et al., causal strength decreased from one to four:

Level
1. Joey's big brother punched him again and again.
   The next day his body was covered with bruises.

2. Racing down the hill, Joey fell off his bike.
   The next day his body was covered with bruises.

3. Joey's crazy mother became furiously angry with him.
   The next day his body was covered with bruises.

4. Joey went to a neighbor's house to play.
   The next day his body was covered with bruises.

Reading times for the second sentence were recorded and the hypothesis of Keenan et al. (1984) was confirmed since reading times for the second sentence increased from scenarios one to four. Further investigation found that a stronger memory connection was established for the high-causal relation sentence compared to low-causal pairs. Taken together, these investigations suggest that readers automatically make causal antecedent inferences between adjacent sentences when the causal relation is strong in memory. When the causal relation is weak, the processing becomes shallower. Looking at the results of Keenan et al. (1984) from the perspective of van den Broek (1994), we can say the following. Readers have little problem instituting *connecting* causal antecedent inferences across sentences. However, the strength or shallowness of the *elaborative* causal antecedent inference is dependent on the strength of the causal relation in memory. This is in line with Vonk and Noordman (1990) above, that is, coherence inferences become shallower the less the material leads to accessing of familiar background knowledge. An important corollary follows from all of this. Earlier (7.2.2), I said that causal antecedent inferences are necessary for coherence and so would be habitually generated.

This needs to be qualified: while connecting causal antecedent inferences are automatic, elaborative causal antecedent inferences depend for their automaticity on familiar information being accessed in memory.

7.2.4 Causal Consequent Inferences and the Likelihood of Their Generation

In 7.2.2, we saw that the elaborative inference that the actress had died was only weakly identified or, put another way, was produced shallowly. This inference is, more specifically speaking, a *causal consequent* inference. McKoon and Ratcliff's minimalist hypothesis position that causal consequent inferences are not usually generated if the situation is unfamiliar is in consensus with the position of the *later constructionists* Graesser, Singer and Trabasso (1994), a response to McKoon and Racliff's minimalist hypothesis. The following is from Graesser et al. (1994: 382) on why causal consequents are *not* usually constructed:

> because there are too many alternative hypothetical plots that could potentially be forecasted, because most of these alternatives would end up being erroneous when the full story is known **or because it takes a large amount of cognitive resources** to forecast a single hypothetical plot (Graesser and Clark 1985; Johnson-Laird 1983; Kintsch 1988; Potts, Keenan and Golding 1988; Reiger 1975). [my bold]

Moreover, causal consequent inferences are shallowly generated at best when a reader has little vested interest in a text, that is, a reader who is not prepared to invest 'a large amount of cognitive resources'. Of course, a reader with more vested interest, and thus one more willing to invest cognitive effort, can generate a causal consequent inference strategically. Having said this, there are conditions where the automatic generation of causal consequent inferences is more likely. One of these relates to the degree to which the context is constrained; I come back to this in more detail in 8.4.3.[3] I now move on to consider another type of elaborative inference: *instantiation*.

7.2.5 Instantiation Inferences and the Likelihood of Their Generation

Instantiation transpires when a superordinate/general category is processed more specifically from its context. 'Vehicle' in 'The vehicle hovered over the crowd' is most probably processed as a helicopter, balloon or such like and is unlikely to be processed as a car, a bus and so on (Garnham 1985: 162). Investigators into instantiation inferences have commonly constructed sentences with general and specific categories:

1. Julie was convinced that spring was near when she saw a cute red-breasted **bird** in her yard.
2. Julie was convinced that spring was near when she saw a cute red-breasted **robin** in her yard.

When a sentence such as 'The robin pecked the ground' followed sentences like the two above, reading times for this ensuing sentence have been shown to be about the same (Garrod et al. 1990; McKoon and Ratcliff 1989b; O'Brien et al. 1988). This suggests that 'bird' is automatically instantiable in the first sentence above. Singer's (1994) synoptic treatment of recent work in 'discourse (1) inference processes' also avers that there is strong support for automatic instantiation of general categories on-line when scenarios are familiar. Moreover, for McKoon and Ratcliff (1989b: 1,143), the statement that general object categories are automatically instantiated on-line is in line with the minimalist hypothesis: 'If a specific inference is provided by easily available general knowledge from long-term memory, then it will be constructed even if it is not required for coherence.'

Processing and the Order of General Category/Instance

Finally, in this section, I want to consider how the order in which an instance and a general category noun are expressed in a text affects processing time. In an investigation of superordinate category instantiation, Garnham (1981) used a measure known as 'self-paced reading time' where:

> If subjects are allowed to control the rate at which text is
> presented to them, the time which they spend reading a particular
> portion of that text can be used as a measure of on-line processing
> load.
>   (Garnham 1981: 377)

Consider the following:

1. a) The denim would fade in the sun. b) The cloth was kept in big rolls.
2. b) The cloth was kept in big rolls. a) The denim would fade in the sun.

Garnham found that there was no difficulty in processing in the first example [when (b) followed (a)] but that, in the second set of sentences, (a) was read much more slowly when it followed (b). Garnham (1981: 383) concluded that subjects take a longer time reading a sentence with an instance noun if it follows a sentence in which its referent is a general category. Garnham does qualify these results by indicating that they only hold if co-text for the first sentence does not hint what type of instance the category member is. So, for example, if in the second set of sentences above, (b) was replaced by 'the cloth was made into jeans', the general category 'cloth' receives some instantiation towards the specific category of 'denim'. This point applies to the example of instantiation of 'bird' as 'robin' above. That is, although a general category 'bird' precedes an instance category 'robin' which comes in the succeeding sentence, 'bird' is all the same constrained by the information 'cute, red-breasted'.

To sum up, the results of Garnham and McKoon and Ratcliff and others indicate that instantiation is for the most part an automatic process when appropriate knowledge is readily accessible, appropriate contextual information is present, and when instances precede superordinates. As a corollary, text that introduces a superordinate term which is then followed by an instance (and in the absence of appropriate contextual information) could then be said to be *inconsiderate* (Sanford and Garrod 1981: 196–8). I now move on to discuss one more elaborative inference.

7.2.6 Instrument Inferences and the Likelihood of Their Generation

Consider the following sentence: 'The accountant dried his hands'. A reader may infer that the accountant was using a towel to dry his hands. In other words, 'towel' is an *instrument inference*. Early investigations into instrument inferences suggested that they were not automatically produced during reading. In the experiments of Singer (1979a, 1979b), verification times for the instrument word were longer with an implied rather than explicit instrument, indicating that they are not inferred automatically. Later research suggested, however, that an instrument has a higher probability of being inferred when it has been referred to already in the text (Lucas et al. 1990) or when context constrains towards a specific instrument. To investigate the latter, O'Brien et al. (1988) had subjects read the following:

(1) All the mugger wanted was to steal the woman's money.
(2a) But when she screamed, he **stabbed** her with his **weapon** in an attempt to quiet her.

[(2b) But when she screamed, he **assaulted** her with his **weapon** in an attempt to quiet her.]
(3) He looked to see if anyone had seen him.
(4) He threw the **knife** into the bushes, took her money, and ran away.
[my bold]

O'Brien et al. considered reading times for sentence (4) above when the passage was read by different subjects when either (2a) or (2b) was included. When the passage was read with (2b), the last sentence took longer to read. O'Brien et al. deduced that this was because the inference that the weapon was a knife was produced only while (4) was being read. In contrast, after finding a quicker reading time for (4) when (2a) was used, they deduced that this was because 'knife' had already been generated before (4) was read via the more constraining co-textual information of 'stabbed'. Processing of (1) and (2b) was, then, more shallow than with (1) and (2a).

Garrod and Sanford (1982) also produced evidence that implied instruments are automatically generated on-line. Sanford (1990: 518–19) attempts to answer the question why the results of Singer (1979a) differ from those of Garrod and Sanford (1982). Sanford (1990) draws attention to the fact that a subsequent experiment by Cotter (1984), using both sets of materials, showed that the Garrod-Sanford and Singer results were replicable within the same study, ruling out spurious explanations. Sanford (1990) reasons that the difference appears to be that with the Garrod-Sanford set, the instruments are 'part of the meaning' of the verbs (for example, *key* is 'part of the meaning' of *unlock*), whereas for Singer's verbs, this is not the case. A similar set of reasoning is provided in Sanford and Garrod (1994: 703).

7.2.7 Summing-Up of the Psycholinguistic Research on Inference Generation

I have drawn attention to the minimalist hypothesis. This states that in the absence of specific goal-directed strategic purposes, only two types of automatic inferences are produced: (1) local coherence inferences, and (2) elaborative inferences that rely on information that is readily and easily available. When a reader is specifically goal-directed and willing to spend more time and effort in processing, then other elaborative inferences generated are not automatic but strategic. The inferences I have referred to above will inform the idealised reader framework in Section C for the analysis of mystifying text. The above evidence will provide a more consistent basis than found in current CDA for the appreciation of inference generation in text comprehension and how inference generation relates to mystifying text. For the sake of clarity, I list in tabular form, in Figure 7.1, the inferences that will inform the reader framework in Section C.

AUTOMATICALLY GENERATED:	AUTOMATICALLY GENERATED:	USUALLY HAVE TO BE STRATEGICALLY GENERATED:
Necessary for local coherence	When information is quickly and easily available	
1. connecting causal antecedents	1. elaborative causal antecedents 2. instantiations 3. instruments	1. causal consequents
	Strength of 1, 2 and 3 relies on ready availability of information	

Figure 7.1 Inference generation in text comprehension

In this section I have highlighted the issue of shallow generation of inferences. The issue of shallow processing is continued into the next section where, instead of inferences, I look at how *top-down* processing can lead to shallow processing of lexis and syntax.

7.3 SHALLOW PROCESSING OF TEXT THROUGH TOP-DOWN PROCESSING

7.3.1 Sanford and Garrod's Primary Processing Principle

Sanford and Garrod (1981) argue that a central aspect of comprehension is that when it is possible, and as soon as possible, linguistic input will be related to background knowledge, the resulting representation being used to assist the comprehension of subsequent text. This is known as the *primary processing principle*. The primary processing principle, then, has much in common with the minimalist hypothesis in this respect.[4] For Sanford and Garrod (1994), the need to link linguistic input quickly to background knowledge accounts for the fact that it is common for top-down processing to prevail over the processing of syntax and lexis. As examples of this phenomenon, Sanford and Garrod offer the common misperceptions of 'Can a man marry his widow's sister?' and 'This book fills a much-needed gap'. Sanford and Garrod (1994: 710–11) conclude:

> the problem seems to be that existing stereotyped knowledge of
> the situations seems to override sufficient processing detail to

enable the anomaly to be detected ... processes necessary for true
coherence can be incomplete, and that a sense of coherence is
achieved on the basis of a good fit between some elements of the
sentences concerned and stereotyped knowledge. This is
consistent with the primary processing principle of mapping ...

Sanford (1990) and Barton and Sanford (1993) make use of a well-known puzzle to illustrate how top-down processing can prevail over lexical registration leading to shallow processing. So as to better understand the points that Barton and Sanford make, it might help if you try this puzzle yourself:

There was a tourist flight on its way from Vienna to Barcelona.
On the last leg of the journey, it developed severe engine trouble
over the Pyrenees. The pilot lost control, and it crashed, right on
the border. Wreckage was equally strewn in France and Spain, and
one question facing the authorities was where the survivors
should be buried. What was the solution?

In Barton and Sanford's (1993) experiment, a two-thirds majority (67 per cent) did not detect the anomaly that 'survivors should be buried'. This could be explained by invoking the potency of top-down driven expectation, in this case that dead people result from crashes. So since 'survivors' is part of the semantic field of air crash, readers might admit it as a legitimate filler for the patient of 'bury'. To test the argument that the anomaly is *not* detected because of the potency of top-down-driven expectation, Barton and Sanford (1993) conducted a similar 'detection experiment' this time using the scenario of a bicycle accident instead of an air crash. Detection rates for 'survivors being buried' following bicycle accidents averaged 80 per cent compared with 33 per cent for the air crash. It seemed, then, that top-down processing influences detection rate since one would not usually expect death to accompany a bicycle accident, while one *would* expect it to follow a plane crash.

In a further study of the plane crash text, 'survivors' was replaced by 'surviving dead', clearly in this context contradictory. Since this phrase is irregular the detection rate should be high, if the meaning of 'surviving dead' is fully analysed by subjects when they read the text. Barton and Sanford (1993) found the opposite, however, with only 23 per cent detecting the anomaly. The result seems to suggest that if one element of the noun phrase, in this case 'dead', is able to fit expectation to an adequate degree, then the noun phrase is in effect only analysed in a shallow manner. A possible objection to this experiment is that it is not so much that readers fail to notice that survivors would not be buried or that they cannot be dead, but that readers edit such phenomena in real discourse (1), treating them as mistakes. However, the strength of the objection still rests on the fact that top-down has precedence over bottom-up processing. See also the outline of Reder and Kusbit (1991) in the next section (7.3.2).

Now, consider the following from Sanford (1990: 522) on the partial processing of the 'burying the survivors' text:

> If the processing of inferences is incomplete, in what way is it incomplete? Linguistic elements can fill roles that they do not really fit on the basis of partial matches. What kind of relation can be said to result? In terms of **conventional AI, the role could be said to be an IS-AN-INSTANCE-OF relation**. Yet this may not make much sense. With the airplane scenario, if one asks explicitly, 'do you bury survivors?' subjects recognise how silly the problem was. An alternative to the full relation is that the pattern match produces the equivalent of a link, but one that does not have a semantic value (i.e. *survivors* is simply *associated* with the slot for patient). **This is very different from the classical view of inference, of course, which would require the derivation of a predicate with a semantic value.** [my bold]

Evidence from Sanford (1990) and Barton and Sanford (1993) indicates that readers are often shallow with regard to the construction of *semantic value*. Since on the classical picture, the derivation of a predicate requires 'whole' semantic value, the classical theory is directly confronted by Barton and Sanford's (1993) experimental evidence.

7.3.2 'Moses Illusion'

Erickson and Mattson's (1981) investigations into partial processing led to the coinage of the 'Moses Illusion'. They asked their subjects to respond to 'How many animals of each sort did Moses put on the ark?' Erickson and Mattson found that a large number of subjects processed this in a shallow manner since they did not detect the anomaly. Erikson and Mattson argued that this was because of the closeness between Moses and Noah in memory. From the perspective of Sanford and Garrod's primary processing principle, this would be accounted for as follows: readers make an effort to immediately relate textual information to the familiar (familiar, in this case, to those with some knowledge of the Old Testament); the necessary partiality that ensues means that anomalies often go undetected. Indeed, Erickson and Mattson go on to state that the Moses Illusion suggests that natural language processing involves incompleteness on a more general level. In other words, readers are likely to embrace a particular term providing there is a *high degree of fit* with their expectations in that context, and a full analysis of the meanings of terms usually does not occur.

Reder and Kusbit (1991) performed a series of experiments in order to try to ascertain explanations for the Moses Illusion. One explanation might be that readers do notice the anomaly but do not report it, assuming the text is *co-operative* in the Gricean sense (see 9.2.1). To test this, Reder and Kusbit asked one group of respondents to spot irregular items in sentences, and another group to ignore anomalies and answer questions as if they were semantically adequate. However, subjects who had been requested to detect anomalies *still* erred, overlooking many of them. Reder and Kusbit noted that the detection tasks were time consuming, suggesting the difficulty of such a process. This in turn suggested the high degree of overriding capacity of top–down processing over bottom–up analysis. Overall, for Reder and Kusbit, these results lent support for the following: subjects who originally did not report the Moses Illusion most probably had *not* noticed the anomaly.[5]

7.3.3 Flores d'Arcais

Evidence that registration of syntax is not necessarily prominent in processing comes from Flores d'Arcais (1987). He makes a distinction between computation and use of the results of computation. On the basis of findings, he argues that while readers make full computation of syntax, the results of this computation are not necessarily used. This is because 'what makes good readers good is their ability to deal more efficiently with "higher order" kind of strategies, thus relying less on the results of syntactic computation' (Flores d'Arcais 1987: 632). For Flores d'Arcais, readers rely first on top–down strategies and use bottom–up strategies when top–down sources are impoverished. Indeed, from the results of one experiment, Flores d'Arcais (1987: 632) suggests that 'readers who are good at extracting information from rapidly presented texts seem to be less sensitive to syntactic violations than less efficient readers'. This supports the results of experiments we have seen above. On a similar point, evidence cited in Garnham (1985: 138–41) suggests that what people remember about a sentence is not its syntactic structure, nor its semantic meaning verbatim, but its *message* constructed through an interaction between the sentence and the reader's cognitive resource.[6]

7.3.4 Summing-Up

From the evidence discussed in 7.3, top-down processing can prevail over the registration of syntax and lexical items such that they are processed in a shallow or partial manner. So we should also be sceptical of the symbolic assumption that mental representation of lexical items in a sentence is necessarily compositional. In the Barton and Sanford (1993) experiment, while a two-thirds majority (67 per cent) did not detect the anomaly 'burying survivors' in the air crash scenario, 33 per cent *did* detect this irregularity. We cannot, then, take it as an absolute that top-down expectancy always overrides the semantic meaning of a lexical item for every reader. However, to detect the anomaly, the reader has to be able to analyse 'survivors' and 'buried' compositionally or 'fully', something that the majority patently did not do. We saw also that Reder and Kusbit (1991) reported that detection of anomalies, which would necessarily involve compositional analysis, was time-consuming. To sum up: (1) it would appear that it is more usual for the mental representation of a reader to be non-compositional with regard to lexical items in a text; and (2) to detect anomalies, the necessary compositional analysis is in line with extra cognitive effort.

Returning to the Erickson and Mattson (1981) experiment, the evidence is generalised to apply to all readers when, of course, the processing presupposed a particular kind of reader: one familiar with the Old Testament. The danger with generalising the results of such experiments is that inter-individual variation as well as intra-individual variation is downplayed. For example, if Reder and Kusbit (1991) had offered large cash awards for all the anomalies that their subjects were able to spot, these subjects would have had a greater vested interest and so would have been more likely to engage with the text with greater cognitive effort. It is a basic assumption, however, of this book that degrees of reading scrutiny and vested interest in texts can vary both inter and intra-personally. As we shall see in 7.5, I argue that a CD analyst *has* a vested interest in the text they examine. This can lead them to derive a different discourse (1) from a reader with no specific reading goal for the same text because they are more likely to derive strategic inferences than the latter.

Let me now turn to the last section on psycholinguistic evidence for shallow processing.

7.4 SELECTIVE PROCESSING OF NARRATIVES

7.4.1 Main versus Secondary Characters

Various studies have shown how references to *main* and *secondary* characters are treated differently in reading. Anderson, Garrod and Sanford (1983) investigated the differences in processing of 'main' and 'scenario-dependent' characters. The latter were characters which depend upon a particular scenario. So, for example, if John visits the cinema and is shown to his seat by the usherette, then John would constitute a main character since he is outside the limits of the cinema, whereas the usherette is bound to the scenario of the cinema. Using a self-paced reading approach, Anderson et al. ascertained that sentences containing pronominal anaphoric references to main characters were read more quickly than those with references to scenario-bound characters. This suggests that readers are more 'involved' in processing with main characters than with secondary characters. In a similar experiment, Morrow (1985) explored the processing of a main character, a character which was the theme of the first three sentences of a short narrative. Below is the narrative used by Morrow (1985), where different subjects were presented with the text in its different variations [with (A) or (B) or (C)]. For whatever variation, subjects were asked at the end of the text the following question: 'Whose feet are referred to?'.

> Paul caught the flu and was feeling pretty awful. He told his eldest son Ben to keep the house quiet. He got up from bed to go to the bathroom, irritated by the noise. Traffic was rushing by the house. The kids were arguing in the den.
> (A) That noisy Ben was messing up the kitchen.
> or
> (B) Noisy Ben was tramping around in the kitchen.
> or
> (C) Ben was wondering when his father would feel better as he ate in the kitchen.
> The floor felt cold on his feet.
> Whose feet are referred to?

The narrative presents the main character (Paul) and the secondary character (Ben). (A) introduces Ben from Paul's attitude, (B) is similar to (A) but presents the secondary character as being more active, while (C) allows Ben to have a perspective. With (A) and (B), the secondary character is backgrounded while it is more foregrounded in (C). In response to the probe question 'Whose feet are referred to?', Morrow found that choice of main character (Paul) as referent was high in (A) (97 per cent) and (B) (84 per cent), but low in (C) (34 per cent). Morrow concluded that when the secondary character is backgrounded from the perspective of the main character, the reader's perception of states is bound up with the perspective of the main character. A straightforward objection to this experiment is that the reader's perception of states is generated after the probe question and so we cannot infer that the experiment indicates what transpires normally in the heads of readers. An experiment where this objection does not apply, because it is *on-line reading* which is being gauged by measurement of reading time, is included in the following section.

7.4.2 Proper Names versus Role-Descriptions

Garrod and Sanford (1988) performed a reading-time investigation into how contextual information affects the processing of characters (see also the experimental evidence of Sanford, Moar and Garrod 1988). Below is an example of a text used by Garrod and Sanford (1988):

> *Lunch at the cafeteria*
> Alistair hung up his coat and picked a tray.
> The waitress smiled as she poured the coffee.
> The atmosphere was hot and sticky. (optional)
> He took the cup   or   *She* offered the cup. (character mention)
> He mopped his brow   or   *She* mopped *her* brow. (target sentences)

The main character is Alistair since he has a proper name and is not bound by the scenario, whereas 'the waitress' is the secondary character since it is a role description of a character bound by the scenario. The target sentence can refer to either the main or the secondary character. In order that the referent of the target sentence does not surprise the reader, the same referent is mentioned in the previous sentence. So when the character-mention sentence is 'He took the cup', the target sentence is 'He mopped his brow'. The reading times of subjects were ascertained for the target sentence 'He mopped his brow' referring to the main character (Alistair) and the target sentence 'She mopped her brow' referring to the secondary character (waitress). This was done with the atmosphere sentence either present or absent. Consequently, there were four sets of reading times, shown in Figure 7.2.

When the atmosphere sentence is absent, reading times are signifi-

	Main character (*Alistair*) Target: He mopped his brow	Secondary character (*waitress*) Target: She mopped her brow
With *Atmosphere* statement	1,379	1,430
Without *Atmosphere* statement	1,650	1,463

Figure 7.2 Sample reading times (ms) for the target sentences in Garrod and Sanford (1988)

cantly slower when the main character (Alistair) is referred to in the target sentence, but this is not the case when the secondary character (waitress) is referred to in the target sentence. Here are Sanford and Garrod (1994: 709):

> The results thus fit intuitions that the behaviour of the main character needs causal explanation, not that of the secondary characters. Certainly, the actions of main characters are typically either explained or motivated directly in stories and narratives, whereas those of secondary characters are not. The present results suggest that this goes hand in hand with an **automatic selective process** which seeks the formation of richer structures around main characters. [my bold]

For Sanford and Garrod (1994), the experiment showed that subjects focused more on the main character since they were actively seeking to supply a causal explanation for *why* he mopped his brow in the absence of information that the atmosphere was hot and sticky. When the target sentence referred to the waitress, the absence of the 'atmosphere sentence' did not affect processing time, indicating that the behaviour of the secondary character did not lead the reader to seek causal explanation.

The expectation that the actions of main characters in narratives should be explained is in line with other experiments cited in this section, in the sense that main characters are an automatic focus for readers (see Sanford and Garrod 1994). The corollary of this is that inferences surrounding secondary characters in narratives are normally generated in a more shallow manner compared to that of main characters (see also Stevenson (1993: 119) on the issue of reader-focus on characters in narrative).

I now move on to the implications of all the above psycholinguistic evidence for CDA.

7.5 IMPLICATIONS OF THIS CHAPTER FOR CDA

7.5.1 Orientation

In 7.5, I am concerned, broadly speaking, with the following. In chapters 5 and 6, I showed that what symbolic CDA identifies as mystifying text was not the case from the perspective of connectionism and cognitive linguistics. In 7.5.2, I show that the psycholinguistic evidence for shallow processing I have amassed in this chapter also conflicts with symbolic assumptions in CDA, and in turn also problematises what CDA regards as mystifying text.

Secondly, I make the assumption that a *resistant* reader, in the parlance of CDA (Fairclough 1992), makes a good deal of cognitive effort. An assumption in socio-cognitive analysis in CDA is that non-resistant readers can allow texts to position them into particular interpretations. I assume then that, for CDA, readers who are positioned into particular interpretations make much less effort. This is especially if they are merely reading for gist. Below I also make the idealised assumption that non-resistant readers make uniform minimum cognitive effort and that they are characterised by the psycholinguistic evidence of this chapter for automatic processing. While this is an idealised assumption, it can, all the same, have a certain utilitarian value. This is because it can be used to check whether critical discourse analyses make strategic inferences, and thus can *over-interpret* texts on behalf of non-analysts who, in reading for gist, do not make so much effort and so are less likely to make strategic inferences. This is the subject of 7.5.3.

7.5.2 Problematising what CDA Regards as Mystifying Text

As we saw in Chapters 2 and 4, the agentless passive is a feature which CDA has often isolated as being salient because of its associations with mystification. In relation to this, consider again the texts Keenan et al. (1984) used, outlined in 7.2.3. The second sentence in all of the texts, 'The next day his body was covered with bruises', has similarities with the passive voice. That is, although in this context 'covered' is functioning as a stative adjective, there is an absence of agency in this sentence similar to agency deletion in a passive such as 'The dog was run over'.[7] Even though 'was covered', in Keenan's et al.'s (1984) texts, describes a state and not an action, this experimental evidence enables us to say more precisely why use of the passive *can* be mystifying and sometimes not. In the experiments of Keenan et al. (1984), the agent was readily inferable across the first pair of sentences ('Joey's big brother punched him again and again. The next day his body was covered with bruises.') because the causal relation was strong in memory. Not only could a connecting causal antecedent inference be instituted (which we saw earlier is usually effortless for readers) but a strong elaborative causal antecedent inference could also be inferred since background knowledge was strong. However, agency was less strongly inferred in the fourth pair of sentences ('Joey went to a neighbor's house to play. The next day his body was covered with bruises.') since the causal relation in memory was not so strong. That is, while the *connecting* causal antecedent inference was inferred, the *elaborative* causal antecedent was weak since causal relation in memory was weak. So what do we conclude? By analogy, passives accompanied by agent deletion can be mystifying (to varying degrees) at least to the identity of causal antecedence if the causal relation in memory is not so strong. But, crucially, mystification has nothing to do with the fact that agency has to be inferred across clauses or adjacent sentences. This is shown more clearly below with the aid of an example.

Consider again Trew's (1979: 98–9) analysis (backed up by Toolan 2001; Montgomery 1995; Lee 1992 and Simpson 1993) that the identity of the agent of the killing is only weakly implicated in 'Eleven Africans were shot dead and 15 wounded when Rhodesian police opened fire on a rioting crowd of about 2,000 . . .' There are two points to note here. First, as Keenan et al. (1984) show, agency is inferable across sentences and so by extension across clauses. Secondly, the causal relation between 'police' or anybody else 'opening fire' and people being 'shot dead' is, I would assert, a fairly strong causal relation for many people, and so the causal antecedent is not 'identified weakly'. Not only is a connecting causal antecedent inference likely to be instituted but so is a strong elaborative causal antecedent inference. In other words, what Trew regards as being mystifying of agency is not the case from the perspective of the psycholinguistic research above.

Again, Trew's analysis is predicated upon a symbolic over-emphasis on sentential structure (as well as internalist assumptions of mental representation) over consideration of the contribution of the human understander. In this particular case, the contribution of the human understander is his or her strength of causal relation in memory and his or her capacity to generate inferences across clauses and sentences. Indeed, if what makes good readers, as Flores d'Arcais (1987: 632) says, is their ability to rely less on the results of syntactic computation, Trew and others in CDA are again misguided in focusing so much on sentential structure. Full use of syntactic computation is not the norm for people reading quickly for general information, with otherwise little vested interest in the text, since they are relying much more on 'higher-order' or top-down strategies.

As another example, consider the following sentence from a story for five-year-olds analysed by Hodge and Kress (1993: 48) (see 4.2.2): 'As time went by, the rain fell on the seeds and the sun shone down on them, and the turnips began to grow.' They argue that the non-transactives used in the young children's story mystify the nature of the causality whereas the transactives do reveal the causality. I highlighted in 4.2.2 how Hodge and Kress (1993) neglected the issue of how language cues background knowledge. The psycholinguistic evidence of Keenan et al. (1984) supports this perspective, discriminating background knowledge as strength of causal relation in memory. Since a young child, I presume, would not have rich knowledge of the cause-effect relations involved in respiration, germination, photosynthesis and so on, we can suppose that in their discourse (1) they would not make rich, elaborative causal antecedent inferences but merely make connecting causal antecedent inferences. In other words, they would connect turnip growth to the rain and the sun but not really know why. Again, the psycholinguistic evidence conflicts with the symbolic over-emphasis on sentential structure in CDA, as well as internalist mental representation, over considerations of the contribution of the human understander.

In Chapters 5 and 6, I showed how the symbolic postulates in Clark (1992) and Simpson (1993) were problematised by connectionism and cognitive linguistics respectively and thus what these authors regarded as mystifying text. Below, I show how psycholinguistic evidence relating to *instantiation* inferences and *selective processing of main characters* also conflicts with Simpson's (1993) and Clark's (1992) symbolic analyses and with what they regard as being mystifying text.

Consider again Clark's (1992: 215) argument (see 4.7) that the perception of Steed as rapist is reduced by using the euphemism 'attacked' to mask the terrible details of rape. We have seen that instantiation takes place automatically when it is based on familiar background knowledge. In the minimalist hypothesis, this includes information already established in the text (McKoon and Ratcliff 1992: 440). Thus, it is likely in reading the Steed text that there would be instantiation of 'attack' in sentence 2. ('His third victim, a 39-year-old mother of three, was attacked at gunpoint after Steed forced her car off the M4') via the more specific and basic-level 'rape' information from sentence 1. ('Two of Steed's rape victims – aged 20 and 19 – had a screwdriver held at their throats as they were forced to submit'). This is especially the case given that when Steed 'attacks', he is attacking his *third* victim, having raped his first and second (this point also applies to Fairclough (1992: 182–3) and what I said about instantiation of the category 'abnormalities' (see 4.7)). In looking at the text via the psycholinguistic phenomenon of instantiation, the following symbolic assumptions are problematised: (1) all the information should be 'in' the sentence, that is, the structure of the sentences should mirror reality regardless of the processor's (inferential) input; and (2) 'attacked' is compositional in mental representation irrespective of how co-text affects its processing.

In the news report, Steed is a proper name and the other referents, apart from Jacqueline Murray, are role descriptors: 'rape victims' and 'mother of three'. News reports can be regarded as a type of narrative and so if we go back to the psycholinguistic evidence for *name/role descriptor*, we see that Steed can be treated as the 'main character'. The psycholinguistic experiments we saw in 7.4 dealt with short narrative texts. These are akin to extracts from 'literary stories' where interest in the psychology of main characters is usually motivated because the reader has a vested interest in being entertained, wanting to know what happened next (see also 9.4.2). So applying the results of psycholinguistic evidence of very short narrative texts to news reports/stories, where the reader may be less concerned to understand psychological motivation because they are reading for general information, is not so straightforward. However, what we can say from the experiments in 7.4 and on the basis of other experimental evidence in this chapter, is that readers are likely to focus on proper names in news text in relation to establishing causal antecedence. Given this, Steed as 'main character' in the above extract, is unlikely to be absent in discourse (1) when sentence 2. is processed, *pace* Clark and Simpson. Thus, again, the psycholinguistic evidence from this chapter conflicts with the symbolic assumption that a sentence should fully represent events independently of the human understander. In turn, the interpretation of sentence 2. as one which is mystifying is problematised.

Finally, let us return to Simpson's (1993: 170) analysis that 'so obscured is the relationship between attacker and victim that it allows a possible reading wherein someone else attacks the woman at gunpoint while Steed only forces her car off the road'. Since 'someone else' is not given a name, 'someone else' would have to be a *secondary* character. But if there is automatically more focus on main characters, it follows that the alternative interpretation that Steed forced the 'victim' off the road while 'someone else' attacked her is a purely *strategic* elaborative inference, generated by an analyst with a vested interest in the text.

7.5.3 Over-Interpretation in Socio-Cognitive Analysis in CDA

Recall from 2.5.2 Fairclough's line (2001: 67–8) that if the textual material is unfamiliar, then readers would commit themselves to inferential labour to 'fill in' 'implicit links'. Now, let me reproduce part of a television documentary text which Fairclough (1995a: 122–3) analyses, and then some of Fairclough's analysis:

[*MIX to pipes in slum area of Manila, pan to wide-shot slums*]
[Narration]
(1) Everywhere in the Third World life in rural areas gets harder – and poor people flock to the city.
(2) The urban poor get poorer.
[*Close-up child standing in pipe; Slum area, mother and child*]
(3) When rice prices go up, hunger and unrest grows.
(4) In the city, the people can usually be kept in their place.
 (from 'A New Green Revolution?', a documentary programme in the science series *Horizon*, broadcast in January 1984 on BBC2)

Cohesion relations are largely implicit in this sequence. For example, I interpret the clauses of the first three sentences as in relations of enhancement, and more specifically cause-effect relations, but they lack markers of causal cohesion. In sentence 1, the two clauses are linked by the all-purpose conjunction *and*, which leaves implicit the cause-effect relation (poor people flock to the city *because* life in rural areas gets harder). I also see an unmarked cause-effect relation between the second clause of sentence 1 and sentence 2 (the urban poor get poorer *because* so many people flock to the city). Again, although the first clause of sentence 3 is marked with a temporal conjunction (*when*), there is an implicit causal relation between the two clauses (hunger and unrest grow *because* rice prices go up). **It takes quite an inferential leap on the interpreter's part to establish a coherent meaning relation between sentences 3 and 4.** I interpret this as an extension-type relation of an adversative type (unrest grows, *but* the people can usually be kept in their place; or *although* unrest grows, the people can usually be kept in their place). The connection between these sentences rests upon a 'bridging assumption' (Brown and Yule 1983, Fairclough 1992): that popular unrest gives rise to a problem of order, and the need for official action to try to contain it. [my bold]

Before I continue with quotation from Fairclough, let me highlight his point above that 'it takes quite an inferential leap on the interpreter's part to establish a coherent meaning relation between sentences 3 and 4'. I will come to the significance of this highlighting shortly. In the meantime, Fairclough continues:

Overall, this part of the extract addresses an ideal interpreter who is familiar with a particular preconstructed 'script' (Montgomery et al. 1989) that is being evoked here: a predictable sequence of events leading from rural poverty to urban squalor and unrest and consequential problems of order. **The ideal interpreter** is relied upon to fill in the gaps, make explicit what is left implicit, and construct a coherent, preferred, meaning for the text . . . the text takes the script as universally given for its audience, and so positions audience members that they are induced to draw upon it to arrive at a coherent interpretation. [my bold]

Examining the above, we can suppose that Fairclough has a reader (that is, a non-resistant reader) in mind, gleaned from what Fairclough also says about it being a 'moot point how many real audience members might, if asked, actually agree with the stereotypical narrative of Third World urban problems which constitutes the script'. That is, if such a reader were prompted to think about the stereotypical narrative of Third World urban problems, they might not agree with it, given the extra cognitive effort incurred by the prompting. But without such prompting they might be compliant with the way in which the text 'positions' them.

For Fairclough, the absence of cohesive markers is significant since readers are induced to draw upon a particular script of the Third World in order to 'arrive at a coherent interpretation'. For him, 'the ideal interpreter' (see text in bold) will invest the necessary cognitive labour to make the 'bridging (coherence) assumption' he outlines between sentences 3 and 4. As I have highlighted, Fairclough is explicit that this involves a fair amount of cognitive labour ('quite an inferential leap'). But as we saw in the experimental work of Vonk and Noordman (1990) (see 7.2.2), even if cohesive markers are present, if the reader is unfamiliar with the textual material, then coherence will inevitably be shallow, readers satisfying themselves that the text is coherent because it is cohesive. Indeed, I would argue that for many readers, 'problems of order following popular unrest and the need for official action to try to contain it' is hardly an everyday, familiar scenario. So Fairclough over-estimates the amount of cognitive work many readers would be prepared to invest since the 'inferential leap' would not be made, at least, by a reader with no specific goal, with little vested interest in the text, and largely unfamiliar with subject matter. Finally, Fairclough's explanation itself, it could be argued, rests on a conceptual tension. In being willing to make the cognitive effort, to make 'quite an inferential leap', one could assert that Fairclough's 'ideal interpreter' is someone *with* a vested interest in the text. But at the same time, for Fairclough, the 'ideal interpreter' is someone who accepts the positioning of the text and thus is someone who presumably does not make a great deal of cognitive effort.

Fairclough's (2001: 67–8) distinction between *automatic gap-filling* and *inferences which require work* (and thus the idea that readers are willing to invest in such inferential work even if they are unfamiliar with the subject matter) is found in Brown and Yule (1983). From chapter 7 of their book, here are Brown and Yule (1983: 266): 'the more interpretive "work" the reader (hearer) has to undertake in arriving at a reasonable interpretation of what the writer (speaker) intended to convey, the more likely it is that there are inferences being made'. Indeed, Fairclough (2001: 89; 1989: 108) cites and endorses Brown and Yule's (1983) chapter 7 as 'a helpful discussion of inferencing, and its relation to "automatic gap filling"'. Gough and Talbot's (1996) position on inferences (see 2.5.2 and below) derives from Fairclough (1989), which also suggests it derives from Brown and Yule (1983). Brown and Yule (1983) was published before the papers associated with the minimalist hypothesis and the later constructionists, since these were published in the late 1980s and early 1990s. Consequently, Fairclough's sources are not up-to-date and grounded in consensus thinking on inference generation. Brown and Yule's position, and in turn Fairclough's, is contradicted not only by the minimalist hypothesis and the later constructionists but by Sanford and Garrod's (1981, 1994) primary processing principle and by Vonk and Noordman (1990).

Section 2.5.2 referred to the problem-page advice commented upon by Gough and Talbot (1996: 226). The notion of a reader here is more implicit than in Fairclough's text but, all the same, the phrase 'the reader's complicity' indicates Gough and Talbot do have a (compliant) reader in mind. The assumption was, as we saw in 2.5.2, that readers will 'work', even if they are 'unfamiliar with problem pages', to produce the inference that 'interest in homosexuality (in this context, by adolescent males) is useful inasmuch as it reinforces this separate heterosexual identity'. In doing so, the reader becomes ideologically positioned. But the inference that heterosexual identity is reinforced by interest in homosexuality is a causal consequent inference. As we saw in 7.2.4, causal consequents are normally weakly generated since they are not required for coherence. Furthermore, like 'popular unrest leading to problems of order etc.', the above inference is a rather non-everyday, abstract one that the minimalist hypothesis would regard as unlikely to be generated unless the reader had quite a specific goal in mind. The psycholinguistic evidence, then, contradicts Gough and Talbot's line at least for a reader without a specific goal, that is, one close in disposition to a reader reading for gist. What Gough and Talbot have produced is a strategic inference, one less likely to be generated by such readers. This strategic-inference generation most probably reflects Gough and Talbot's (1996) own vested interest in the text, their own specific goal.

Gough and Talbot's position (as well as Fairclough's position earlier) seems akin to that of the early constructionists (7.2.2) where there are few restrictions placed around the types of elaborative inference produced, a position which the later constructionist position has moved away from (7.2.4). In their review of different models of inference generation, Graesser at al. (1994: 384) indicate that the types of inference that are generated on a model of reading which subsumes Schank and Abelson (1977) include elaborative inferences such as causal consequence:

> This model asserts that reading is expectation-driven in addition to explanation-driven. That is, readers generate expectations about future occurrences in the plot, and these expectations guide the interpretation of clauses in a top-down fashion (Bower et al. 1979; DeJong 1979; Dyer 1983; Schank and Abelson 1977). Expectations are formulated whenever higher order knowledge structures are activated, such as a script or a theme. For example, if a story activates a RESTAURANT script and the text mentions that two characters entered a restaurant together, then the reader would form expectations that the characters will eat, talk and be served food. If a story activates a REVENGE theme and the text specifies that character A hurts character B, then the reader would form the expectation that character B will hurt character A.

However, the fact that Schank and Abelson's (1977) model includes fully formed causal consequent inferences is in direct conflict with both the later constructionists and the minimalists. Schank and Abelson (1977) is cited in Gough and Talbot (1996: 228) which is unsurprising when we consider that Schank and Abelson's script theory is drawn upon in Fairclough (1989), a source work for Gough and Talbot (1996). I am speculating here but perhaps Gough and Talbot (1996) take for granted that causal consequents are readily produced since Fairclough (1989) draws directly upon Schank and Abelson (1977).

In 4.5, I discussed Fairclough's (1995a: 113) argument that 'flock' in 'Poor people flock to the city' is 'usually associated with sheep – notoriously passive', thus reinforcing the perspective in the rest of the text that the 'poor' are not agents of their circumstances. We saw, in 4.5, that an assumption which facilitates this is the symbolic one of compositionality where symbols are discrete and enduring. Compositionality, then, facilitates the choice of the ovine sense of 'flock' so as to suit Fairclough's line.

However, in 5.3.3, I indicated how a connectionist perspective conflicted with Fairclough's explanation.

What about the psycholinguistic evidence in relation to Fairclough's explanation? The low detection rates of lexical anomalies in the experiments of Barton and Sanford (1993) (7.3.1) as well as Reder and Kusbit (1991) (7.3.2) suggest that it is automatic for the mental representation of a reader to be non-compositional with regard to lexical items in a text. For a reader not investing so much effort, 'flock' is likely to have *partial* value and not the 'full' semantic value of 'collection of sheep'. This psycholinguistic evidence then also conflicts with Fairclough's analysis of 'flock'. In conclusion, Fairclough has produced a strategic inference to suit a particular line which is likely to be at odds with the discourse (1) of non-analysts. All of the above applies to other instances of CDA treating lexical items as mentally compositional.

7.6 SUMMARY

There is not much citation of recent psycholinguistic work on inferencing in the CDA literature. By drawing on such evidence, I have been able to show a number of things in 7.5:

1. Psycholinguistic data from this chapter conflicts with symbolic CDA and thus with how it highlights mystifying text.
2. This psycholinguistic evidence indicates that mental representation necessarily goes beyond the semantico-syntactic structure of a sentence and so is not as implied in CDA, and warranted on a Hallidayan outlook, a facsimile of semantico-syntactic structure.
3. Different levels of cognitive investment in a text can lead to different discourses (1) being derived from the text. In the previous section, the different discourses (1) were the non-shallow discourse (1) generated by proxy for non-analysts by CD analysts, and the more shallow discourse (1) likely to be generated by readers reading for gist. (See 2.2.2 for a definition of discourse (1). Note that from now on all references in this book to 'discourse' are to discourse (1) unless otherwise stated.)
4. Fairclough (2001: 139) asserts (see 2.5.1) that there is essentially little difference between what the analyst does and what the non-analyst does (other than the analyst being 'concerned to explicate *what* she is doing'). With regard to

inferences, this assumes that inferences that non-analysts make implicitly are made explicit or visible by analysts. But this assumption does not take into account the fact that analysts characteristically make more effort than non-analysts. The greater effort of analysts is much more likely to lead to the generation of strategic inferences which would be much less forthcoming from a reader who, in reading for gist, is investing something akin to minimum effort.
5. Some CD analysts have *over-interpreted* by proxy for such a reader.
6. Since different levels of vested interest and thus different levels of cognitive labour lead to different interpretations, Widdowson's principle of 'partiality of interpretation' (see 2.7) for the same text has thus been demonstrated.
7. The psycholinguistic evidence of this chapter also has implications for CDA which does not take account of the non-analyst. Here, for example, is van Leeuwen (1996: 39) in relation to the *Times* news text analysed by Trew (1979: 98–9) (see 2.4.1):

> When the activities (e.g. the killing of demonstrators) are included, but some or all of the social factors involved in it (e.g. the police) are excluded, the exclusion does leave a trace. We can ask 'but who did the killing?' or 'but who was killed?', even though the text does not provide the answers.

Van Leeuwen does not try to make a distinction between interpretation by an analyst and by a non-analyst. So the analysis lacks a certain cognitive significance. It tells us that the analyst was able to notice certain text absences. But it does not tell us whether these text absences are likely to go unnoticed by a non-analyst or whether such text absences would not be absences from the discourse of a non-analyst because they are likely to be generated as inferences. For example, causal consequent inferences ('but who was killed?'), as we saw, do not stand a great chance of being generated if the reader has general goals and little vested interest in the text.

In Chapters 5, 6 and 7, I have used connectionism, cognitive linguistics and psycholinguistics separately to problematise the symbolicism of CDA and, in turn, how CDA highlights mystifying text. But we can now go further than 'problematising'. That all three paradigms conflict with symbolicism indicates real difficulties with using symbolic assumptions in CDA in the analysis of mystifying text. It would seem that mystification analysis based on symbolicism should be avoided. Given their non-symbolic nature, there is much potential for cross-over between the three paradigms. There is also, as we shall see, potential for cross-over between the three paradigms on the issue of minimum effort processing. In 7.5.3, I used the device of an idealised reader based on the psycholinguistic evidence for automatic processing in this chapter. The purpose of this device was to highlight over-interpretation in CD socio-cognitive analysis. In Section C, I will go on to explore the potential for cross-over between the three paradigms in order to construct a more comprehensive idealised reader framework which will be used instead for the highlighting of mystifying news text. Because it will be based on *non-symbolic* assumptions, in contrast to most of the CDA work which has been reviewed in this book, a certain theoretical robustness will be afforded to it.

NOTES

1. When an inference is necessary in order to connect a pronoun with a preceding noun, for example '*Sheila* takes a bow. *She* deserves the applause', then this is a case of *anaphora* or anaphoric inference. Although I do not deal with anaphoric inferences in this chapter since they do not inform the reader framework in Section C, there is ample evidence that coherence anaphoric inferences are made on-line (for example, Dell, McKoon and Ratcliff 1983).
2. Vonk and Noordman's (1990) experiments highlight one essential difference between cohesion and coherence.
3. The other relates to 'topicalisation'. Sanford (1990: 519–20) draws attention to how sentences with different attentional foci can affect the likelihood that automatic elaborative inferencing (a causal consequent below) can occur. For the sentence 'The husband had been unable to control his anger, and he hurled the extremely delicate and very valuable antique porcelain vase at the brick wall', the combination of the verb 'hurled', suggesting more intensity, and the richness of the modification in emphasising the significance of the object (see also Sanford and Garrod 1981: 171–85) makes the causal consequent – the vase broke – more likely. The inclusion of the material of the wall may also contribute to this likelihood.
4. Sanford and Garrod (1994: 704) point out that the 'primary processing principle' differs from the minimalist hypothesis 'in philosophy' since it makes 'the assumption that grounding incoming text in background knowledge is necessary to achieve a sense of understanding and to achieve coherence in many instances'. However, Sanford and Garrod (1994: 704) also acknowledge that 'once possible elaborative inferences are based on the availability or accessibility of general knowledge, the minimalist position and the primary processing accounts are not so easy to distinguish'.
5. In a way similar to Sanford (1990) in note 3, Bredart and Modolo (1988) showed that error detection in the Moses Illusion can depend on topicalisation. In the sentence 'It was Moses who put two of each kind of animal on the Ark', the cleft transformation highlighted 'Moses' and led to higher detection rates.

6. Of course, there are occasions when sections of texts are remembered verbatim, for example, texts of personal significance, or statements of high interactional value (see Keenan et al. 1977). This can apply also to highly patterned language read for the first time, for example, lines from a poem or a song, or some newspaper headlines. But since CDA has tended to deal with news text of a reasonable length, rather than just headlines, I make the assumption in this book that such texts will usually hold little personal significance for the reader, or are so unpatterned and of such length that they would not ordinarily be remembered verbatim.

7. Take 'The window was broken'. How are we to analyse this? Is this a description of an *action* – an *agentless passive* where 'was' is an auxiliary verb? Or is it a description of a *state* where the past participle is an *adjectival complement* and 'was' a copula? The answer is that analysis must take into account context and human motivation, that is, features of *discourse*. For example, for 'The window was broken' where the context is a burglary, a detective may be more interested in the person who was responsible for the breakage rather than the state of the window, and so see the form 'was broken' in terms of an agentless passive. Alternatively, imagine the context of a car-safety experiment which is testing whether a particular windscreen glass is strong enough for a certain impact. In a report that 'The window was broken', 'broken' would be understood in terms of a stative adjective since the state of the window is more important than the agent of the breaking.

SECTION C

The Idealised Reader Framework

This section comprises three chapters. The purpose of these chapters is to construct an *idealised reader* framework to be used as a guide as to whether the absences from a news text, for a non-critical reader, are likely to be mystifying of the events and participants being reported. I demonstrate this application in Chapter 10. By non-critical reader, I mean a reader who is largely unfamiliar with the events being referred to and who does not invest the effort to notice absences from a news text because they are reading for gist. I highlight, in Chapter 8, compatibilities with regard to inference generation in minimum effort processing across *three* paradigms: connectionism, cognitive linguistics and psycholinguistics. In effect, I construct an idealised reader framework as a guide to the kinds of inferences actual non-critical readers are likely or unlikely to generate from news text. In Chapter 9, the framework is given a more obvious pragmatic dimension. I thread the compatibilities demonstrated in Chapter 8 through another paradigm concerned with least effort: relevance theory. By the end of Chapter 9, the idealised reader framework will be complete and will thus consist of compatibilities from *four* paradigms. I explain in Chapter 8 and in Chapter 9 why I focus on news text in my use of the framework.

CHAPTER 8

Constructing the Idealised Reader: Compatibilities between Connectionism, Cognitive Linguistics and Psycholinguistics

8.1 INTRODUCTION

Consider the following from Brown and Yule (1983: 266):

> While . . . it is, in principle, impossible to predict the *actual* inferences a reader will make in arriving at an interpretation of a text, we may be able to make predictions regarding particular aspects of individual texts which readers will generally have to interpret on the basis of inference. Such predictions will be closely related to some concept of 'depth of processing'. Clearly, the reader who casually skims across the news article . . . while sitting in the dentist's waiting room, is likely to be 'reading' the text in a qualitatively different way from the reader who is anticipating being asked comprehension questions after he has finished the text.

While the psycholinguistic data reviewed in Brown and Yule (1983) is at least twenty years old now, the basic principle above remains a valid one: predictions about the actual inferences a reader makes will be closely related to some concept of 'depth of processing'. It is on this basis that I construct a reader framework. In this chapter I shall indicate compatibilities between what I have outlined of connectionism, cognitive linguistics and psycholinguistics. As we shall see, these compatibilities are not only related to a common non-symbolicism but also shallow/minimum effort processing. In threading compatibilities from these three paradigms with regard to minimum effort processing, in effect I construct the following: a framework to act as a guide to the kinds of inferences *non-critical readers* are likely to generate from news text. By non-critical reader I mean a reader who (1) is largely unfamiliar with the events being referred to; (2) in reading for gist and so something akin to minimum effort, does not invest the effort to notice absences from a news text. The guide to the processing of this non-critical reader, I call the *idealised reader* framework. The capacity to act as a guide as to how actual non-critical readers generate inferences from text is useful in mystification analysis, as will become apparent.

Before I go on to construct the idealised reader framework, it would be useful to do the following. I want first in this chapter to refer back to aspects of Sections A and B, to make clear why an idealised reader framework would, I think, be useful in the interpretation stage of CDA.

8.2 WHY A READER FRAMEWORK IS USEFUL IN THE INTERPRETATION STAGE OF CDA

8.2.1 The Need for a Reader Framework which Recognises the Distinction Between Analyst and Non-Analyst Reading

In 2.7, I highlighted a number of criticisms of CDA. Let me briefly recap. We saw, for example, that the need in CDA to conceptualise the reader has been signalled for some time (Richardson 1987). However, while there has been endorsement in CDA of using the idea of a non-analyst reader in conducting analysis of a text (for example, Hodge and Kress 1993: 175) as well as further calls for this reader to be conceptualised (Fowler 1996a; Stubbs 1997), there has as yet been little movement in taking this forward. Moreover, these observations are not made with regard to distinctions in effort made by analysts and non-analysts. Consider now the following from Widdowson (1997: 153):

> Text does not signal its own meaning, so linguistic analysis, no matter how detailed, cannot result in understanding of how and why a text means what it does.
>
> Indeed I would argue that the more detailed the linguistic analysis, the further one is likely to get from the significance of the text. And this follows because only some of the semantic meaning encoded in linguistic form is activated as contextually appropriate on a particular occasion.

We can apply what Widdowson says about how 'the more detailed the linguistic analysis, the further one is likely to get from the significance of the text' to critical discourse analysts who either (1) regard the processes of analyst reading and non-analyst reading as the same or (2) analyse the text merely from their own perspective. Because they highlight absences from a text, analysts expend effort which is not forthcoming from readers under conditions where the latter are likely not to notice absences: when reading effort is something akin to a minimum in line with general goals such as in reading for gist. So in expending such effort in analysis, while not taking account of the smaller amount of effort invested in reading for gist, the critical discourse analyst moves away from the significance of the text for the gist reader. As we saw, critical discourse analysts are likely to generate strategic inferences which a reader who is investing something close to minimum effort is less likely to do. A reader framework that is based on minimum effort in reading is necessarily idealised but it would nevertheless go some way to addressing where the significance of absences from a news text could be very high, that is, under gist reading. It would help to accord more validity to the analysis and thus avoid the kind of over-interpretation that we saw in the previous chapter.

8.2.2 The Need for a Reader Framework which Draws on Empirical Evidence

I indicated in 2.7 that Stubbs (1997: 106) criticises CDA for not making use of independent empirical evidence on the relationship between language and thought. Any reader framework would indeed need to address this criticism. This is especially the case since, as we saw in Chapter 2, attitudes to inference generation in the interpretation stage of CDA are inconsistent with one another and there is little awareness in CDA of inference typology from psycholinguistics. Furthermore, when inference theory *is* drawn upon in CDA (as, for example, in Fairclough 2001), the age of the sources in discourse analysis (for example, Brown and Yule 1983) means important work on inference generation which has transpired in the late 1980s and afterwards is absent. The idealised reader framework I begin to construct in this chapter draws on the psycholinguistic evidence of Chapter 7 and so is based, at least in part, on independent empirical evidence which is recent. Since, as I noted in 7.1, this evidence has a certain validity in that it consists largely of consensus evidence in current psycholinguistics, the idealised reader framework consists of the same. And since, as I also noted in 7.1, the evidence of Chapter 7 is unobscure, being readily available in standard psycholinguistic and cognitive psychology reference books (Gernsbacher 1994; Eysenck and Keane 2000; Harley 2001), the idealised reader framework is also based on unobscure empirical evidence.

8.2.3 The Need for a Reader Framework which Recognises that Absences from a Text are not Always Absences from Discourse

One problem with a number of the critical discourse analyses we have seen is that they presume that just because there is an absence in the text, so this translates into an absence in the discourse of a reader. We saw, contrary to some CD analyses, that just because there is an absence of agent-process-affected structures, this does not necessarily mean that there is an attenuated appreciation of the agency of an event in discourse. We also saw that although a sentence may only contain general categories and thus has an absence of specific information, more concrete co-textual information can instantiate the general category in that sentence. Once more, absences from sentences do not necessarily translate into absences from discourse. Indeed, if sufficient effort is made, then a whole host of elaborative inferences is likely to be generated. Therefore, for such an investor of effort, absences from a text are less likely to translate into absences from discourse. But my focus is on a reader who only invests something akin to minimum effort because he or she is reading for gist, and thus for whom absences from a text could be significant. There is a need for a framework that can indicate the kinds of inference which are likely to be made by such a reader and so can indicate whether absences from a text are unlikely to lead to absences from the discourse of this reader. But if such a reader framework can indicate absences from text which are unlikely to be absences from discourse, it can also do the converse: indicate absences from a text which *are* likely to be absences from discourse because they are not generated as inferences. This would be useful since it could provide a better idea of whether a text is likely to be mystifying, for a particular kind of reader, of an event or its participants because significant information is not likely to be generated as inferences. As will be seen in Chapter 10, I use the idealised reader framework constructed in Section C to do this.

8.2.4 The Need for a Reader Framework to Help Prescribe Non-Mystifying Text

Toolan (1997) is a constructive critique of CDA. Among a number of points he makes, he (1997: 88–90) argues 'that prescription not only ought to but must be part of the armoury of CDA'. For him, CDA would become more compelling if it could prescribe how a manipulative text might have been constructed so as to be non-manipulative. I agree with this, at least as regards mystification. But in order to be able to make a critique and prescribe an alternative, a framework is needed, in order to indicate why there is something wrong with the original text and why the reformed version is better. A framework, in the form of the idealised reader, based on compatibilities from different paradigms will allow more systematic articulation of intuitions as to how a text is likely to mystify what it reports for a reader who is investing something close to minimum effort. In consequence, the prescription for how the text should be constructed so as to be non-mystifying is more likely to carry conviction. Moreover, the non-symbolic nature of the idealised reader framework will usefully *prohibit* symbolic-based CD analysis which, as we saw, is problematic. Since the idealised reader framework has such a prohibitive function, prescriptions on the basis of this framework for helping to remove the mystifying properties of a particular text are then likely to carry greater conviction.

I now move to indicating compatibilities, with regard to minimum effort processing, between the three paradigms of connectionism, cognitive linguistics and psycholinguistics, and this in turn yields the major part of the idealised reader framework. I do this as follows. In 8.3, I demonstrate compatibilities between connectionism and cognitive linguistics. Then, in 8.4, I indicate compatibilities between cognitive linguistics and psycholinguistic evidence in minimum effort processing. In 8.5, I show the compatibilities between connectionism and psycholinguistic evidence in minimum effort processing. In 8.4 and 8.5 the compatibilities demonstrated are with regard to shallow processing, something which is more likely to occur when minimum effort is invested.

8.3 COMPATIBILITY OF CONNECTIONISM WITH COGNITIVE LINGUISTICS

8.3.1 General Compatibilities

There are many parallels between cognitive linguistics and connectionism. The cognitive linguist Langacker (1987a) argues that it is unhelpful to treat syntax as autonomous and thus separate from semantics, and, as we have seen in Chapter 5, connectionist models do not treat syntax and semantics in this way. Cognitive linguistics and connectionism also intersect in their eschewing of logical reasoning and rule application as being central to an understanding of language performance. On this comparison and on the shunning of 'propositional formats' and transformational derivation (such as those inherent in the derivational theory of complexity, a performance theory similar to that used in Hodge and Kress 1993 – see 4.2.2) and the notion that linguistic systems are recurrent patterns of activations, here is Langacker (1987b: 6):

cognitive grammar (at least my own formulation of it) is basically compatible with the connectionist philosophy. First, cognitive grammar makes no qualitative distinction between rules and their instantiations – rules are simply schematized expressions; moreover, the 'schemas' in question are thought of as being 'immanent' to their instantiations, not as separate or discrete structures. Second, only elements with semantic and/or phonological content are permitted, and they are characterized directly in terms of such content, not in a propositional format. Third, analyses are based on the overt form of expressions; derivation from abstract, 'underlying' representations is precluded, as is any sort of algorithmic computation. Finally, a linguistic system is viewed as simply an inventory of 'cognitive routines', which are interpretable as recurrent patterns of activation that are easily elicited by virtue of connection weights; the construction of complex expressions reduces to the co-activation of appropriate routines and 'relaxation' into a pattern of activation that simultaneously satisfies all constraints.

Langacker explicitly recognises compatibility between cognitive linguistics and connectionism. Similar explicit recognition of these compatibilities is found in the connectionist philosophers Churchland and Churchland (1996: 238), who draw parallels with the work of the cognitive linguists (Lakoff, Langacker, Bates, Fauconnier) and show how they, like connectionists, have not treated syntax and semantics as being separable; see also Harris (1990), Langacker (1987a: section 12.3), Langacker (1997), Regier (1996) and Schopman and Shawky (1996) for discussion of cognitive linguistics in the context of connectionism. As we saw in 5.2.5, one of the pioneers of cognitive linguistics, Rosch, endorses the connectionist view that symbols are 'approximate macro-level descriptions of operations whose governing principles reside at a subsymbolic level' (Varela, Thompson and Rosch 1991: 101–2). The cognitive linguist George Lakoff has also been involved since the late 1980s in a research group (at the International Computer Science Institute, University of Berkeley, California) which aims to provide connectionist modelling of learning and use of human concepts (Lakoff and Johnson 1999: 569–83).

8.3.2 Linguistic Input Not Equivalent to Process Output

Another area of compatibility between cognitive linguistics and connectionism is in the notion of *accommodation*. For the cognitive linguist

Langacker (1987a: 76–7), accommodation refers to the adjustment of the meaning of a lexical item according to the lexical company it keeps. For example, 'ball' in 'The toddler kicked the ball' and 'The final ball of the over was hit for six' are likely to be different. The connectionist Elman (1992: 170), makes explicit mention of Langacker's concept of accommodation, quoting Langacker (1987a: 76–7). Indeed, Elman's connectionist model was able to simulate accommodative effects (Elman 1992: 170). Langacker's concept of accommodation also dovetails with the capacity of McClelland and Kawamoto's (1986) connectionist network to shade meaning, which we saw in 5.3.2.

The connectionist Elman (1990: 378) offers the 'safe-combination' metaphor as an explanatory metaphor for language processing in connectionist networks:

> A metaphor that captures some of the characteristics of this approach is the combination lock. In this metaphor, the role of words is analogous to the role played by the numbers of the combination. The numbers have causal properties; they advance the lock into different states. The effect of a number is dependent on its context. Entered in the correct sequence, the numbers move the lock into an open state . . . The numbers are 'present' insofar as they are responsible for the final state but not because they are still physically present.

The safe-combination metaphor contrasts with the symbolic 'building-block' metaphor, referred to in Chapter 3. In the building-block metaphor for language processing, process output still 'contains' the building blocks of linguistic input. However, in the safe-combination metaphor for language processing, linguistic input is responsible for the final state and so is not present in this final state. Linguistic input is not the same as the process output. Langacker (1987a: chapter 12), offers a 'scaffolding' metaphor which has much in common with Elman's 'safe-combination' metaphor. Langacker views the (linguistic input) components of a compound as scaffolding, that is, they are disposable when no longer needed. The cognitive linguistic scaffolding metaphor and connectionist safe-combination block metaphor are similar, then, in emphasising how cognition output does not necessarily mirror linguistic input as well as in both being the antithesis of the building-block approach. Another cognitive linguist, Lakoff (1987a: xiv) also, like Langacker, positions against the notion of cognitive 'building blocks'.

In Chapter 6, I highlighted Barsalou's notion that many concepts are actually created 'on the fly', being ad hoc categories formed according to specific goals and as a function of context dependence, for example, 'things to take with you in event of a fire' (see 6.2.1). For Barsalou (1989), humans possess in long-term memory a large amount of loosely organised knowledge associated with a category. The connectionist philosopher Bechtel (1990: 266) sees Barsalou's perspective as compatible with that of connectionism:

> It is somewhat difficult to make sense of this [Barsalou's] view within a rule-based account of cognition, since concepts would seem to be the atoms of such systems, but much easier to make sense of it from a connectionist perspective where what exist in long-term memory are only connections. These enable the subject to produce representations that play the role of concepts and may be used in solving problems for which even rules might be invoked, but the concepts need not be fixed, atomic structures as they are in most rule-based accounts. Thus, implementing concepts in a connectionist system might allow us to explain in a straightforward manner some characteristics of concepts that might otherwise be difficult to explain.

Stillings et al. (1995: 96–7) also make the link between Barsalou's dynamic theory of concepts and connectionism.

8.3.3 The Functionalism of Cognitive Linguistics and Connectionism

The connectionist Elman (1990: 378–9) highlights the *functional* aspect of the connectionist approach to language comprehension:

> This view of language comprehension emphasizes the functional importance of representations and is similar in spirit to the approach described in Bates and MacWhinney 1982; McClelland, St John, and Taraban 1989; and many others who have stressed the functional nature of language. Representations of language are constructed to accomplish some behavior. Obviously, that behavior may range from daydreaming to verbal duels, from asking directions to composing poetry. The representations are not propositional, and their information content changes constantly over time in accord with the demands of the current task. Words serve as guideposts that help establish mental states that support this behavior; representations are snapshots of those mental states.

As Elman says, the functional importance of language is something which other connectionists, McClelland, St John and Taraban (1989) (see 5.4), have emphasised also. But the prominence of this aspect of language is compatible with a similar emphasis in cognitive linguistics where, in contrast to classical semantics, it draws attention to the interactional properties of an object. That is, language may be used not just to institute a conceptual state in a reader's or listener's mind but to institute a functional state. Section 6.3.2 gave the example of the mouse pad on a laptop computer which has different inherent properties to an external mouse. Referring to this item as a 'mouse', that is, employing a basic-level category, enables the hearer to realise the particular motor-interactionality associated with a laptop; in other words the actual function of the mouse. The hearer experiences no difficulty in activating the referent's function and allowing it to prevail over its form; the hearer perceives there to be no conflict.

As we saw in 7.2.6, humans have the ability to generate instrument inferences readily but only if the context constrains sufficiently. In 5.4.2, we also saw that connectionist networks are successful in replicating this human ability. McClelland, St John and Taraban's (1989) connectionist network was able to generate readily the instrument inference 'with a knife'. In addition, McClelland and Kawamoto's (1986) network (see 5.3) was able to fill in the 'missing instrument argument' for 'The boy broke the window', 'inferring' that the boy broke the window 'with something hard'. So connectionist models can replicate human ability to generate instruments. What about the relationship between instrument generation and cognitive linguistics? Recall the experiment from 5.2.2 of Taraban and McClelland (1988). The experimental evidence bore out Taraban and McClelland's supposition that 'with the broom' is the most expected role for 'The janitor cleaned the storage area with the . . .'. This can be explained from a cognitive linguistic perspective. In 6.4.2, we saw that, for Lakoff (1987a: 54–5), prototypical causality is understood in terms of a cluster of 'interactional properties' since it involves a high degree of direct physical manipulation, agents using their hands, body or some instrument. The *function* of the janitor also cues in that direction. It is not surprising, from the perspective of cognitive linguistics, that people choose the instrument 'broom' more readily than 'manager' or 'odour', and why Taraban and McClelland regard 'broom' as the most expected.

8.3.4 Prototypes

In 6.4, I highlighted the relationship between basic-level categories and prototype effects, for example, that prototype effects are more readily generated from basic-level categories than superordinate ones. Although the provenance of prototype theory is the cognitive linguistics of Rosch and others, connectionism and prototype theory are not incompatible. Here is Harley (2001: 303):

> [Connectionism] . . . is not necessarily a competitor to other theories such as prototypes; one instance of a category might cause one pattern of activation across the semantic units, another instance will cause another similar pattern, and so on. We can talk of the prototype that defines a category as the average pattern of activation of all the instances.

Let me flesh out this relationship between connectionism and prototypes. In essence, because of the distributed encoding of a set of exemplars, the microfeatures common to the exemplars become strongly associated. In other words, common microfeatures form strong mutually excitory links. A prototype emerges thus, an automatic consequence of connectionist networks. Interestingly, the prototype does not need to coincide with any concrete instance exposed to the system. This is because the prototype is the statistical central tendency of the various microfeature dimensions of the exemplars (Clark 1993: 22). Prototype emergence goes hand in hand with generalisation. A net is said to be able to generalise if it can handle novel cases. For example, McClelland, Rumelhart and the PDP Research Group (1986: chapter 17) were able to produce a 'dog-recognition network' which recognised a three-legged dog as a dog, something that would seem to negate against 'dogness' on the classical perspective where meaning is predicated upon necessary features. From a connectionist point of view, a tri-ped dog is still a dog because it still shares the vast majority of microfeatures of the prototypical dog. The fact also that prototypes emerge in connectionist networks dovetails with the averring of the cognitive linguist Rosch (1978) (see 6.2.1) that prototypes are not stored representations.

I have outlined some general compatibilities between connectionism and cognitive linguistics. In sections 8.4 and 8.5 respectively, I outline how cognitive linguistics and connectionism relate to the psycholinguistic evidence for shallow processing I outlined in the previous chapter, this type of processing being more likely to occur when minimum effort is invested.

8.4 COGNITIVE LINGUISTICS AND SHALLOW PROCESSING

8.4.1 Cognitive Linguistics, Shallow Processing and Instantiation

As we saw in 7.2.5, instantiations are elaborative inferences where a general category is made more concrete. For instance, in 'The vehicle hovered over the crowd', likely instantiations for 'vehicle' are that it is a balloon or a helicopter. In line with the minimalist hypothesis of McKoon and Ratcliff (7.2.2), in the absence of specific reading goals, instantiations will be readily generated when information is quickly and readily available. Recall now from 6.6.3 the text from Bransford and Johnson (1973: 400) which starts, 'The procedure is actually quite simple. First you arrange things into two different groups . . .'. We saw in 6.6.3 also that in referring to this text, Rosch (1978: 45) makes the point that:

> what Bransford and Johnson call context cues are actually names of basic-level events (e.g., washing clothes) and that one function of hearing the event name is to enable the reader to translate the superordinate terms into basic-level objects and actions.

First, we can now see that what Rosch terms 'translation' is actually the generation of *instantiation* elaborative inferences via the basic-level event category, 'washing clothes'. Secondly, as to why basic-level categories lead to instantiation and ready comprehension, and also why the superordinate categories (for example, 'procedure', 'groups', 'things' in the Branford and Johnson text) lead to shallow comprehension, we can go further than in 6.6.3 by relating cognitive linguistic explanation to the minimalist hypothesis. Since prototypes are by definition familiar, and since they are linked to the basic level, the use of basic-level categories facilitates instantiation because, from the minimalist hypothesis, instantiation is dependent on accessible knowledge.[1] Furthermore, such instantiation can be taken as being automatically generated (that is, with minimum cognitive effort) in line with the cognitive economy principle. Superordinate categories are not associated with prototypes and not characterised by cognitive economy. To yield a large amount of information from them, a higher degree of cognitive effort is required in contrast to processing of basic-level categories. And so, in line with the minimalist hypothesis, if a reader has no specific goal (that is, he or she does not invest high cognitive effort), in the absence of sufficient basic-level categories for their instantiation, superordinates do not lead to ready accessing of information. Of course, with the inducement of a cash prize for the 'answer' to Bransford and Johnson's (1973) text, a higher degree of cognitive effort is prompted, leading to a greater likelihood of the general categories being instantiated regardless of the absence of basic-level categories. However, these would be instantiations generated strategically rather than automatically.

As a caveat to the above, I should say that basic-level categories are not necessarily all that is needed to instantiate a general category. The context will also need to be sufficiently constraining. But at least basic-level categories, which exist in relationships of cognitive interdependence with other basic-level categories, are more likely to contribute to instantiation. Indeed, contexts which indicate *motor-interactionality* (that is, are associated with basic-level categories) are more likely to lead to instantiation of a general category. For example, McKoon and Ratcliff (1989b: 1,145) found that the superordinate category 'furniture' was readily instantiated by experimental subjects in the following: 'While the movers took a break, Betty went to her room for a quick nap, thankful that at least one piece of furniture had not been loaded yet.' From a cognitive linguistic perspective, this can be explained by Betty's motor-interactional behaviour.

8.4.2 Cognitive Linguistics, Shallow Processing and Instrument Inferences

Section 7.2.6 covered instrument inferences. An instrument has a higher probability of being generated when it has been referred to already in the text (Lucas et al. 1990) or when context is sufficiently constraining (O'Brien et al. 1988). We saw that O'Brien et al. (1988) showed that instruments can be readily generated, that is, 'knife' can be generated from 'He stabbed her with his weapon' but not from 'He assaulted her with his weapon'. Cognitive interdependence explains the ready generation of an instrument here. 'Stabbed' gives rise to extra information since it suggests motor-interactionality, and leads to the generation of a gestalt and, in turn therefore, ease of understanding. The second sentence, however, did not strongly suggest 'knife' to subjects since 'weapon' and 'assault' are superordinate categories. That is, these superordinate categories led to shallower processing since the instrument inference is not generated. The same reasons as outlined in 8.4.1 apply for shallow processing with these superordinate categories.

In Chapter 7, I outlined Sanford's (1990) reason why Garrod and Sanford's (1982) experiments supported the generation of implied instruments on-line whereas Singer's (1979) experiments did not. For Sanford (1990), the difference appears to be that with the Garrod-Sanford set, the instruments are 'part of the meaning' of the verbs (for example, *key* is 'part of the meaning' of *unlock*), whereas for Singer's verbs, this was not the case. In cognitive linguistic terms, 'part of the meaning' is as follows. 'Key' and 'unlock' exist in a relationship of cognitive interdependence. Given that 'key' is basic-level and yields high information for minimum cognitive effort, the instrument 'key' is readily generated from the verb 'unlock'.

8.4.3 Cognitive Linguistics, Shallow Processing and Causal Consequents

I indicated in 7.2.4 that, where a situation is not highly familiar, causal consequent inferences are likely to be only shallowly generated at best by a reader with no specific reading goal, given the extra processing effort involved in forecasting possible outcomes. Conversely, a causal consequent inference is only likely to be generated on-line, by a reader with no specific goal, if it is highly constrained by a context which is very familiar, and few if any other consequences would occur. Consider the following from Keefe and McDaniel (1993: 454) as an example of a highly constrained context: 'After standing through the three-hour debate, the tired speaker walked over to his chair. He realized that his valiant effort was probably in vain.' When that text was given to subjects, Keefe and McDaniel (1993) found that the causal consequent inference – *the speaker sat down* – was inferred a significant number of times. This was put down to the high level of semantic association between 'chair' and 'sitting'. But a cognitive linguistic explanation can also be furnished here. In the above, there is cognitive interdependence between the basic-level category 'chair' and the verb 'sit' since 'sitting' is a motor-interactional property of a chair. Thus, the information 'sitting' becomes available readily with the information 'chair', with only a small investment of cognitive labour (again basic-level categories are characterised by cognitive economy). In terms of the minimalist hypothesis, the causal consequent is generated because necessary information can become available quickly and there is only one obvious consequence.

Imagine now that in the above text from Keefe and McDaniel (1993: 454), 'his chair' is replaced by the superordinate 'the furniture'. In terms of the minimalist hypothesis, superordinate categories do not make necessary information available, for reasons we saw in 8.4.1. The causal consequent of 'sitting' is unlikely to be generated automatically with little effort. In the absence of sufficient information to instantiate them, and for a reader who makes minimum cognitive effort, superordinates are only likely, at best, to lead to automatic shallow generation of causal consequents. (Naturally, however, the causal consequent of 'sitting' could be generated strategically.)

8.5 CONNECTIONISM AND SHALLOW PROCESSING

8.5.1 Connectionism, Shallow Processing and the Moses Illusion

In 7.3, invoking psycholinguistic experimental work, we saw that because of commonplace top-down driven expectation in language processing, mental representation is likely to be non-compositional. Conversely, compositional analysis of a sentence is in line with a greater investment of cognitive effort. In connectionist networks, sentence processing is also non-compositional. In the connectionist network of McClelland, St John and Taraban (1989), there was a tendency for the network to be too sensitive to context, particularly with the sentence 'The adult ate the steak with daintiness':

> in that in fact it [the connectionist network] allows context
> sometimes to override the correct interpretation of a word...
> After the presentation of *with daintiness*, the activation of *steak* on
> probing for the patient is weakened. In fact, at earlier points in
> learning, the model actually activates soup more strongly than
> steak after *with daintiness* is presented.
> (McClelland, St John and Taraban 1989: 322–3)

McClelland et al. (1989) point out that while this behaviour can be seen as erroneous, it is nevertheless compatible with a common type of human error where top-down processes of script expectation override bottom-up processes, that is, with the psycholinguistic evidence I outlined in 7.3. Indeed, McClelland et al. (1989: 323) explicitly cite Erickson and Mattson's (1981) psycholinguistic evidence (highlighted in 7.3.2) for the common shallow processing of sentences such as 'How many animals of each kind did Moses take on the ark?'. For McClelland et al., errors of the Moses Illusion type indicate that the classical theme of compositionality misconstrues the contributions of words to how sentences are processed, and the frequency of the Moses Illusion implicitly lends support for the connectionist stance which eschews output compositional representations. Similar points concerning the compatibility of connectionist processing and the routineness of shallow processing of the Moses Illusion type are made in St John (1992).

One of the drawbacks of connectionist models is that if they are taken as providing some kind of simulation of brain networks, then this is only one of automatic brain processing rather than more consciously directed strategic brain processing. However, since I will only be concerned with automatic/minimum effort processing in line with the processing profile of an idealised reader, this drawback is not significant for my purposes. So, irrespective of this disadvantage, the non-compositional processing of McClelland, St John and Taraban's (1989) connectionist network still lends support to the psycholinguistic evidence that non-compositional language processing is also automatic in humans. I should qualify this, however, from a cognitive linguistic perspective. When a sentence contains basic-level categories, familiar background knowledge is more likely to be activated because basic-level categories can lead to the generation of prototypes. So processing of the sentence will likely go beyond its compositional input. Conversely, an absence of basic-level categories and a presence of superordinate or abstract categories is less likely to activate familiar background knowledge. In this respect, the output of such sentences is likely to be compositional to some extent. As illustration, first consider the following from Kress's (1989: 1) *Linguistic Processes in Sociocultural Practice*:

> I had tried to think of a title which did not separate 'language' from 'society' or 'culture', or language from its 'context', or talk about language and its social functions, or any of these formulations. The fact that I have not succeeded in my wish will be everywhere apparent in the book. Indeed the very structure of the English language, with its preference for nominal, object-like forms rather than for the process-oriented forms of verbs, makes it a difficult and perhaps impossible task. So, quite often where I have used ungainly and awkward circumlocutions, that has been my reason: to try and invent ways of talking in which the linguistic and the social appear as one (though this last formulation signals yet another failure!).

I would argue that Kress's 'failure' lies not with the propensity for object-like forms in English but with the difficulty of conceptualising 'language', 'society', 'culture'. They are *supra*-basic-level and so it is difficult to generate prototypes (that is, familiar and 'graspable') from them. In being supra-basic-level, there is little, if any, cognitive interdependence between these categories. So while 'culture', 'society' and 'language' may be linked together grammatically or morphologically ('sociocultural'), conceptualising them in unison, going beyond the original compositional input, is another thing all together. To sum up, in the absence of a fair amount of effort/familiarity with literature in this area, a book title like *Linguistic Processes in Sociocultural Practice* stands a good chance of being understood in a compositional manner.

8.5.2 Connectionism, Shallow Processing and Sanford and Garrod's Primary Processing Principle

We saw in 5.5.2 how in connectionist systems, 'connections between actions and the facts of the world can be represented as statistical correlations' (Waltz 1989: 58). There is an emphasis on a *good fit* between language and the world rather than an *exact match*, the latter being a facet of symbolicism. In 7.3.1, we saw that Sanford and Garrod (1994: 710–11) place emphasis on coherence being achieved 'on the basis of a good fit between some elements of the sentences concerned and stereotyped knowledge'. It is this common need of readers merely to find a 'good fit' which accounts for the error in the 'air crash survivors' puzzle (see 7.3.1). In a reference to the puzzle, Sanford and Garrod (1994: 713) state, 'Because *survivors* is a word which **fits** with an air crash, it is accepted as a filler for the patient slot of the verb *to bury*' [my bold]. In fact, Sanford and Garrod (1994: 715) are explicit about the link between the shallow processing of the connectionist network of McClelland, St John and Taraban (1989), alluded to in the previous section (see also 5.4), and the shallow processing of the 'survivors puzzle':

> Our interpretation of the survivors problem data is as follows. First, the data show that in the presence of sufficient expectation of accident victims who are dead, the analysis afforded to items which should be consonant with that expectation receives relatively shallow processing. Another way to think of it is that these items exert little bottom-up impact because contextual inferences are so strong. The kind of mechanism we have in mind is that described by **McClelland, Taraban, and St John (1989)**. [my bold]

See Sanford (1990: 527) for other endorsements of connectionism.

8.5.3 Connectionism, the Minimalist Hypothesis and Shallow Generation of Forward Elaborative Inferences

Orientation

In 7.1, I quoted Sanford (1990: 515) who said that 'the ubiquity of inferences in text comprehension makes the study of text comprehension look like a subset of the study of inference making'. The first point to make is that connectionism is in line with the prominence of inference generation in psycholinguistics indicated by Sanford, since in connectionist networks inferences are not ancillary to processing (*pace* symbolicism) but are an inherent aspect of language processing coterminous with the processing of syntax and semantics (5.4). In 7.2.4, we saw how there was a consensus in psycholinguistics (among the minimalist hypothesis/later constructionists) that causal consequent inferences are, at best, only partially generated for a reader with little vested interest. For minimalists and later constructionists, causal consequent inferences are much less likely to be generated than causal antecedent inferences. This is in contrast to Schank and Abelson (1977), referred to in 7.5.3, where inference generation is regarded as an *all-or-nothing* process, that is, inferences are not generated partially.

Now consider the following from the connectionist authors St John and McClelland (1992: 122):

> In parallel constraint satisfaction . . . as in sentence comprehension, inference-making is inherent to processing the explicit text . . . The reader's hope is that by the end of the story, sufficient constraints have been provided by the text for a complete interpretation to be computed. The interpretation would, at that point, contain fully activated coherence inferences, **partially activated prediction [elaborative] inferences**, and resolved pronouns. [my bold]

Because the processing of connectionist nets is based on weights, 'the constraints in a parallel constraint satisfaction model can represent the **likelihood of information**. Interpretations can then be activated according to their degree of support from the text and their likelihood to occur' (St John and McClelland 1992: 123) [my bold]. Owing to its capacity to capture probabilities, a connectionist network seems suitable for capturing the probabilistic nature of inference generation which we saw in the psycholinguistic evidence from Chapter 7. Indeed, in St John and McClelland (1992: 121), there is explicit reference to McKoon and Ratcliff (1986), the originators of the minimalist hypothesis, and their experiment where the death of the actress after a fourteen-storey fall was only weakly inferred as a causal consequent inference (see 7.2.2).

St John's (1992) Short Text Processing Model and the Minimalist Hypothesis

In what follows, I outline a model for the processing of a simple text from St John (1992) to indicate how a connectionist model is suited to what the minimalist hypothesis predicts, that is, that forward-elaborative or predictive inferences are generated in a more shallow manner than backward coherence inferences. Before I do so, let me highlight some preamble of St John. After he cites similar psycholinguistic evidence to evidence I cited in 7.2 (for example, McKoon and Ratcliff 1986; Potts et al. 1988), St John (1992: 274) goes on to say that 'prediction inferences are activated only weakly according to their support from the text'. Coherence inferences are a different matter and again St John (1992: 274) cites Potts et al. (1988) (as I did in 7.2) for the relative ease of activation of coherence inferences: 'Coherence inferences, on the other hand, are fully activated and inferred (Potts et al. 1988; Singer 1990). Following the same line of argument, the strength of coherence inferences results from their stronger support in the text.' Both of these positions are in tandem with the minimalist hypothesis. St John's (1992: 274) conclusion from all this is as follows: 'To simulate this interpretation of the empirical results, models of text comprehension should incorporate a mechanism that uses the degree of support provided by the text to determine the activation level of inferences.'

Now to the model. The connectionist model is inputted with a short text consisting of the following three sentences:

Albert and Clement decided to go to a restaurant.
The restaurant was expensive.
Clement paid the bill.

The model uses information from the training corpus to respond to questions such as 'Who ordered?', 'Who paid?', and so on (see below). For example, the model infers that Clement will order cheap wine and that this restaurant is far away, since, in the corpus, expensive restaurants are usually far away. Inferencing as to tip size is more complex. Its size depends on three factors: who tips (based on who paid), whether that person is generous or not and the quality of the restaurant since in the training corpus, tips were not left in cheap restaurants. As in his preamble, St John (1992: 284) makes a distinction between coherence inferences and prediction (forward-elaborative) inferences in the model:

> Coherence inferences concern propositions that lie between explicit text propositions. Prediction inferences concern propositions that lie after the final explicit text proposition. For example, **ordering** is a coherence inference because it occurs before the explicit proposition about **paying**. **Tipping** is a prediction inference because it occurs after **paying**. In the Story Gestalt model, all inferences are processed the same way. Any information correlated with the explicit text is activated immediately as the text is read.

I would agree with St John (1992) that *ordering* by the *agents* is a (causal antecedent) coherence inference (see 7.2.3) since it leads to the paying of the bill. I also agree that tipping is a forward-elaborative or predictive inference since it elaborates on the text and so is not necessary for coherence. Figure 8.1 gives St John's (1992: 283) simulation of inference generation:

Input Text
Albert and Clement decided to go to a restaurant.
The restaurant was expensive.
Clement paid the bill.

Questions

DECIDED TO GO				ORDERED			
agent:	Clement	.9		agent:	Clement	.8	
	Albert	.4			Albert	.1	
	and	.9					
destination:	restaurant	.9		patient:	cheap wine	.6	
					expen. wine	.1	
QUALITY				PAID			
patient:	restaurant	.9		agent:	Clement	.9	
value:	expensive	.9			Albert	.1	
				patient:	bill	.9	
DISTANCE				TIPPED			
patient:	restaurant	.9		agent:	Clement	.9	
value:	far	.9			Albert	.1	
				patient:	waiter	.9	
				manner:	small	.4	
					big	.1	
					not	.0	

Figure 8.1 Degree of inference activation in St John's (1992) connectionist network

The numbers in Figure 8.1 indicate the probability activation of active concepts following questions relating to the headings in capitals. In DECIDED TO GO, there are two agents, as indicated by the *and* unit, whereas elsewhere there is only one agent. When we inspect TIPPED, the lower probabilities for *manner* do reflect the fact that predictive (forward-elaborative) inferences should have more shallow activation levels than coherence inferences. In other words, this is in line with the psycholinguistic evidence of the previous chapter.[2]

We saw in 7.2 that the prospect of instrument inference generation is proportional to how readily familiar background knowledge can be accessed and to the degree of contextual constraints on this scenario. St John and McClelland (1992: 100) are aware that instrument inferences are related to a high degree of contextual constraint:

> Psychological evidence indicates that missing constituents, when strongly related to the action, are inferred and added to the description of the event. McKoon and Ratcliff (1981) found, for example, that 'hammer' was inferred after subjects read 'Bobby pounded the boards together with nails'.

However, absent from St John and McClelland (1992), as well as from St John (1992), is the notion that instruments are more likely to be generated when they rely more on familiar background knowledge. Nor do they try to simulate the fact that elaborative causal antecedent inferences are stronger when the causal relation is stronger in memory, that is, more *familiar*, as the experiments of Keenan et al. (1984) showed (see 7.2.3). But the probabilistic nature of connectionist models could, in principle, capture this. Sanford and Garrod point to the possibilities of something like this direction (1994: 704):[3]

> The primary processing account assumes that a text is easy to read if it can be mapped onto familiar background knowledge structures and that the writer should try to make such mappings possible. It does not assume that all background knowledge representations will be equally rich or detailed (Sanford and Garrod 1981: 125–31). Furthermore, with the advent of connectionist realizations of schemata, it is easy to envisage how various aspects of a scenario may be differentially accessible at various points in processing, which is not unlike McKoon and Ratcliff's [minimalist hypothesis] views on incomplete inferences.

8.5.4 General Corollary

Connectionist models, because they deal in probabilities and because they deal in constraint satisfaction, can handle a graded approach to inference generation inherent within the minimalist hypothesis. Moreover, since the difference between coherence and predictive inferences is one of probability (predictive inferences being more likely to be shallowly generated than coherence inferences), it is quite unrealistic to see a clear dividing line between coherence and predictive inferences. As St John and McClelland (1992: 131) indicate:

> One process, activating the story based on constraints from the input, is used to produce a complete interpretation. Representing the explicit text, **drawing prediction inferences, drawing coherence inferences**, and resolving pronouns all result from this same process. [my bold]

All this ties in with Smolensky's (1987) connectionist notion that the term *inference* is merely a higher-level description, a useful label that bears 'only approximate relations to the underlying computational structure' (cited in Clark 1989: 111–12). Moreover, this is in concert with the psycholinguistic work of Vonk and Noordman (1990) (see 7.2.2) which shows that the coherence (necessary) inference/predictive (forward-elaborative) inference distinction does not have a readily definable boundary, a notion which is supported by Sanford (1990: 521), the co-originator of the primary processing principle.

8.6 THE IDEALISED READER FRAMEWORK

8.6.1 The Idealised Reader Framework and Gist Reading

Threading together compatibilities, with regard to minimum effort processing, of the three paradigms dealt with in this chapter, yields, in effect, the following: a framework that can act as a guide to the kinds of inference actual gist readers are likely to generate in reading, on the assumption that such readers invest something akin to minimum effort. I call this framework guide the *idealised reader* (IR). This reader is idealised particularly because of its uniform minimum effort. And IR is connected with gist reading not only because gist readers are likely to invest something close to minimum effort, but because reading for gist is a general goal. Since the psycholinguistic evidence of the minimalist hypothesis is based on readers who are largely unfamiliar with the text's subject matter and have general goals, then IR too is largely unfamiliar with the subject matter of a text, and also has general goals.

8.6.2 Processing Principles of the Idealised Reader Framework

For the sake of clarity and the reader's convenience, I now outline the set of principles from the source components which make up the IR framework. They are in no particular order:

1. IR is a relatively parsimonious processor. Since IR has general reading goals, having little vested interest in a text, IR thus reads in line with the minimalist hypothesis; IR's reading only involves *automatic* inferences. These include coherence inferences as well as elaborative inferences generated where information is quickly and easily available.
2. IR's reading does not involve generation of *strategic* inferences since these involve work.

3. Instantiations of superordinate/general/abstract categories are a type of elaborative inference which are automatic for IR if relevant background knowledge is readily available.
4. Causal-antecedent inferences are automatic for IR. They can be divided as follows:
   connecting – IR establishes a link between the current focal event and prior information thus instituting a causal antecedent for the new event.
   reinstatement – information from prior text which is currently not activated can be reactivated by IR in order to establish a causal antecedent.
   elaborative – IR utilises background knowledge to establish a likely but unmentioned causal antecedent.
   Connecting causal-antecedent inferences are readily instituted by IR. But the strength of *elaborative* causal-antecedent inferences is dependent on the strength of causal relation of the particular scenario in memory, for example:
   A punches B. The next day B is covered in bruises [inference – *the punching caused the bruises* – is strong]
   A goes to a neighbour's house to play. The next day A is covered in bruises [inference – *playing caused the bruises* – is less strong].
5. Causal consequent inferences are *not* generated by IR or generated only weakly by IR when the situation is *not* highly constrained and very familiar, given the processing effort incurred in forecasting potential consequents.
6. For IR, causal *antecedent* inferences are much more probably generated than causal *consequent* inferences.
7. IR relates textual material as soon as possible to background knowledge (in line with the primary processing principle).
8. Lexical items in a sentence are unlikely to figure compositionally in mental representation when context is rich and constraining and especially when basic-level categories are present.
9. Instrument inferences are only likely to be generated by IR when knowledge is quickly and readily available such as when the instrument is part of a well-known *semantic field*, for example, unlock (with a key), stab (with a knife), shoot (with a gun).
10. IR is largely unfamiliar with the subject matter of the textual material under analysis, but otherwise possesses default adult background knowledge.

11. Linguistic input is not equivalent to process output.
12. Inferences are inherent to processing, so syntax, semantic and inferential processing are interactional, that is, the 'syntax-first' approach is prohibited.
13. Inferences are not weak representations *per se*. They can, however, be *weakly* generated, for example, causal consequent inferences. Connectionist models capture the strength/weakness aspect of inference generation because of their capacity to capture probabilities.
14. The basic level is the category level where the largest amount of information about an item is understood with the least cognitive labour, that is, basic-level categories are characterised by *cognitive economy*.
15. Basic-level categories are more directly understood with minimum cognitive effort since they lead to generation of prototypes, and thus the familiar, through being associated with neurophysiological capacity for motor-interaction, gestalt perception and image generation. The converse of this is that a context where motor-interactionality and so on is emphasised (although perhaps without use of basic-level categories) will also be 'directly understood'.
16. Superordinate/general/abstract categories are not characterised by cognitive economy. To yield more information, they require more cognitive effort than with basic-level categories. On their own, or in context where there is an absence of sufficient basic-level categories or sufficient constraints, and when minimum cognitive effort is invested, they are unlikely to lead to elaborative inference generation.
17. Prototypical causality involves 'direct manipulation' by an agent.
18. The IR framework prohibits the notion that use of a basic-level nominal produces objectifying effects since basic-level object categories and basic-level action categories are cognitively interdependent.

8.6.3 The Utility of the Idealised Reader Framework in CDA

I said in 8.6.1 that IR can act as a guide to the kinds of inference actual gist readers are likely to generate in reading. How might the ability to do this be useful in CDA? One use is with regard to identifying mystifying news text (as I alluded to in 8.2.3). I make the assumption that a specifically goal-oriented approach to reading such as critically analysing a news text for its absences, expends much more effort than the more general goal-oriented approach of reading a news text for gist. On the assumption that actual *non-critical readers* – that is, those who have the general goal of reading for gist rather than critically assessing absences from a news text – are likely to invest something close to minimum effort, the IR guide can serve a useful purpose. Because IR is based on general reading goals and minimum effort, it can help to assess whether or not the absences from a news text are unlikely to be generated as inferences by actual non-critical readers. In other words, it can help to assess whether the absences from a news text are likely to be mystifying, for a non-critical reader, of an event or its participants because significant information is *not* likely generated as inferences. I show this in Chapter 10 in a comprehensive mystification analysis of a news text. The primary focus of the IR framework is with regard to causal relations in news text (see 9.6). Why does IR, however, focus on news text?

8.6.4 Why Use the IR Framework in Mystification Analysis of News Text?

There are a number of reasons for using the IR framework in mystification analysis of news text. The first is for the same reason that news texts are a common source of data in CDA: news text has cultural salience. Another reason is that the IR framework is based on a reader who has general goals, general goals being common in the reading of news text. This is echoed by Graesser et al. (1994: 377):

> When readers comprehend a text, they are motivated by one or more goals. In some contexts, the goals are ill defined and general. This is the case when an adult reads the morning newspaper to become informed about current events and when a person reads a novel to be entertained. The reader must understand the meaning of the text under these conditions. In other contexts, the reader's goals are specific. This is the case when a reader tries to determine whether it is a good time to invest some money in the stock market (while reading a newspaper) and when a reader tries to form a mental picture of what a character looks like (while reading a novel).

Typical reading of ('current events') news text would come under what Graesser et al. (1994: 377) call the 'default' goal specificity where 'the reader's goal is to construct a meaningful situation model that is compatible with the text'.

Another reason for applying IR to news text is that IR does not generate strategic inferences. Strategic inferences are less likely to be generated when reading goals are general. Since general reading goals are common with news text, strategic inferences in the reading of news text have a lower chance of being generated compared with when reading goals are more specific (for example, trying to form a picture of a character in a novel). Indeed, McKoon and Ratcliff (1992: 440), whose minimalist hypothesis informs much of IR, suggest news text processing as a likely scenario where little strategic processing will take place:

> For different readers, minimalist processing with little strategic processing will occur in different situations. For some readers, it might be a rare occurrence; for others, it might happen in such situations as reading a magazine on an airplane, reading the newspaper through the morning fog over breakfast . . .

Of course, one can never say that readers will never make strategic inferences even in 'morning fog' reading of news text; one can say only that with general goals and reading a news text for gist, there is a low chance of strategic inferences being generated.

There are other reasons why strategic inference generation is likely to be low in the reading of news text and thus why IR is suitable for application to news text. Since news exists to provide new information, there is a good chance that many readers of a news text will be unfamiliar with the event being reported (this is particularly so if the event is a 'one-off' rather than being part of a chain of recent events and/or if the event is not a local or national one, which is then likely to be less familiar). The prospect of strategic inferences being generated because of the ready accessibility of background knowledge relating to the events being reported is then also likely to be low. So I build in the assumption in the framework that while IR has the general default background knowledge that would be expected of an adult, at the same time IR is unfamiliar with the specific events being described in a news text. This is far from being an implausible notion. People do read news texts, after all, for *new* information.

It is also worthwhile to consider the following from Graesser et al. (1997: 183): 'The minimalist hypothesis is probably correct when the reader is very quickly reading the text, when the text lacks global coherence, and when the reader has very little background knowledge.' The minimalist hypothesis is a central part of the IR framework and this, in turn, fits in with the latter's application to news text given that the best conditions for its validity are where the reader has very little background knowledge of the events being reported. (Of course, even though readers may have no specific background knowledge of the events being reported, they will nevertheless relate these new events to their general background knowledge.) That the minimalist hypothesis fits in with quick reading also connects well with application of IR to news text given that people commonly read quickly when they have general goals such as extracting gist from news text (rather than the specific goals of searching for absences from a text). Furthermore, that Graesser (a constructionist and thus someone the minimalists critique) should say this about the minimalist hypothesis augments the credibility of the statement.

Let me also address the other condition Graesser et al. (1997: 183) indicate where the minimalist hypothesis is valid: 'when the text lacks global coherence'. Bell (1991: 172) writes about the confusion that 'results from the fragmented structure of news writing', going on to say 'the ideal news story is one which could be cut to end at any paragraph. It is thus common for cohesion between paragraphs to be unclear or non-existent . . .' Given this ideal, it is not surprising that news texts, and particularly long news texts, are not written so as to facilitate the ready construction of a global coherence by the reader. Again, since the minimalist hypothesis is a basis of IR, news text is appropriate for application of IR. There is one more point as to why news text is suitable for IR application. Widdowson (1996) contains a critical examination of Fairclough's analysis of a text that supplies information to pregnant women. He criticises Fairclough for 'interpretation by proxy' arguing that Fairclough should enquire as to the perlocutionary effect of the text on mothers rather than estimating what it may be. Analysts cannot be expected to be reliable in interpreting by proxy for discourse communities they do not belong to. But since the IR framework is suitable for use with news texts, these are texts for which analysts could be considered potential addressees.

I shall provide other reasons for applying the IR framework to news text towards the end of Chapter 9. I should, however, finally qualify 'news text' and indicate more specifically the type of news text I will apply the IR framework to: *hard news text*. To make clear what this is, here is a definition of hard news from Bell (1991: 14):

> Newsworkers' basic distinction is between hard news and features. Hard news is their staple product: reports of accidents, conflicts, crimes, announcements, discoveries and other events which have occurred or come to light since the previous issue of their paper or programme. The one-off, unscheduled events such as fires and disasters are sometimes called 'spot news'. The opposite to hard news is 'soft' news, which is not time-bound to immediacy. Features are the most obvious case of soft news. These are longer 'articles' rather than 'stories' covering immediate events. They

provide background, sometimes 'editorialize' (carry the writer's personal opinions), and are usually bylined with the writer's name . . . For both newsworkers and researchers, the boundaries between hard and soft news are unclear . . . journalists spend much of their energy trying to find an angle which will present what is essentially soft news in hard news terms. Journalists and media researchers both recognize hard news as the core news product, the typical against which other copy will be measured. Hard news is also the place where a distinctive news style will be found if anywhere.

A reason for choosing hard news texts is that, in detailing events and actions, they handle causal relations. This then connects with the basis of the IR framework since much of it is concerned with types of causal inference.

8.6.5 Some Comments on How I will Use the IR Framework

Since the IR framework is made up of compatibilities from non-symbolic paradigms, use of it implicitly *prohibits* the kind of problematic CDA which is predicated on symbolicism, for example, the syntax-first approach (see Chapter 4). Use of IR also implicitly helps to prevent over-interpretation on behalf of the reader. This is because IR does not make strategic inferences, inferences that are in line with vested interest in a text, that is, as exhibited in CDA. When I use the IR framework in the next two chapters, I recognise that the vocabulary of the framework mediates between the text and my analyses. For instance, I use the terms 'coherence' and 'elaborative' even though there is no absolute distinction between these inferences. However, I retain the use of these terms in order to make it easier to articulate the probability of inference generation. For similar reasons of ease of articulation, I also continue to use the term 'inference'. This is despite the fact that inferences, on a connectionist perspective, are *inherent* to processing, being high-level descriptions which approximate underlying processing.[4]

In previous chapters I have criticised work in CDA for its sentential focus. This was in relation to CDA asserting that a certain kind of semantico-syntactic form was the best representation of events, that is, agent-process-affected. Like CDA, I too focus on sentences in my analysis. However, sentences are merely the starting point of my analysis. Where I differ from previous CDA is that I am interested in the holistic processing output of sentences (that is, including inference generation). I follow the connectionist and cognitive linguistic principle that treats syntactic and semantic information as well as inferences interactively and so I do not make an equation between sentential form and mental representation (*pace* much work in CDA). The same applies to compositional analysis. In contrast to much of CDA, I lock on to lexical items compositionally as input but not in terms of output. That is, I do not make an equation between my analysis of a category and compositional mental representation in the discourse of a reader.

The IR framework, so far, is based on compatibilities from three paradigms: connectionism, cognitive linguistics and psycholinguistics. In the next chapter I complete the IR framework by adding a more obvious pragmatic dimension. I thread the compatible aspects of connectionism, cognitive linguistics and psycholinguistics, shown in this chapter, through *relevance theory*, another paradigm which has least effort processing as a feature, and also conflicts with symbolicism. At the end of Chapter 9, the idealised reader framework will be complete and so will be based on compatibilities from *four* paradigms.

NOTES

1. The relationship between prototypicality and instantiation is often exploited in 'trick questions'. Consider the *Trivial Pursuit* question – 'What mammals can jump the highest?' Instantiations are automatic when they rely on familiar knowledge. So automatically, 'mammal' is likely to be instantiated as one with legs, since 'jump' is prototypically associated with 'legs'. But it is the automatic relating to familiar knowledge in instantiations that can lead the player astray. 'Whales', the answer, are neither prototypical 'jumpers' since they have no legs, nor are they prototypical mammals.
2. However, the high activation of Clement as tipper is out of step with tipping as a predictive inference. The activation level of Clement as tipper would, all the same, be greater than for Albert, as reflected in the model, since Clement ordered and paid the bill.
3. If, with the implementation of connectionist realisations of schemata, the richness of background knowledge can be made 'differentially accessible', this lends support to the idea that differential accessibility in a connectionist network could in principle be configured according to the nature of the cognitive categories employed. In other words, (1) basic-level categories would lead to a readier accessing of familiar knowledge and familiar scenarios, so as to generate implied instrument inferences (for example, hammer from the basic level in 'Bobby pounded the boards together with nails'), and (2) superordinates would make the accessibility of well-known knowledge and familiar scenarios more difficult.
4. The connectionist background to the framework suffers in being selective, drawing principally on work by McClelland and his collaborators. This selectivity is unavoidable given the constraints of what I am able to accomplish in this book. However, my choice of McClelland is significant in that he is one of the fathers of connectionist approaches to language processing.

CHAPTER 9

Further Constructing the Idealised Reader: Compatibilities with Relevance Theory

9.1 INTRODUCTION

First, consider the following from Widdowson (2000: 22) where he comments on practice in CDA:

> Texts are analysed in reference to grammatical and lexical categories without regard to the way they are discoursally realized: the signification of linguistic forms is carried intact into text to be recovered as significance. The process whereby these forms inter-relate co-textually with each other and contextually with the circumstances of their use is left largely unexplored. Text is treated as a kind of static semantic patchwork, existing as an object for analysis in its own right . . . [P]eople do not consume texts unthinkingly, nor subject them to linguistic analysis, but process them in normal pragmatic ways, inferring meanings which have not been explicitly spelled out by reference to what they have already read and what they know of the world.

The dynamising of a text in making inferences from it – pragmatically realising meaning in line with reader goals/effort from part of the semantic potential of a text – is something I deal with more specifically in this chapter. I indicated, in the previous chapter, that IR has rather general goals since it does not have a vested interest in the hard news text being read. This may have given the impression that the reading behaviour of IR or actual readers is unfocused. This is far from the case since typical reading, regardless of how much effort is invested, is in line with a pragmatic principle. That is, typical reading takes place in line with expectations of relevance.[1] In this chapter, I draw on the *relevance theory* of

Sperber and Wilson (1995), which also has minimum effort processing at its centre. The purposes of this chapter are as follows:

1. to detail this relevance principle so as to thread it into the IR framework-so-far and thus provide a clearer pragmatic dimension to the framework
2. to provide a better sense of how goals with regard to causal relations are likely to be actualised for a non-critical reader who is processing hard news text
3. in drawing upon another compatible framework with regard to minimum effort processing, to strengthen the IR framework for use in the interpretation stage of CDA.

As the spirit of this book is positive, in that I want to contribute to moving CDA forward, I also show later in this chapter how the IR framework, then based on compatibilities from *four* paradigms, can enhance a valid critical discourse analysis of a hard news text by providing a richer account of how mystification can take place for a non-critical reader.

9.2 RELEVANCE THEORY

9.2.1 Orientation

The relevance theory of Sperber and Wilson (1995) can be seen as a development of Grice's (1975) inferential model of communication, itself an alternative to the classical code model. In the code model, the intended message is encoded by the sender into a signal. Since the receiver shares the code with the sender, the receiver is able to decode the intended message. Grice's (1975) model of communication does involve decoding but crucially involves pragmatic inferences. Take the following example:

A: Was there a fiddler at the bar last night?
B: There was a man scraping a bow across a violin.

B's response evaluates the skills of the musician. The evaluation, however, is not explicit: we do not have an evaluative adverb such as in the sentence 'He played the fiddle badly'. The evaluation has to be inferred, so how is this achieved? For Grice (1975) communicators operate on a co-operative principle, observing four basic maxims (*quality*: be truthful; *quantity*: give as much information as is required; *relation*: be relevant; *manner*: be clear and brief). 'There was a man scraping a bow across a violin' does not, on the surface, seem so co-operative since it imparts more information than is needed. But, for Grice, since the hearer naturally assumes the speaker's intention is to be co-operative, they seek significance in the *flouting* of the quantity maxim – that there is more information than is needed. In doing so, they form an inference that the fiddler was not very good. This type of inference Grice terms an *implicature*. On Grice's account, such verbal comprehension involves, first, decoding the literal meaning of the sentence. This then becomes an input to the inferential process which yields an interpretation of the speaker's meaning.

How is Sperber and Wilson (1995) a development of Grice? The two fundamental differences between Sperber and Wilson's position and that of Grice is that Sperber and Wilson argue that only one of Grice's maxims is necessary: that of *relevance*. Secondly, they question the need for a *co-operative principle*. For Sperber and Wilson (1995: 260), there are two *principles of relevance*. The first, which they call the *cognitive principle of relevance*, is as follows: (1) *the cognitive principle of relevance*: human cognition tends to be geared to the maximisation of relevance.

Owing to this universal tendency to maximise relevance, people will only attend to a stimulus that appears relevant. For Sperber and Wilson, humans automatically tend to maximise relevance because constant, Darwinian selection pressure on human cognitive systems has led to increasing efficiency. As a result, our perceptual systems have an automatic tendency to locate relevant potential input stimuli and our systems of memory retrieval have an automatic tendency to cue relevant background knowledge. An utterance is relevant when it connects with the background information available to the hearer or reader to yield conclusions that matter to him or her. In contrast to Grice, Sperber and Wilson (1995: 162) do not assume that speakers *follow* a 'relevance maxim' since the principle of relevance 'is a generalisation about ostensive-inferential communication' that 'applies without exception'. Therefore, communicators 'could not violate it even if they wanted to'.

Ostension refers to the act of drawing attention to something. Pointing and shouting are acts of ostensive behaviour and can serve as ostensive stimuli. In creating an ostensive stimulus, a communicator encourages the audience to assume it is relevant enough to be worth processing. This brings us to the second principle in Sperber and Wilson (1995: 260), which they call the *communicative principle of relevance*: (2) *the communicative principle of relevance*: every act of ostensive communication communicates a presumption of its own optimal relevance.

By 'optimal', Sperber and Wilson (1995) mean that the audience will understand the relevance of a particular stimulus in terms of yielding the greatest effects in return for the smallest processing effort. The greater the effort of perception, memory and inference that is needed for processing an input, the less rewarding it will be to process, and hence the less deserving of our attention. In other words, for relevance theory, all other things being equal, the greater the processing effort required, the less relevant the input will be. In relevance theory, this explains why we allow only particular stimuli to become inputs to processing and why the mass of potential stimuli is dormant for us. Sperber and Wilson (1995: 266–78) sub-divide the *second* or *communicative principle of relevance* as follows:

(a) The ostensive stimulus is relevant enough for it to be worth the addressee's effort to process it.
(b) The ostensive stimulus is the most relevant one compatible with the communicator's abilities and preferences.

We need an example to illustrate Sperber and Wilson's take on the relationship between cognitive effect and processing effort, so here is one I have taken from Wilson and Sperber (2004):

Mary, who dislikes most meat and is allergic to chicken, rings her dinner party host to find out what is on the menu. As chicken is on the menu, the host could truly tell her any of three things:
(a) We are serving meat.
(b) We are serving chicken.
(c) Either we are serving chicken or $(7^2 - 3)$ is not 46.

In relevance theory, all of the above would be relevant for Mary. However, (b) would be more relevant than (a). Since (b) entails (a), it yields more information (or more cognitive effects) than (a) for a similar processing effort. In addition, (b) is more relevant than (c). The same information is yielded from both (they are logically equivalent) but (c) requires more processing effort. In conclusion, (b) is the most relevant utterance for Mary because of a combination of effort and effect. Summing up, here are Wilson and Sperber (2004) on the relationship between effect and effort: 'More generally, when similar amounts of effort are required, the effect factor is decisive in determining degrees of relevance, and when similar amounts of effect are achievable, the effort factor is decisive.'

Given clause (b) of the definition of optimal relevance above, Sperber and Wilson argue that it is reasonable for receivers to follow a path of least effort until the resulting interpretation meets their expectation of relevance. This is because of the expectation that senders would (within the limits of their abilities and preferences) make their utterances as easy as possible to understand. Here are Wilson and Sperber (2004) again:

> when a hearer following the path of least effort arrives at an interpretation that satisfies his expectations of relevance, in the absence of contrary evidence, this is the most plausible hypothesis about the speaker's meaning. Since comprehension is a non-demonstrative inference process, this hypothesis may well be false; but it is the best a rational hearer can do.

What Sperber and Wilson mean by non-demonstrative is that the pragmatic inferences involved in verbal communication cannot be deduced or 'demonstrated' logically.

9.2.2 Other Differences from Grice

Relevance Theory versus the Co-Operative Principle

While Grice assumes co-operation between speakers, clause (b) of the *second principle of relevance* allows for the possibility that communicators may not want to be totally co-operative or, for example, fail to be sufficiently co-operative because they are unable to think of something at the time. This is covered by the reference to 'abilities and preferences'. It also allows for the fact that the communicator may be lazy, or may want to frame communication with particular moral and aesthetic preferences which might rule out utterances that would be easiest to process. Nevertheless, for Sperber and Wilson (1995), the audience of an ostensive stimulus is entitled to have high expectations that the communicator would prefer to minimise the addressee's effort; 'no unjustified or gratuitous effort' should be demanded from the hearer (Sperber and Wilson, 1995: 268).

Another difference from Grice is as follows. Because Grice's approach assumes that people are naturally co-operative, when they remain silent after being asked a question they in effect violate his co-operative principle. And so in this case since the co-operative principle is suspended, it is impossible for any conversational implicatures to be communicated. The relevance-theoretic approach, however, captures the fact that silence could be ostensive and thus carry the presumption of relevance. Thus, under the appropriate contextual conditions, silence can carry the implicature that the questionee is, for example, unwilling to answer, or unable to answer because they do not speak the language of the questioner.

Explicatures

Grice discusses the co-operative principle and maxims mainly with regard to the generation of implicatures. Because the focus of Gricean pragmatics is on implicature recovery, there is a suggestion in Grice's work that it is possible to differentiate between implicatures and explicit speaker meaning where explicit meaning is the thoughts of the speaker encoded into the utterance. So while Grice's focus on implicatures takes him away from the code model, in terms of his assumptions about explicit meaning he still operates with the code model. For Sperber and Wilson (1995), the code model is unfeasible here since any linguistic representation underdetermines the thought behind it: every representation is incomplete. A sentence can only serve as a set of clues to the sender's meaning to help 'the audience infer what' the sender means. A sentence is not a full representation of the thoughts of the sender (Sperber and Wilson 1995: 27). Indeed, other more recent contributions to pragmatics recognise that it is not just implicatures that go beyond the linguistic encoding but the explicitly communicated content of an utterance also (see Kempson 1996; Levinson 2000). Sperber and Wilson (1995: 182) refer to an 'explicitly communicated assumption' as an *explicature*, a proposition recovered by a combination of decoding and inference, and which can go on to provide input for the generation of contextual implications and other cognitive effects. Crucially for Sperber and Wilson, explicatures are also generated in line with both principles of relevance. As an example of an explicature and of the relationship between explicatures and implicatures, consider the following, derived from Wilson and Sperber (2004):

> Peter: Did John pay back the money he owed you?
> Mary: Well, he forgot to go to the bank.

Although Mary's response is an incomplete representation, her utterance is optimally relevant to Peter, since Peter expects an explanation as to why John has not repaid the money he owed her. The presumption of relevance which entails maximum cognitive effect for minimum effort obviates any mental dallying over whether bank could be, say, a river bank. Thus Peter is able to produce the possible explicatures that 'bank' refers to an institution that deals with private individuals rather than say the World Bank; that 'going to the bank' is not visiting a friend in a bank who illegally passes money to John (unless this was an extant background assumption), and so on. Because of the presumption of optimal relevance and because Peter, we can assume, will have the background knowledge as to what banks are and how they operate, the incomplete representation of Mary's utterance is able to provide easy access to the background assumption that people go to banks to withdraw money. For Sperber and Wilson, explicature generation is a flexible process, flexible to the extent that it may involve narrowing or loosening of encoded meaning. Above, 'bank' is narrowed to the ad hoc concept BANK*, for example the local bank John uses for withdrawing money. But John may not need to enter the bank to get his money and instead could withdraw it from a cashpoint machine outside the bank. Cashpoint machines, of course, need not be outside banks and can be found in supermarkets and train stations and other places. So 'bank' could be understood as the looser ad hoc concept BANK** which shares with 'bank' the attribute of being a place where money can be withdrawn from an account.

Implicatures

I have dealt with explicatures but what of implicatures in Sperber and Wilson's pragmatics? For Sperber and Wilson, an implicature is a proposition which may be *more or less* implicated by an utterance. If it is strongly implicated (that is, it is a strong implicature), then its generation is necessary for an interpretation that satisfies expectations of relevance which the utterance excites. It is weakly implicated (that is, it is a weak implicature) if its construction assists an interpretation that satisfies expectations of relevance but is not itself essential since the utterance suggests a number of similar potential implicatures, any one of which would do. So Mary's utterance, 'He forgot to go to the bank' yields the strong implicature that John could not repay Mary. Without this strong implicature, Mary's utterance cannot function as a relevant response to 'Did John pay back the money he owed you?'. As Wilson and Sperber (2004) point out, Mary's reply can also suggest the further implicature that John might pay Mary back after his next visit to the bank. But this is a weaker implicature since it is not necessary for an interpretation that satisfies expectation of relevance. A final point: since relevance-theoretic comprehension procedure involves following a path of least effort in yielding cognitive effects, interpretative hypotheses are tested according to the theory in order of accessibility. The receiver stops when expectations of relevance are satisfied. Thus, the decoding of the representation, the construction of explicatures and derivation of implicatures are arrived at in parallel with mutual adjustment, hypotheses being considered in order of accessibility.

I have only given a sketch of relevance theory, but it is sufficient for my purposes. I now thread relevance theory through the IR framework constructed so far (from three paradigms) so that the IR framework will be based on compatibilities from four paradigms. In doing so, we gain a better sense of how reading goals with regard to causal relations are likely to be actualised for a non-critical reader reading hard news text. This is taken up specifically with regard to hard news text in 9.4 and the application of the IR framework to hard news text is demonstrated in 9.5. First, I highlight compatibilities between relevance theory and compatibilities from connectionism, cognitive linguistics and psycholinguistic evidence for inference generation.

9.3 THE COMPATIBILITIES OF RELEVANCE THEORY WITH CONNECTIONISM, COGNITIVE LINGUISTICS AND PSYCHOLINGUISTIC EVIDENCE FOR INFERENCE GENERATION

9.3.1 Relevance Theory and Non-Symbolicism

Clearly with its concept of explicature, relevance theory regards words as *cues* for meaning formation. This is similar to: connectionism, where words are cues to scenarios; cognitive linguistics, where basic-level categories cue information about gestalts, motor-interactions and so on; and psycholinguistic theory on inference generation where words cue familiar background knowledge, which in turn facilitates the generation of an inference. Where relevance theory is different is that it treats the process of lexical narrowing as a type of pragmatic process, that is, one driven by the search for relevance. Explicatures involve a combination of decoding and inferencing to realise lexical narrowing or loosening. Thus, explicature generation does not involve compositional decoding of a sentence, again in consonance with the other three paradigms; relevance theory is also non-symbolic in this respect. Since explicatures also involve both decoding and inference generation in a mutual parallel-adjustment process, the inferencing involved cannot be thought of as a secondary process to the primary process of decoding. Decoding and inference generation in explicature derivation is a holistic process. Again, this is very much in line with the general non-symbolicism of the other three paradigms, particularly connectionism. Given this non-symbolicism of relevance theory, the symbolicism of CDA which was problematised by connectionism, cognitive linguistics and psycholinguistics is also problematised by relevance theory. Similar problematising of how CDA highlights mystifying text also ensues.[2]

9.3.2 Relevance and Category Type

We saw in 9.2.1 that 'We are serving chicken' is more relevant than 'We are serving meat' in the earlier example of the dinner party. Sperber and Wilson reason that this is due to the derived cognitive effects since for the same investment of effort 'We are serving chicken' supplies more information than 'We are serving meat'. But this reasoning can be enhanced from a cognitive linguistic perspective. 'We are serving chicken' is more relevant because it is bound up with a prototype for the basic-level event of 'having a dinner party' (see 6.5.2), where we would expect the type of meat to be specified by the host. 'Chicken' also is more bound up with motor-interaction, gestalt formation and image generation as compared with the superordinate 'meat'. This is why 'chicken' provides a larger amount of information for minimum effort than 'meat'. And so we can see that 'chicken' is more relevant in the above.

9.3.3 Relevance, Barsalou and Explicatures

In Chapter 6, I highlighted Barsalou's position that many concepts are actually created 'on the fly', being ad hoc categories formed according to specific goals and as a function of context dependence, for example, 'things to take with you in event of a fire' (see 6.2.1). The work of Barsalou (for example, 1983, 1989) thus suggests that understanding of lexical items varies considerably across situations. In 8.3.2, I also indicated how there was connectionist support for this (Bechtel 1990; Stillings et al. 1995). For Barsalou, his results are best explained by the assumption that lexical items do not give access to ready-made prototypes but instead give rise to non-conventional categories which are created 'on the fly' but have, all the same, prototypical structure. Wilson and Sperber (2004) criticise Barsalou's work because he makes no clear proposal about how the generation process operates and when it finishes. Alluding to Barsalou's work on ad hoc concepts, they suggest that 'the relevance-theoretic comprehension procedure may be seen as a concrete hypothesis about how such a flexible, relevance-governed lexical interpretation process might go'. So with a non-conventional category such as 'things to take from one's home during a fire', people would be guided by expectations of relevance. Using contextual assumptions made accessible by the encyclopedic entry of the linguistically encoded concept, people would start deriving cognitive effects. When they had enough effects to satisfy their expectations of relevance, they would finish.

9.3.4 Relevance Theory and Sanford and Garrod's (1981) Primary Processing Principle

In 7.3.1 I explained Sanford and Garrod's (1981) primary processing principle: that a central aspect of comprehension is that when it is possible, and as soon as possible, linguistic input will be related to background knowledge. The resulting representation is used to assist the comprehension of subsequent text. We also saw for Sanford and Garrod (1994: 710) the following: the need to link linguistic input quickly to background knowledge means 'a sense of coherence is achieved on the basis of a good fit between some elements of the sentences concerned and stereotyped knowledge'. As a result, it is common for top-down processing to prevail over the processing of both syntax and lexical items. Echoes of Sanford and Garrod's position are apparent in relevance theory except that for Sperber and Wilson, coherence can be 'incomplete' because expectations of relevance have been satisfied. Wilson and Sperber (2004) allow too for the fact that being attuned to expectations of relevance means that comprehension can be 'false' in the way in which Sanford and Garrod have indicated in their research, for example, with their 'survivors' text.

9.3.5 Relevance Theory Inferences and Psycholinguistic Inferences

Relevance theory tends to talk of inferences in terms of explicatures and implicatures only. But threading through work on psycholinguistic inferencing can provide more discrimination of explicatures and implicatures. In the following, I locate the psycholinguistic inferences we saw in Chapter 7 under the categories of explicatures and implicatures.

Explicatures

1. Instantiations – these take place in the narrowing of lexical meaning (for example, 'The fish attacked the swimmer') and so could be a type of explicature.
2. Instrument inferences – these also involve the narrowing of lexical meaning (for example, 'He stabbed her with his weapon') and so could also be located under explicatures.

Implicatures

But what about implicatures? Sperber and Wilson (1995) make a distinction between strong and weak implicatures, strong ones being necessary for communication and weak ones not. Let me now relate these notions to *causal antecedent* inferences and *causal consequent* inferences.

On *causal antecedents*, let us return to two short texts from Keenan et al. (1984) (see 7.2.3):

1. Joey's big brother punched him again and again.
   The next day his body was covered with bruises.
4. Joey went to a neighbor's house to play.
   The next day his body was covered with bruises.

The second sentence for both 1 and 4 would raise expectations of relevance for the reader and in expending minimum effort they would seek the reason for the bruises. Because in 1 the causal relation is likely to be strong in memory, this is accessed readily and a strong 'bridging implicature' (that is, bridging two sentences) would be generated. (I take the concept of bridging implicature from Wilson and Sperber 1986.) In Chapter 7, the above bridging implicature was called an *elaborative* causal antecedent inference. A weak elaborative causal antecedent inference is generated from text 4, however, since the causal relation is likely to be much weaker in memory. Bridging implicatures, as should be clear, are a type of coherence inference.

There is another bridging implicature which is generated across both sets of sentences but this time is strong for both 1 and 4. This is, using the parlance of Chapter 7, a *connecting* causal antecedent inference. That is, we automatically connect the information in the second sentence with the first by inferring that the punching caused the bruises. We will make a causal connection between the two sentences in each text regardless of whether the causal relations are weak in memory. To sum up: for text 1, there are two strong bridging implicatures while for text 4, there is a strong and a weak bridging implicature. Consider now the following from Wilson and Sperber (1986: 69–70) on bridging implicatures:

> The general principle, for bridging implicatures as for all other implicated assumptions, is that they should – at least in the estimation of the speaker – be virtually instantaneously accessible, and more accessible than any alternative assumption likely to lead to an acceptable interpretation. If not, a speaker observing the principles of relevance should have done something to increase their accessibility – for example by directly mentioning them in the utterance – and thus save the hearer some unnecessary processing costs.

On this rationale, text 1 is more *relevant* than text 4 since it more readily accesses causal relations in memory and thus leads to more cognitive effects for the same amount of effort.

On *causal consequents*, let us return to the example given in Wilson and Sperber (2004):

> Peter: Did John pay back the money he owed you?
> Mary: Well, he forgot to go to the bank.

We saw that Wilson and Sperber (2004) indicate that Peter may formulate the weak implicature that John would pay back Mary after next going to the bank but that this was a weaker implicature since it is not necessary for an interpretation that satisfies the expectation of relevance. Wilson and Sperber (2004) also indicate that the hearer would need to take some responsibility for its generation. Here, we can clearly draw parallels with causal consequent inferences which we looked at in Chapter 7. Paying back Mary at some date is a forward inference just like causal consequents are. On the psycholinguistic perspective I gave in Chapter 7, they are not necessary for coherence and are normally not generated because of the effort needed to forecast and explore alternatives and so on. On a relevance theory account, we know that the greater the effort of memory and inference, the less rewarding processing is, and so the less deserving of attention is the item being processed. And so this is why, on a relevance-theoretic account, causal consequents are not readily generated and usually only weakly at best. When Sperber and Wilson indicate that the receiver needs to take some responsibility for the generation of the above inference, it is because this causal consequent inference would have to be generated *strategically*.

Previously I have said that the IR framework will be applied to hard news text. Having related the three paradigms of Section B to relevance theory, I now broaden out the threading through of relevance theory into the IR framework in relation to hard news text.

9.4 THE IR FRAMEWORK, RELEVANCE AND CAUSAL RELATIONS IN HARD NEWS TEXTS

9.4.1 Relevance, Causal Antecedent Inferences and Hard News Texts

Given that hard news text involves the detailing of actions and events, their causes and their results, it can be treated as a kind of narrative text.

Graesser et al. (1994) carry out a major review of empirical evidence for the processing of narrative text, and contend the following (1994: 379) for narrative text:

> Comprehenders attempt to explain *why* episodes in the text occur and *why* the author explicitly mentions particular information in the message. Thus, comprehension is typically guided by why-questions rather than other types of questions (e.g. what-happens-next, how, where, or when). There is extensive evidence that causal explanations of actions, events, and states play a central role in our understanding of narrative (Black and Bower 1980; Bloom et al. 1990; Bower et al. 1979; Fletcher 1986; Graesser 1981; Rumelhart 1975; Schank 1986; Singer 1990; Trabasso and Sperry 1985; Trabasso et al. 1989; van den Broek 1990).

Indeed, as Graesser et al. (1994: 379) indicate, seeking causal explanation is especially significant given that it is a focus in so many other disciplines:

> The importance of causal explanations is also bolstered by theories outside of the discourse-processing arena. For example, it is compatible with theories of causal attribution in social psychology (Hastie 1983; Hilton 1990; McLaughlin 1990; Pennington and Hastie 1986; Read 1987; Read and Marcus-Newhall 1993) and with theories of planning and mundane reasoning in artificial intelligence (Kuipers 1985; Mooney 1990; Schank 1986).

In the first principle of relevance (9.2.1), Sperber and Wilson (1995) argue that human cognition tends to be geared to the maximisation of relevance for minimum effort, and so humans only attend to a stimulus that appears relevant. Our perceptual systems have an automatic tendency to locate relevant potential input stimuli, and our systems of memory retrieval have an automatic tendency to cue relevant background knowledge. For Sperber and Wilson, humans automatically tend to maximise relevance because constant Darwinian selection pressure on human cognitive systems has led to increasing efficiency. An evolutionary basis for inference is also espoused by the cognitive linguists Lakoff and Johnson (1999: 4):

> reason is evolutionary, in that abstract reason builds on and makes use of forms of perceptual and motor inference present in 'lower' animals. The result is a Darwinism of reason, a rational

Darwinism ... reason is not completely conscious, but mostly unconscious.

So we can see how the pragmatic principles of relevance and causal explanation can be linked, given the latter's centrality in human affairs and especially in light of what Graesser et al. (1994: 379) indicate: 'that comprehension is guided by why-questions rather than other types of questions substantially narrows down the set of inferences that readers normally construct'. In other words, comprehension for why-questions is less 'wasteful' of effort. Because of wiring for efficiency of cognition as a result of Darwinian selection, when presented with information as to the result of an action, we *automatically* expect other presented information to be relevant for ascertaining causal antecedence (rather than, say, causal consequence, which would involve more effort in forecasting). Indeed, in the same section on causal explanation in narrative texts, Graesser et al. (1994: 379) allude to the pragmatic theory of Sperber and Wilson in relation to the comprehension of actions and events in a text:

> A pragmatic level of explanation must also be considered when readers comprehend explicit actions, events, and states in the text. The reader considers why the author would bother mentioning the information conveyed in each explicit clause. Readers normally follow the Gricean postulate that whatever the author expresses is relevant and important (Grice 1975; Roberts and Kreuz 1993; Sperber and Wilson 1986).

But Graesser et al. (1994) go no further in linking pragmatic principles of relevance with psycholinguistic theory or evidence.

In Chapters 5, 6 and 7, I applied connectionism, cognitive linguistics and psycholinguistic evidence respectively to the Clark (1992)/Simpson (1993) analysis of the 'Steed text' (see 4.2.1). I now do the same with relevance theory but this time weaving in the psycholinguistic evidence for selective processing of characters from 7.4. When presented with information as to the result of an action, readers automatically expect other presented information to be relevant for ascertaining causal antecedence. We saw in 7.4 that it is common in reading for there to be a focus on main characters in relation to causality. As we saw, proper names which have topic focus are likely to be deemed relevant in establishing this. Because of the presence of the proper name 'Steed' in the 'Steed text', it follows that the alternative interpretation that Steed forced the 'victim' off the road while 'someone else' attacked her is pragmatically aberrant. Conjuring up a 'secondary character' would take more effort than just focussing on 'Steed'. It would then be less relevant than the interpretation where Steed forces his third victim off the road and *also* attacks her at gunpoint. Again, we can see how Simpson over-interprets the text when viewed from the perspective of someone reading for gist and so investing something akin to minimum effort.

To sum up this section, given that hard news text is a form of narrative text, readers will automatically assume that the information presented to them is maximally relevant for establishing, if it is not already explicitly mentioned, the causal antecedence of an action. This is a fundamental pragmatic principle with regards to understanding causal information and is then a fundamental pragmatic principle in the idealised reader framework. But if causal antecedent inferences are bound up with the maximisation of relevance, conversely other inferences which require more effort to generate will be less relevant. This is what I address in the next section.

9.4.2 IR and Less Relevant Inferences

Graesser et al. (1994) is a detailed later-constructionist response to critique from the founders of the minimalist hypothesis, McKoon and Ratcliff (1992), that constructionist theories often fail to specify the kinds of inferences drawn upon in comprehension. From a review of experimental evidence, Graesser et al. (1994) agree with the minimalists that the following inferences are normally drawn because they are necessary for coherence: (1) referential inferences (to what previous words does this word apply?); (2) role assignment inferences (for example, what is the agent, object and so on in the clause?); (3) causal antecedent inferences (what caused this?). With regard to inferences that are *not* habitually generated, Graesser et al. (1994) also agree with the minimalists that these include two elaborative inferences: causal consequent inferences and instrument inferences (that is, they are not generated when information is not quickly and easily available and context is not sufficiently constraining). Another elaborative inference, one we have not met yet, which for the same reasons both later constructionists and minimalists hold would not habitually be drawn, is the following: *subordinate goal-action* (how was the action achieved?). So, for the sentence 'The soldiers killed the demonstrators', the inference – that they did so by firing bullets at them – would not usually be inferred in the absence of constraining information, just as in the same way that 'with guns', for the same conditions, would not usually be inferred as an instrument inference in the above sentence. Where the later constructionists and the minimalists *do* differ, however, is with regard to the generation of another inference: *superordinate goal inferences*, that is, why did someone do something, and what was their goal? While this is not predicted by minimalists, it *is* predicted by later constructionists.

More recently, Graesser et al. (1997: 183) have made an accommodation between their later constructionist perspective on inference generation and that of the minimalists:

> We suspect that each of the . . . models is correct in certain conditions. The . . . minimalist hypothesis [is] probably correct when the reader is very quickly reading the text, when the text lacks global coherence, and when the reader has very little background knowledge. The constructionist theory is on the mark when the reader is attempting to comprehend the text for enjoyment or mastery at a more leisurely pace, when the text has global coherence, and when the reader has some background knowledge.

Eysenck and Keane (2000: 351) evaluate this as a 'reasonable conclusion'. On the basis of the above, since (1) both later constructionists and minimalists predict that causal antecedent inferences (what caused this?) are normally generated; and (2) later constructionists predict that superordinate goal inferences (why did someone do this?) will usually be generated and the minimalists do not, the latter must be because superordinate goal construction is in line with the investment of more effort compared with causal antecedent inference generation. This is not surprising since it is rather obvious that the reasons why people perform particular actions can be complex and often unfathomable. With the example in Keenan et al. (1984):

> Joey's big brother punched him again and again.
> The next day his body was covered with bruises

an elaborative causal antecedent inference is more readily generated than a superordinate goal inference since accessing knowledge of events in the world is easier than trying to understand the psychological motivation here. From a relevance point of view, then, superordinate goal inferences are less relevant than causal antecedent inferences given that extra processing effort will usually be required for the former. The same must be said also for subordinate goal-action inferences (that is, how was the action achieved?).

It is revealing that the texts examined in Graesser et al. (1994) in relation to predictions of inference are very short 'story-like' narratives. Indeed, as we saw in 7.4, in such narratives readers focus on main characters in trying to ascertain their superordinate goals. It is also revealing that other inferences that the later constructionists Graesser et al. (1994)

predict would normally be made on-line, but are not predicted on the minimalist hypothesis, relate to the literary genre as well. These are as follows: (1) *thematic inferences* – what is the main point or moral of a text?; and (2) *character emotional reaction* – inferencing an emotion experienced by a character in response to an action or an event. Graesser et al. (1994: 377) point out that while 'goals are ill defined and general . . . when an adult reads the morning newspaper to become informed about current events', the goal is more specific while reading a novel and forming a mental picture of what a character looks like. The more specific the reading goal, the more effort invested. And investment of effort in a character in a novel will bring its own rewards, such as emotional pay-off for the reader. Indeed, if cognitive benefits match the cognitive costs, on a relevance outlook it would be worth the investment of effort. Given this 'literary' genre focus in Graesser et al. (1994), and the relationship between costs and benefits, it is not surprising that later constructionists see the three inferences – superordinate goal, thematic and character emotional reaction – as being normally generated on-line. The psycholinguistic evidence of Vonk and Noordman (1990) in 7.2.2 on costs and benefits in inference generation would appear to support this.

To sum up, it would seem that the minimalist hypothesis is in keeping with general goals in reading, when reading is quick and where little background knowledge of the events being reported is expected. On the other hand, the later constructionist perspective is in keeping with more specific goals and thus where more cognitive effort would be invested. Because I focus on hard news reports where general reading goals are common and where the purpose of the reports is to provide new information, this is why IR incorporates the minimalist hypothesis and not the predictions of inference generation based on the later constructionist position of Graesser et al. (1994). Thus, IR does not seek to infer superordinate goals in the reading of hard news text (if this information has not already been explicitly mentioned in the text). Neither does IR seek to generate thematic inferences or character emotional reactions.

In relation to one of the inference types I have just introduced, I now highlight another example of how CDA can veer into over-interpretation. This is from Goatly (2000: 4–5). First, I reproduce the news text (*International Express*, June 1995) he examines and then his commentary:

'SUPERMAN' MAY NEVER WALK AGAIN
(1) *Superman* star Christopher Reeve is in hospital with a suspected broken back.
(2) His family ordered hospital officials not to give out any information – but sources say he is partially paralysed.

(3) The actor's publicist, Lisa Kastelere, was plainly upset as she revealed that horse-mad Reeve was hurt show-jumping in Virginia.
(4) Witnesses saw him hit the ground hard as his horse shied.
(5) As doctors evaluated his condition in the acute-care ward at the University of Virginia's Medical Centre in Charlottesville, it was not known whether he will walk again.
(6) Reeve, 43 and 6 ft 4 in, was flown to the hospital by air-ambulance after doctors at the competition decided he needed special care.
(7) Reeve, who stared in 4 *Superman* movies, lived with his British lover Gael Exton for 11 years.
(8) They had two children.
(9) Reeve then began a relationship with singer Dana Morosini.

... it's quite clear that we have to make several inferences in order to understand this passage. We would infer, for example, that the events described in the last two sentences took place before those in the first six. Or that Reeve's hitting the ground hard (sentence 4) was the cause of his suspected broken back (sentence 1), since this is not actually stated. These two inferences are quite uncontroversial, but inferencing is a risky business and a more controversial inference may be suggested by the information in sentences 8 and 9. These may imply that Reeve somehow deserved this 'punishment' for abandoning his British lover and their two children and striking up a relationship with Dana Morosini ... the only nationality adjective used in the passage is 'British', used to describe Gael Exton. We can explain this if we know the ideological position of the newspaper. Express Newspapers are British with a capital 'B', unashamedly nationalistic, featuring the Union Jack flag and a medieval crusader as masthead adjacent to their title. Reeve's former partner – who was a 'lover', by the way, not just someone like Dana Morosini with whom he had a 'relationship' – was British. This might make Britain somehow more important, or at least enable the British reader to relate more closely to the story. Such a nationalistic background also provides an ideological explanation for the doubtful interpretation – that the accident was deserved as a punishment for infidelity.

From the perspective of IR (which incorporates the minimalist hypothesis), Goatly is right to be circumspect about the possibility of the 'controversial' inference being produced. In having a moral basis, this inference could be cast as a type of *thematic inference*. As I indicated, this is an inference more likely to be generated in the reading of literary narratives where benefits can match effort costs but is much less likely in the reading of hard news text. For the reading of news text, it requires more effort than another inference Goatly refers to: the *causal antecedent inference* that hitting the ground hard was the cause of the suspected broken back. In other words, the thematic inference that Goatly generates is less relevant than the causal antecedent inference he also generates. In being less relevant, it is strategically generated by the analyst here but most likely not by a reader reading for gist and so investing something close to minimum effort.

The idealised reader framework, being based on compatibilities from four different paradigms, is now complete. Now, I have in this book gone through analyses from CDA at different points in order to try to indicate problems in these analyses. Many problems have derived from not having a developed and consistent approach to inference generation (or text processing generally). One purpose of this book is to try to move forward mystification analysis in CDA. This can be done not only by pointing out how many CD mystification analyses are based on problematic symbolic assumptions, but also by providing a richer perspective on where analysts are correct in their interpretations. The latter is what I do in the next section.

9.5 PROVIDING A MORE COMPREHENSIVE EXPLANATION OF A CRITICAL DISCOURSE ANALYSIS

I would like to endorse most of the following analysis by Trew (1979: 100–1) (an analysis which has been commented upon many times, for example, in Toolan 2001: 208–9; Lee 1992: 101–3; Montgomery 1995: 240) by showing how the IR framework can provide a richer perspective as to why the text in question is mystifying. In 2.4 I provided an extract from *The Times* of 2 June 1975:

> *The Times*
> RIOTING BLACKS SHOT DEAD BY POLICE AS ANC LEADERS MEET
> Eleven Africans were shot dead and 15 wounded when Rhodesian police opened fire on a rioting crowd of about 2,000 . . .

Below is an extract from *The Times* of the following day (3 June 1975), as well as some of Trew's (1979) analysis:

> *The Times*
> SPLIT THREATENS ANC AFTER SALISBURY'S RIOTS
> After Sunday's riots in which 13 Africans were killed and 28
> injured, a serious rift in the ranks of the African National Council
> became apparent today.

And here is Trew (1979: 101):

> In *The Times* report itself there is a reference to the killing, but in
> a way that is significant. It is in this clause:
> After Sunday's riots in which 13 Africans were killed.
> Once again, it is in passive form, and the agent is deleted. But
> more than this, the description is changed from 'shot dead' to
> 'killed' so that any reference to the manner of death is deleted.
> The new description gives no hint of the agent or the manner of
> death – there is only a suggestion of a cause resulting from the
> way the 'riots' are made focal and made the context of the deaths.

Trew does not regard as particularly strong the causal antecedent inference that the riots killed the thirteen Africans. But we now can 'translate' his analysis into something more systematic via the IR framework. In line with least effort investment, it is likely that non-critical readers (that is, readers who (1) are largely unfamiliar with the events referred to in a news text, and (2) do not invest the effort to hunt for absences because they are reading for gist) will presume that information presented is optimally relevant for use in establishing causal antecedence. A strong connecting causal antecedent inference would thus be instituted between 'riots' and 'killed' so that, on relevant least effort processing, riots caused the deaths of the thirteen Africans. The textual configuration which leads to the generation of this connecting causal antecedent inference thus exploits the principle of expectation of relevance. What Trew means by 'only a suggestion' is in fact that a fairly weak elaborative causal antecedent inference would also be produced. This is weak since the causal relation for how riots lead to deaths would be fairly fuzzy for many people. It does not correspond to a prototypical and well-defined gestalt.

From a semantic point of view, the first clause of the text body is truthful. The author of the news article could claim they represented the event since the Africans did die while rioting took place. But from a pragmatic point of view the configuration of information in the text is exploitative. In using the IR framework in this way to highlight manipulation, the realism–idealism dichotomy highlighted in 5.5.2, is avoided. The sentence from the hard news text analysed by Trew is not problematic because it does not mirror the world (realism) nor because it mediates between the world and what we can know of it (idealism). It is problematic because understanding of the event comes about through an interactive process between the reader's cognitive procedures and the input. That is, the reader is likely to *enact* a misleading understanding because of default expectations of relevance for causal antecedence.

Finally, consider the following from Montgomery's (1995: 240) commentary on the second extract from *The Times* (3 June):

> The *agent* now remains completely unspecified. This vagueness is reinforced if anything by the selection of 'were killed' rather than 'were shot' which would at least have implied someone to do the shooting.

Again Montgomery's point is essentially correct but can be extended via the IR framework. Subordinate goal-action inferences as to how an action was executed and inferences for instruments used in the execution of the action are usually generated only when the context is sufficiently constraining. Basic-level categories can provide such constraint but a superordinate category such as 'kill' helps to background the nature of the subordinate goal action and thus the instrument. Since the context is not constraining and expectations of relevance are based on least effort processing, the subordinate goal-action 'were shot' will most likely not be generated for a non-critical reader.

As we saw in 6.4.2, prototypical causality is understood in terms of a cluster of 'interactional properties'. This involves an agent that does something using his or her hands, body or some instrument. Because 'were shot' will be related to prototypical causality, 'were shot' thus implies an agent did something. In introducing 'were shot', Montgomery uses the basic-level verb 'shoot'. Because of the cognitive interdependence at the basic level, itself associated with motor-interaction and gestalt formation, 'with guns' can be more readily generated as an instrument inference from 'were shot'. To sum up, 'were shot' would imply a subordinate goal-action involving a human agent(s) rather than the more nebulous 'riot' as cause of the deaths. Indeed, 'were shot' is more relevant than 'killed' because it yields more cognitive effects for the same processing effort.

I finish this chapter with some general comments relating to the IR framework.

9.6 GENERAL COMMENTS RELATING TO THE IR FRAMEWORK

9.6.1 The Primary Focus of IR is Causal Cognition

In IR there is no attempt to model the social situatedness of a reader. The main reason for this is that IR is a device to assist mystification analysis rather than socio-cognitive analysis. In addition, the primary focus of IR is, as we have seen, on causal cognitive processes. These are processes which can be regarded as *universal* in human cognition. In other words, the actual mechanisms of causal processing exist regardless of social situation. All three paradigms I drew on in Chapter 8 to begin the construction of IR carry the presumption of universality and generalisability. This is no different for relevance theory: relevance theory 'is concerned with the basic, universal principles that underlie utterance interpretation rather than the content of interpretations' (Christie 2000: 169).

Another reason why there is no social-situatedness of IR is as follows. In Chapter 10, I use IR as a guide to highlighting (1) whether absences from a text are likely to be conveyed into the discourse of a gist reader and thus result in mystification of the events being described, and (2) whether absences from a text could be generated by a gist reader as inferences on the basis of other information already in the text and thus not result in mystification of the events being described. The focus of IR with regard to mystification is then principally on what is *absent* from hard news text rather than what the reader *brings to* the news text in terms of his or her social-situatedness. This perspective suits hard news text, especially given that one of its main functions is to provide specific knowledge which it assumes readers do not know and thus would not likely bring to the text. One more reason why social-situatedness does not feature with IR is the nature of hard news text. By their very nature, the events described in news are highly ephemeral. The shelf-life of a hard news article is *one day* which can make empirical socio-cognitive analysis more difficult. Empirical socio-cognitive analysis would involve investigation of how actual readers understand the events via the discourses (2) they inhabit. But the longer empirical socio-cognitive investigation takes place after the appearance of the news article, the more likely subjects may activate, as being relevant, general background knowledge which was acquired *subsequent* to the appearance of the news article. The relating of textual cues to accessible knowledge is as likely (if not more likely) to be the relating of textual cues to information in short-term memory as long-term memory (this is all in line with the principles of relevance and primary processing). Clearly, this leads to misleading results. Instead, an empirically oriented socio-cognitive focus on representations in news texts of a particular *topic* such as 'sexual harassment' (Christie 1998) or 'poverty' (Meinhof and Richardson 1994) circumvents the extremely time-bound nature of hard news text (I will allude to Meinhof and Richardson (1994) in the next section).

9.6.2 IR and Empirical Testing

Cameron (2001: 140) argues that analysis in CDA can be enriched through exploring actual interpretations of texts by readers. The case study she focuses on is an investigation of a television documentary series called 'Breadline Britain', where the topic was poverty in Britain in the 1990s (Meinhof and Richardson 1994). Richardson supplemented Meinhof's textual analysis by empirically examining how certain viewers of the programme interpreted its representations of poverty. For different viewer groups, Richardson found different interpretations and thus showed, as Cameron (2001: 140) indicates in her summary of Richardson's work, that 'meaning ... was not only in the text itself, but was affected by what viewers brought to bear on it from their own knowledge and experience'. Cameron (2001: 140) is, then, right to point out that:

> The members of Richardson's groups may not represent 'everyone', but they do represent *someone*, whereas the idealized reader of many purely textual analyses is open to the criticism that s/he represents no one, and has simply been invented for the analyst's convenience.

Cameron, however, is referring to an idealised reader in socio-cognitive analysis. Given the potential variation in socio-cognitive response to text, and in line with Cameron, it is difficult to argue that analysts do not have to seek empirical justification for their socio-cognitive analysis of a text based on an idealised reader.[3] Cameron (2001: 140) also points out that Richardson's study 'tells us only about the interpretations produced by the particular groups in her sample'. In other words, it is difficult to generalise on the basis of empirical socio-cognitive results beyond the social contexts where the data was generated.

What of testing a CDA interpretation of a text where the focus is causal cognition in relation to text mystification? Testing the predictions of such an analysis would be an involved and laborious process in its necessary focus on inference generation. For example, it would have to circumvent the problem that just because readers make inferences in verbal protocols, this does not mean that these inferences would ordinarily have been generated. In verbal protocol analysis, experimenters gain insight into a subject's cognitive processes by getting them to verbalise their immediate responses to a text. On the complexity involved in such testing, consider Graesser et al. (1994: 385–6): 'The fact that an inference is expressed in verbal protocols does not imply that the inferences are normally generated on-line. It is possible that readers adopt unnatural reading strategies when producing the verbal protocols (Nisbett and Wilson 1977). Therefore, it is necessary to test the on-line status of candidate inferences by collecting appropriate measures from a separate group of readers who do not supply verbal protocols. Such measures include sentence reading times, gaze durations on words, lexical-decision latencies or naming latencies on test items in a secondary task, latencies in making recognition memory judgments on words or sentences, and so on.' The complexity here creates problems for anyone doing CDA without a psycholinguistics background. Moreover, the need to always put causal-cognitive analyses to test would be a cumbersome and time-consuming process.

As I said in 9.6.1, compared with socio-cognitive analysis, examining the causal relations in text in a mystification analysis is predicated upon how a text interacts with universal cognitive mechanisms rather than variation of response in accordance with different social-situatedness, background knowledge, experience, and so on. Therefore, unlike the kind of social-scientific evidence collected by Richardson above in her socio-cognitive analysis, empirical psycholinguistic evidence for inference generation, felicitously, is *generalisable*. Given the generalisability of this evidence, and since testing causal-cognitive analyses is so cumbersome and time-consuming, an idealised reader framework for causal-cognitive mystification analysis which is at least based on empirical psycholinguistic evidence would be a useful compromise. And what if the empirical psycholinguistic evidence that a causal-cognitive idealised reader framework was based on was consensus evidence? And what if this evidence was compatible with the perspectives of *three* other paradigms with regard to the same universal cognitive mechanisms? Then such a framework would be less of a compromise than it might first appear. It is because of all this that the IR framework can carry a reasonable level of conviction in the guidance it can offer, without the need for complex and cumbersome testing. As I said in Chapter 8, IR cannot indicate what an actual reader will do. Nevertheless, it can usefully set out reading parameters by highlighting what minimum effort readers will most likely *not* do when extracting a text's gist. Because of this, it can usefully help an analyst avoid over-interpretation of hard news text on behalf of an actual non-critical reader on the assumption that the latter is likely to be investing something akin to minimum effort in reading for gist.

9.6.3 The Compatibility Level of the Four Paradigms for the IR Framework

In casting one's net so wide as to include four separate paradigms, the compatibility level needs to be controlled. This is something I have tried to do in this book. But clearly, in dealing with four different paradigms, the 'deeper' one goes into each paradigm the more likely it is that conceptual tensions will become apparent. So, for example, Sperber and Wilson (1995) adopt a view of the mind based on Fodor (1983) who is one of the co-authors of a critique of connectionism (Fodor and Pylyshyn 1988) (see Bechtel and Abrahamsen (2002) for an outline of this critique as well as connectionist responses to this (for example, Elman 1990)). Having said this, more recently Wilson and Sperber (2004) place distance between themselves and the account of the mind given in Fodor (1983). Consider also the following from Sperber and Wilson (1995: 175): 'The linguistic description of an utterance is determined by the grammar, and does not vary with the interests or point of view of the hearers.' As Bex (1996: 125) points out, 'If we accept this, we are obliged to agree with them that language is "a grammar-governed representational system" (Sperber and Wilson 1995: 173) which exists independently of the purposes to which it is put.' In a note, Bex (1996: 204) goes on to say that 'this, of course, is remarkably similar to the characterisation of I-language offered by Chomsky (e.g. Chomsky 1986)'. The similarities to Chomsky's position would be in tension with the perspective of connectionism and cognitive linguistics. And so on. Such possible tensions, however, relate to ontological issues of language, but ontology does not concern me since this book is concerned with the mechanisms of processing only. In other words, it is through processing issues that I have 'controlled' the four paradigms. So, for example, we have seen the following for all four paradigms: lexical processing, for a reader of text who invests minimum effort, is usually non-compositional if the lexical items are basic-level; secondly, inference generation is an inherent part of processing rather than an extra step which follows semantico-syntactic processing.

9.7 ENDPOINTS

The IR framework is now complete, being based on compatibilities from four paradigms. In the final chapter I apply the complete IR framework in a comprehensive causal-cognitive mystification analysis of a hard news text. I show how IR can be used as a guide as to how a news text can be mystifying of causal relations for a reader making something close to minimum effort. Crucially, however, because IR is not based on problematic symbolic assumptions, the results of its application would not necessarily accord with many of the CD analyses of mystification I have highlighted in this book.

NOTES

1. Proof-reading would come under non-typical reading.
2. So, for example, a relevance-theoretic perspective would also be in tension with the compositional analysis of 'flock' in Fairclough (1995a: 113). See section 4.5 of this book.
3. Similarly, Widdowson (2000: 22) holds that CDA should 'take empirical ethnographic considerations into account and locate texts in their socio-cultural settings. In such an ethnographic approach, how non-analysts go about their normal pragmatic business would be the central focus of study.'

CHAPTER 10

Detecting News Text Likely to Mystify in Reading for Gist

10.1 INTRODUCTION

In this chapter, I use the IR guide in a comprehensive analysis of a hard news report from London's *Evening Standard* to show how its absences are likely to be mystifying of causal relations for a non-critical reader (using the same characterisation of this as before). One reason why the analysis is comprehensive – that is, it includes the whole text – is in response to criticisms by Stubbs (1997: 102) and Fowler (1996a: 8) who criticise CDA for commonly focusing only on fragments of texts. I am also mindful, in this chapter, of the following from Stubbs (1997: 107):

> Since the essential claim [in CDA] concerns differences caused by different language use, it follows that studies of language use and cognition must be comparative. Only very few CDA studies compare individual texts...

I provide, then, comparative analysis of other newspaper reports of the event described by the *Evening Standard*. As a result of this and of the limitations in a book of this size, I am only able to produce comprehensive analysis, including comparative analysis, of one news text.

10.2 USING IR TO DETECT MYSTIFYING TEXT IN TERMS OF ABSENCES FROM DISCOURSE

10.2.1 Widdowson's Criticisms

In Chapter 2 (2.7), I flagged up some of Widdowson's criticisms. Now I revisit them. In essence, Widdowson argues that because CDA is committed to a number of particular values (for example, liberal/left values), it cannot provide analysis but only partial interpretation. In line with this criticism, Widdowson (1995a, 1998) has accused certain critical discourse analysts of selecting presences in a text that merely confirm a line they take on the text which fits in with their value-system. At the same time, according to Widdowson, they often conveniently ignore other presences which could be in tension with this interpretation. Because any interpretation is partial, Widdowson (1995a: 169) argues the following:

> What analysis would involve would be the demonstration of different interpretations and what language data might be adduced as evidence in each case. It would seek to explain just how different discourses can be derived from the same text . . .

Widdowson's point that different readers will select different aspects of the same text is a difficult criticism to dodge as it relates to a perennial problem in any text analysis on behalf of readers: how to move validly from *atomising* a text in analysis to drawing conclusions about how it is *holistically* understood by readers.

10.2.2 Addressing Widdowson's Criticisms

How then can critical discourse analysts guard against the intrusion of subjectivity into diagnosing a text on behalf of readers? How can critical discourse analysts increase the likelihood that the texts they interpret as being manipulative really are likely to be manipulative of readers?

Detecting Absences

Focusing on absences from a text can be a way of accomplishing this. While analysts cannot be sure that the presences they pick up in texts are the ones that non-analysts would pick up with the same emphasis, there is a greater chance that absences from a text would be absences from the discourse of a reader. This is due to the greater amount of effort needed to detect absences and the fact that analysing a text for its absences is not a usual part of reading, especially gist reading. But how do we then guard against the subjective detection of absences? I am mindful here of the commonly reproduced criticism of Critical Linguistics from Sharrock and Anderson (1981: 289) that it locates absences from rather ad hoc, individual perspectives: 'One of the stock techniques employed by Kress and his colleagues is to look in the wrong place for something, then complain that they can't find it, and suggest that it is being concealed from them.'

I want to suggest that using the IR framework can help to guard against the subjective detection of absences. That the prospect of such absence detection is not likely to be subjective or intuitive derives from the cognitive interdisciplinarity of the framework and the fact that it consists only of compatible, and thus mutually supporting, aspects of its source components. Now, not all absences from a text will be absences from the discourse of readers. Indeed, the more effort readers are willing to invest, the more likely that absences from a text will be generated as inferences. But my focus is on a non-critical reader who (1) is largely unfamiliar with the events beng described in a news text, and (2) in reading for gist invests something close to minimum effort, and therefore would not search for absences. Usefully, the IR framework can tell us the kinds of inference that such a reader is *unlikely* to make. If these are inferences necessary for a richer understanding of a particular event or the rationale of a participant featured in a hard news text, then we can treat the absence from the text of information equivalent to these inferences as being significant for such a reader. This is because they are also likely to be absent in the discourse of the non-critical reader, given this reader would not seek absences from the text.[1]

The focus here can derive a certain exegetic privilege since, unlike previous CDA, it explicitly tries to take account of the conditions under which absences from a news text are more likely to lead to mystification: that is, when reading effort is something akin to a minimum in line with general goals such as in reading for gist. In addition, when I highlight presences in my analysis of a news text in this chapter, this analysis of presences is subordinate to absence detection. This is because I show how presences in texts help to *reinforce* absences. And because of this, my highlighting of presences is not done arbitrarily or subjectively given that absences are not detected in this way.

On the basis of the IR framework, the elaborative inferences listed below are unlikely to be drawn automatically under the following conditions: when co-text is not highly constraining, where background knowledge cannot be readily accessed, when there is no one obvious inference to be generated, where minimum reading effort is being invested, and where the reading does not have specific goals:

1. Superordinate goal: why did someone do something?
2. Instrument: what did they use?
3. Subordinate goal-action: how was the action achieved?
4. Instantiation: 'filling in' a general category with more specific information.
5. Causal consequent: what were the results of the action?

(Under converse conditions these inferences could be generated, particularly with a fair amount of effort investment. Indeed, causal consequent inferences usually need to be strategically generated.)

In this chapter, I relate my causal-cognitive mystification analysis of a hard news text to these inferences. Throughout my analysis, in employing the IR framework I necessarily prohibit problematic symbolic analysis – that we saw of CDA in previous chapters – as well as over-interpretation on behalf of a non-critical reader.

Causal Antecedent Relevance in Relation to Widdowson's Criticisms

With regard to narrative texts such as hard news texts, I have indicated that there is a fundamental pragmatic principle which readers operationalise, for example, seeking causal antecedence in line with an expectation of relevance. This is not partial in the sense that some readers will seek causal antecedence in a hard news text and some will not. Readers do this naturally when they come to hard news texts given that causal relations are such a prominent part of them. Moreover, we would expect a hard news text that was relevant to lead to *one* possible interpretation with regard to causal antecedence. But texts can be constructed in a vague manner and so possibly lead different readers to operationalise the text in different ways in searching for causal antecedent relevance. Consequently, different interpretations of causal antecedence could result. But in such a case, to paraphrase Widdowson (1995a: 169), if 'different causal antecedence discourses can be derived from the same text', then the text can be diagnosed as problematic as opposed to this being a normal or desirable state of affairs.

I now move on to my mystification analysis of a hard news text taken from the *Evening Standard* (Wednesday, 7 August 1996). The *Evening Standard* is London's only evening newspaper, with different editions appearing earlier in the day. It has a circulation of more than 445,000 with a readership of 1.1 million.[2]

10.3 *EVENING STANDARD* TEXT 1, 'PROTEST MOB STORM TUBE HQ': USING IR IN A MYSTIFICATION ANALYSIS

10.3.1 The Hard News Text

Evening Standard Text 1 begins on the front page of the newspaper and runs on to page 2. The first page is dominated by the report and photograph, and the headline and sub-headline are in large type. Rather than

NEWS TEXT LIKELY TO MYSTIFY IN READING FOR GIST

PROTEST MOB STORM TUBE HQ

Demonstrators fight past security men to occupy chief's office

by LUKE BLAIR, NICK PRYER and ALLAN RAMSAY

PROTESTERS today smashed their way into London Underground headquarters as a mass demonstration on the streets and the Tube strike brought central London to a standstill.

An angry mob overpowered security guards at the LU head offices above St James's station and rushed up seven floors to march into the chairman's office. There they threw papers around and unfurled banners from the windows declaring "Don't squeeze the Tube."

LU chairman Peter Ford said: "I was astonished when they burst into my office. I asked them what they wanted and they didn't seem too sure.

"They started chanting slogans, throwing paperwork around and opening the windows and unfurling banners outside.

"I was worried that they would damage my family photographs so I asked them to respect them and they did. I explained I was a keen cyclist and asked them if there were any points I could clarify about the dispute.

"I even told them how much Underground drivers earn. Then they said they wanted to lock the doors but I told them if this was a non violent protest they would have to play by the rules, which they did."

Police were later questioning a number of the protesters.

At the same time, during the height of the morning rush hour, several hundred cyclists

Continued on Page 2 Col 2

Demonstrating cyclists surround a motorist at Trafalgar Square today   Picture JEREMY SELWYN

Figure 10.1 'Protest mob storm Tube HQ', *Evening Standard* Text 1, 7 August 1996, reproduced by permission of the *Evening Standard*

initially providing context for the report which would help the reader fill in absences, I allow the reader to run through the text 'unaided'. Indeed, I suggest that readers read it as though they were reading the article quickly for gist, one story among a number of other stories they would be reading in the rest of the newspaper. Doing so will make it easier to connect with the analysis that follows.

PROTEST MOB STORM TUBE HQ
Demonstrators fight past security men to occupy chief's office
by Luke Blair, Nick Pryer and Allan Ramsay

[*Page 1*]

1. Protestors today smashed their way into London Underground headquarters as a mass demonstration on the streets and the Tube strike brought central London to a standstill.
2. An angry mob overpowered security guards at the LU head offices above St James's station and rushed up seven floors to march into the chairman's office.
3. There they threw papers around and unfurled banners from the windows declaring 'Don't squeeze the tube.'
4. LU chairman Peter Ford said: 'I was astonished when they burst into my office.
5. I asked them what they wanted and they didn't seem too sure.
6. 'They started chanting slogans, throwing paperwork around and opening the windows and unfurling banners outside.
7. 'I was worried that they would damage my family photographs so I asked them to respect them and they did.
8. I explained I was a keen cyclist and asked them if there were any points I could clarify about the dispute.
9. 'I even told them how much Underground drivers earn.
10. Then they said they wanted to lock the doors but I told them if this was a non-violent protest they would have to play by the rules, which they did.'
11. Police were later questioning a number of the protestors.
12. At the same time, during the height of the morning rush hour, several hundred cyclists

[*Page 2*]

from the same group of protesters – Reclaim the Streets – converged on Trafalgar Square.

13. The protest, ironically aimed at combating car use and supporting public transport, caused massive knock-on effects on routes already overloaded with Tube strike traffic.
14. Scuffles broke out as anarchist cyclists confronted police and angry motorists.
15. They were greeted by shouts of abuse, fist waving, and a cacophony of tooting car horns from cabbies and drivers as they deliberately dismounted and remounted and pedalled slowly around the Square.
16. Edmund King, head of campaigns for the RAC, said: 'I'm

appalled by the action of a bunch of anarchists stopping the traffic.
17. It's ironic they are campaigning against pollution when they've caused 10 times more in Trafalgar Square by blocking the traffic.'
18. After an hour the cyclists peeled off down Whitehall to Parliament Square where they again slowed traffic.
19. Tempers rose to boiling point when several vanloads of police trapped the demonstrators in a bus lane.
20. A stand-off followed, with lines of officers blocking both ends of the street.

10.3.2 Background to the Event

As we will see in this chapter, the IR framework can help to pinpoint whether the absences with regard to the rationale of participants in a news text are likely to be taken in to discourse. But obviously, the IR framework cannot shed light on the *actual* rationale of a particular group of participants. We need to find that out by asking the participants themselves. While this information is not needed for application of IR, it can be interesting and useful to know all the same. This is particularly the case in comparative analysis of other news reports to see how much of the rationale of participants is included.

In email replies to my questions from Reclaim the Streets (http://www.reclaimthestreets.net), I was informed that the purpose of the protest was as follows:

1. to show solidarity with the Tube strikers who were campaigning for a better pay deal and who decided to strike after the London Underground (LU) management withdrew a pay offer. That Reclaim the Streets were supporting the Tube strike is information that was supplied in other newspapers (see below)
2. to highlight how the extra pollution caused by more cars being on the road during the Tube strike was ultimately a result of LU management reneging on a pay deal
3. to support the Tube as a form of public transport preferable to car culture, which leads to pollution, helps to sustain global warming, and so on.

10.3.3 IR's Background Knowledge of Events

In line with what I said in section 8.6, while IR has the general background knowledge that would be expected of an adult, at the same time it is unfamiliar with the specific events described in a hard news text. And as I also said in 8.6, this is far from being an implausible notion. People read hard news texts for *new* information, relating new specific knowledge of events to their general background knowledge. So IR would understand the concept of a strike and know the concept of eco-protest. But they would not necessarily know the specific protest group here, Reclaim the Streets (not in 1996 a household name in London nor now), and so would not know the specific reasons for the organisation's support for the Tube strike. The prospect that readers will be unfamiliar with the event and participants being reported is more likely with a 'one-off' event rather than one which has been part of a chain of events. The fact that this hard news text reports a 'one-off' event, then, sits better with the application of IR.[3]

10.4 USING IR IN A MYSTIFICATION ANALYSIS

10.4.1 Superordinate Goal Absence

Minimum effort readers are unlikely to infer superordinate goals via the IR framework. So, if this information is not present in the text, it could diminish understanding for the non-critical reader of participants in the event being reported. The categories of 'protest mob' (headline), 'protestors' (sentence 1) and 'demonstrators' (sub-headline) and mass demonstration (sentence 1) are general. There are no basic-level categories which would help to lead to their instantiation, for example, a basic-level category like 'cycle', as in 'cycle protestors'. In other words, there are no basic-level categories which would increase relevance and thus lead to a greater yield of cognitive effects for the same effort. While it is somewhat marked by the third sentence that this text is not helpful as to the nature of the protestors, there is nevertheless a photograph which presumably would assist in supplying this information. Strangely, however, the photograph does not relate to the topic of the text (the invasion of the Tube HQ) and this is confirmed by the caption: 'Demonstrating cyclists surround a motorist at Trafalgar Square today'. So there is a very general absence early on in the text which would be likely to make it difficult for the non-critical reader to understand the superordinate goals of the protestors in relation to the invasion of London Underground HQ. Indeed, when LU Chairman says (sentence 5), 'I asked them what they wanted and they didn't seem too sure', the absence of superordinate goals is reinforced.

The mention of cyclists in sentence 8 – 'I explained I was a keen cyclist' – seems anomalous since it does not relate to anything in the preceding text. Readers who are prepared to make the effort may seize on this fragment and relate it to the photograph. But what about readers who are not making so much effort, that is, in line with IR? On this basis, the anomaly of 'I explained I was a keen cyclist' is likely to be overridden. Support for the overriding of anomalies comes from Sanford and Garrod's experiments. As we saw with the 'survivors' text in Chapter 7, global expectation can frustrate anomaly detection at a local semantic level. As Sanford and Garrod (1994: 717) aver:

> processing at a local semantic level, where case assignment and other attachments take place, can be dominated by more global aspects of coherence establishment. In particular, if a text statement fits well with a piece of pre-established knowledge or can be understood easily on the basis of pragmatics, then that link seems to be made, even if there are details of a local nature which are inconsistent with that interpretation.

As we saw in the previous chapter, this is supported by Sperber and Wilson (1995); coherence can be incomplete because expectations of relevance have been satisfied.

To sum up: analysis of the first page reveals that there is no mention of the nature of the protestors. Although there is a passing mention of 'cyclist', via the interviewed London Underground chairman, linking this to the photograph and then going on to generate a superordinate goal inference would require much more effort than is made on the basis of IR. Thus, on the first page, a least effort gist reader is likely to have an attenuated appreciation of events and the rationale of the protestors. On the second page we find out about their rationale, that the protest group is called Reclaim the Streets and that the protest is aimed at combating car use and supporting public transport. We have, then, mention of a general category ('protestors') on page 1 before the instance ('Reclaim the Streets') on page 2. Thus, the text is inconsiderate in another way: it places general categories before instances and this, as we saw in Garnham's (1981) experiments, would likely lead to a processing jolt and extra processing time (see 7.2.5). Extra processing time correlates with a decrease in relevance.

10.4.2 Instrument Absence

Consider the first sentence:

1. Protestors today smashed their way into London Underground headquarters as a mass demonstration on the streets and the Tube strike brought central London to a standstill.

Looking at the sentence via IR, since there is no constrained context on page 1 (that is, that this is a cycle demonstration), this reduces the prospect that the instrument inference – *with bicycles* – would accompany 'mass demonstration on the streets'. In line with expectations of relevance based on least effort processing, it is the most accessible information that will be yielded from memory, and prototypical information is accessible information. Mass street demonstrations are associated with a conventional prototypical gestalt, that is, they involve people marching. Thus, non-critical readers stand a chance of being misled by the first sentence given that it actually refers to a non-prototypical mass demonstration: a cycle demonstration. In other words, processing for this reader is again likely to be shallow with regard to the nature of the protest. Indeed, sentence 1 is something akin to Lakoff's (1987a: 452) examples (see 6.4.1): (1) 'There's a bird on the porch'; (2) 'John hit a ball', which, in being associated with prototypical gestalts, mislead when the scenarios are non-prototypical – (1) the bird is a penguin; (2) John is throwing a rock at a ball. Although, of course, there are cyclists in the picture, this will be in tension with the prototypical gestalt for 'mass demonstration' in sentence 1 of demonstrating on foot. The smoothing-out of this tension would then require more cognitive effort than is invested on the basis of IR.

10.4.3 Subordinate Goal-Action Absence

Without 'bicycles' as an instrument on page 1 of the text, we cannot construct an accurate subordinate goal action of *how* the mass demonstration helped to bring London to a standstill, for example, by riding closely together and thus blocking the passage of cars. The caption does not anchor the photograph in this way and so the generation of this inference is not likely to be forthcoming on something close to minimum effort investment. If a reader were prepared to ponder on the photograph, this subordinate goal action inference could possibly be generated, but this would be a strategic inference and not an automatic inference. The absence of subordinate goal action information means a reader's search to formulate causal antecedent relevance is exploited, something I will take further in 10.5.1.

Since, on page 1, superordinate goals are absent, there is little evidence to suggest that the protestors are supporting the Tube strike. As a result, another subordinate goal action – *how* the invasion of London Underground HQ supported the Tube strike – is unlikely to be realised in cognition. In other words, although the text includes the information – 'unfurling banners', 'declaring "Don't Squeeze the Tube"' – its relevance is unlikely to be activated on least effort processing and thus is likely to be backgrounded in the discourse of the non-critical reader.

On page 2, there is still no explicit mention that the protestors are supporting the Tube strike. The closest we get to an admission that the protestors are supporting the strike is in sentence thirteen: 'the protest ironically aimed at combating car use and supporting public transport'. But 'public transport' is a superordinate category which also embraces the bus and train service. Because of a lack of adequate constraining information in the text, it is unlikely to be easily instantiated as the Tube service. In turn, the lack of more specific context here means that linking 'public transport' with 'Tube strike' requires more than minimum effort. And so, although the non-critical reader knows by page 2 that the protestors are eco-protestors, all the same he or she does not know explicitly that they are supporting the Tube strike. The rationale of the protestors, then, is still likely to be absent from the discourse of the non-critical reader.

10.4.4 Causal Consequent Absence

Let us now examine causal consequence in the text. Consider sentences 13, 17 and 18:

13. The protest, ironically aimed at combating car use and supporting public transport, **caused massive knock-on effects on routes already overloaded with Tube strike traffic.** *[Presence of an actual causal consequent]*
17. It's ironic they are campaigning against pollution **when they've caused 10 times more in Trafalgar Square by blocking the traffic.'** *[Presence of a perceived causal consequent by non-sympathiser]*
18. After an hour the cyclists peeled off down Whitehall to Parliament Square **where they again slowed traffic.** *[Presence of an actual causal consequent]* [my bold]

Here are clearly described causal consequents of the Reclaim the Streets action. The first is not in dispute since it is indicated elsewhere, for example, in an article from *The Guardian*, which we examine later. The second is a *perceived* causal consequent by Edmund King, someone clearly out of sympathy with the protest. But what is absent from the text is a corresponding Reclaim the Streets perceived causal consequent. Judging from the email correspondence I had with Reclaim the Streets spokespeople, the perspective of Reclaim the Streets is the following: the extra traffic pollution was caused by London Underground (LU) management since they caused the Tube strike by reneging on a pay deal, leading to a great increase in the number of commuters going to work by car (see the Reclaim the Streets spokesperson, Reg Wagland, in *The Guardian*'s article below for part substantiation of this). However, this *perceived causal consequent* is not explicitly mentioned in the text.

Certainly, then, at the text level, there is bias. But what of the discourse level? (See: 2.2.1 for the distinction between text and discourse.) Is there *discourse bias*? Does the absence at text level of the Reclaim the Streets perceived causal consequent mean there will be an absence and thus mystification at discourse level? And, as a result, does this mean that the discourse of a non-critical reader is likely to be biased in that it contains the perceived causal consequent by Edmund King but not the one by Reclaim the Streets? I pose this question since, as we saw in Chapter 7, absences from text do not necessarily transfer into absences from discourse (for example, the absence of an agent–process–affected structure in a text does not necessarily mean that agency cannot be inferred). Not all text absences can necessarily be related to mystifying discourse.

From the IR framework, we know that causal consequents are not constructed when the reader has little vested interest in a text or is unfamiliar with subject matter. But they *can* be constructed when the reader is familiar with subject matter. So a reader familiar with the eco-protest (for example, one who has heard a radio report earlier in the day or has eco-protest sympathies) could produce the necessary identification with Reclaim the Streets to generate the Reclaim the Streets perceived causal consequent. And if the subject matter is familiar enough, then the causal consequent might be treated as being automatic (see 7.2.4). Now, consider a second type of reader, one not as familiar with the subject matter but with a vested interest in the text nonetheless. They could also eventually generate the Reclaim the Streets perceived causal consequent if they took the trouble to piece together certain aspects of the text, for example, 'Tube strike brought central London to a standstill' (sentence 1); protestors breaking into LU headquarters (sentence 1); declaring 'Don't squeeze the Tube' (sentence 3); 'combating car use and supporting public transport' (sentence 13); 'campaigning against pollution' (sentence 17), and so on. But, in such a circumstance, the perceived causal consequent would be *strategically* generated rather than automatically. To sum up, despite the text absence, in both cases above the reader's discourse would not be mystifying of the nature of the protestors.

I have mentioned two different types of readers who are able to generate the Reclaim the Streets perceived causal consequent. But IR guides us to ascertain the reading of someone who has general goals when they read news and is largely unfamiliar with the subject matter. Judging the text via the IR guide means this perceived causal consequent is not likely to be generated, or would be weakly generated at best. It is likely to be an absence in discourse. We can say then, using IR as a guide, that with regard to causal consequents the discourse of a non-critical reader is likely to be biased against the protestors. I conclude that, since (1) Edmund King's perceived causal consequent is present in the text, *then* (2) the Reclaim the Streets perceived causal consequent should *also* be present since this also is unlikely to be generated by an actual non-critical reader as it would involve strategic generation.

Why the Text-Based Principle of 'Reporting Both Sides' Needs to be Discourse-Based

In disputes or protests where there are opposing voices/sides, such as in the above, it seems reasonable that a hard news text should report 'both sides of the story' so as to avoid bias. But this is only a text-based principle. Much of this book has tried to show that highlighting a text as being mystifying needs to try to take account of the reader's contribution to the text. As 10.4.4 has tried to show, for absences from a text the principle of reporting both sides has only real significance in the context of readers who are unfamiliar with the subject matter and invest something akin to minimum effort because in reading for gist they do not seek to analyse a text for its absences – that is, a non-critical reader. In effect, I have adjusted the text-based principle of reporting both sides into a discourse-based principle.

Finally, there is the possibility of a weak implicature for IR following on from sentence 18. Because Edmund King says in sentence 17 that the cyclists have caused ten times the pollution, when the non-critical reader gets to sentence 18 and reads, 'After an hour the cyclists peeled off down Whitehall to Parliament Square where again they slowed traffic', it is possible that the weak implicature – *'slowed traffic' equals more pollution* – would be generated. This potentially increases the discourse bias here because information from a purely speculative negative perceived causal consequent (Edmund King could not know that *ten times* the usual amount of pollution has been caused) could be used in deriving an implicature (weak as it would be for someone reading for gist) from an actual

Crawl to work is the worst yet

by LUKE BLAIR
Industrial Correspondent

LONDON today suffered its worst traffic congestion of the summer as the Tube strike and the mass protest by cyclists caused widespread chaos.

At the height of the morning rush hour, parts of central London came to a complete standstill as the protest, ironically aimed at supporting public transport, caused massive knock-on effects on routes already overloaded with Tube strike traffic.

Roads around Westminster, including some of the busiest in London, were blocked solid, according to motoring organisations. Emergency services said the public were doing their best to let them through, but a spokesman for the ambulance service added: "Obviously it gets difficult in a gridlock situation."

A spokesman for the protest group, known only as Chris, said: "The idea was not to block traffic but to get motorists to leave their cars at home."

He said the group supported both the striking Tube drivers and the idea of public transport.

A London Underground spokesman, however, rubbished the protest as "totally self-defeating".

He said: "They are not helping the cause of public transport at all. We need to keep the roads clear on today of all days, if only so that our buses can get through."

As the seventh strike in the current dispute began, only four or five trains were running during the morning rush hour, when 300-400 trains normally operate.

There were single trains running on the Piccadilly, Northern and District lines and two on the Central line.

Between 8am and 9am, the worst-hit routes were all the major roads around Westminster, including Whitehall, the Strand, the Mall and Holborn.

Other routes like the A4, around Hyde Park and parts of the M25 were reported by motoring organisations to be more congested than normal. Another huge queue built up on on the A13 heading into the City through east London.

LU chiefs warned they face a total bill of more than £25 million in refunds and lost ticket sales if all 12 planned strikes in the current dispute go ahead.

Transport protest mob

Continued from Page 1

from the same group of protesters — Reclaim The Streets — converged on Trafalgar Square. The protest, ironically aimed at combating car use and supporting public transport, caused massive knock-on effects on routes already overloaded with Tube strike traffic.

Scuffles broke out as anarchist cyclists confronted police and angry motorists.

They were greeted by shouts of abuse, fist waving, and a cacophony of tooting car horns from cabbies and drivers as they deliberately dismounted and remounted and pedalled slowly around the Square.

Edmund King, head of campaigns for the RAC, said: "I'm appalled by the action of a bunch of anarchists stopping the traffic. It's ironic they are campaigning against pollution when they've caused 10 times more in Trafalgar Square by blocking the traffic."

After an hour the cyclists peeled off down Whitehall to Parliament Square where they again slowed traffic.

Tempers rose to boiling point when several vanloads of police trapped the demonstrators in a bus lane. A stand-off followed, with lines of officers blocking both ends of the street.

Figure 10.2 'Crawl to work is the worst yet', *Evening Standard* Text 2, 7 August 1996, reproduced by permission of the *Evening Standard*

causal consequent. On the basis of this, the following recommendation can be formulated: in a hard news report, there should be spatial distance between any perceived causal consequents and events where actual associated causal consequents are reported. This separation would then prevent the possibility of implicature 'spillage' from the perception, and thus inadvertent discourse bias.

10.4.5 Evening Standard Text 2 (extract)

I now move on to consider an extract from a second text (see Figure 10.2) from the *Evening Standard*, which appeared on the same day as the previous text, on page 2 of the newspaper. This is a related story which reports the problems commuters experienced on the day of the strike. The headline of this text is in smaller type than the first text. Moreover, it is only one of seven articles on page 2 and so does not take up as much space as text 1:

CRAWL TO WORK IS THE WORST YET
by Luke Blair
Industrial Correspondent

1. London today suffered its worst traffic congestion of the summer as the Tube strike and the mass protest by cyclists caused widespread chaos.
2. At the height of the morning rush hour, parts of central London came to a complete standstill as the protest, ironically aimed at supporting public transport, caused massive knock-on effects on routes already overloaded with Tube strike traffic.
3. Roads around Westminster, including some of the busiest in London, were blocked solid, according to motoring organisations.
4. Emergency services said the public were doing their best to let them through, but a spokesman for the ambulance service added: 'Obviously it gets difficult in a gridlock situation.'
5. A spokesman for the protest group, known only as Chris, said: 'The idea was not to block traffic but to get motorists to leave their cars at home.'
6. He said the group supported both the striking Tube drivers and the idea of public transport.
7. A London Underground spokesman, however rubbished the protest as 'totally self-defeating'.
8. He said: 'They are not helping the cause of public transport at all. We need to keep the roads clear on today of all days, if only so that our buses can get through.'

I consider only this part of the text since the rest of the article – another six sentences – does not relate to the cycle protest.

From sentence 1, the instrument of the protest – the bicycle – can be readily inferred. So, unlike *Evening Standard* Text 1, this reference to the basic-level category 'cycle' allows some instantiation of 'protest' early on in the text's reading and potentially then an inkling as to the superordinate goals of the protestors. Relevance is thus increased since a greater number of cognitive effects can be derived for the same amount of effort. However, the impact of this is likely to be reduced since this text is much less salient than *Evening Standard* Text 1. *Evening Standard* Text 1, starting on the front page, is, indeed, much more likely to be read than Text 2. Text 2 may not even be read, then, which of course means these cognitive effects would not be realised. While, in sentences 1, 2 and 8, there is again explicit specifying of negative causal consequents of the cycle protest, there is still no explicitly mentioned perceived causal consequent by the protestors that because LU management reneged on a pay deal, there is more traffic and thus more pollution on the roads. We now know, from sentence 6, the superordinate goal that the 'protest group' supports 'the striking Tube drivers'. But this is in relation to the cycle demonstration around central London rather than the protest in London Underground HQ. And so readers will not readily be able to use *Evening Standard* Text 2 to link the superordinate goal (support for the Tube drivers) to the subordinate goal action (how this might be achieved through the invasion of the London Underground HQ).

10.5 COMPARISON WITH OTHER NEWS TEXTS

In this section, I compare *Evening Standard* Text 1 with hard news texts of the same event in other newspapers. I do this so as to highlight the extent to which *Evening Standard* text 1 is likely to lead to discourse bias. I compare it with reports of the protest on Thursday, 8 August 1996 in two broadsheets in the UK, *The Guardian* and *The Daily Telegraph*. *The Guardian* is centre-left in its politics and *The Daily Telegraph* is on the right of the political spectrum.

10.5.1 Comparing Discourse Bias: *Evening Standard* Text 1 and *The Guardian*

First, here is the text from *The Guardian* (© Alex Bellos):

> Motorists fume over show of support for strikers
> CYCLE PROTEST ADDS TO TUBE DISRUPTION
> Alex Bellos
>   1. Bicycle campaigners ended a rally that brought chaos to London's rush hour traffic yesterday by invading the office of London Transport's chairman and using their bicycle locks to chain themselves to his window.

Figure 10.3 'Cycle protest adds to Tube disruption', *The Guardian*, 8 August 1996, © Alex Bellos, reproduced by permission of *The Guardian*

2. Forty protestors entered LT's headquarters in Westminster after 500 cyclists had brought traffic around Trafalgar and Parliament squares to a standstill.
3. The action was in support of yesterday's strike by Tube drivers.
4. An LT spokeswoman said that the chairman, Peter Ford, was in his seventh floor office when about 10 cyclists came in, started throwing papers around, and hung a banner out the window.
5. They spent 10 minutes having a 'fairly good-humoured chat', in which they all agreed public transport was under-funded, until the police arrived with bolt cutters.
6. Nine protestors were arrested and charged with offences including assault, breach of the peace, criminal damage and theft.
7. Scotland Yard said that protestors punched and kicked a police sergeant.
8. They also grabbed his video camera, police radio and helmet.
9. The event was organised by the anti-car pressure group Reclaim the Streets, which has close links to London's monthly Critical Mass bicycle demonstrations.
10. While participants said the aim was not to infuriate car drivers, an inevitable consequence was that traffic – already slower than normal because of the Tube strike – was brought to a standstill in several places.
11. Many drivers honked their horns in anger and threatened violence at the cheering protestors.

240   CDA AND LANGUAGE COGNITION

12. Groups of cyclists converged on Trafalgar Square at 9am, where a man in his 40s was arrested for breach of the peace.
13. Reg Wagland, aged 62, a retired electrician, said the protest was to highlight transport problems and show solidarity. 'We are here to support the Tube drivers. Their employers reneged on a deal.'
14. Another cyclist said: 'By cycling instead of driving Londoners can show their concern about the chronic underfunding of public transport, which results from placing profits before the environment, the health and safety of workers and quality of life.'
15. Bearing banners saying Squeeze Cars Not Tubes, the demonstration moved on to Parliament Square.
16. In front of the House of Commons the protestors got out of their saddles and held their bikes in the air.
17. The demonstration was criticised by motorists' organisations.
18. The RAC's head of campaigns, Edmund King, said: 'To stage this protest on a strike day when many people have no alternative but to use their cars is selfish and counter-productive.'
19. An AA spokesman, Paul Watters, said: 'Direct action protests really do cause chaos, and some of the more illegal activities can cause disruption to the emergency services and people having to make urgent journeys.'

Using the IR guide we can see that the discourse of a least effort reader is likely to be less mystifying of the superordinate goals of the protestors in the early part of the text than the discourse derived from *Evening Standard* Text 1. IR knows it is a 'cycle' protest from the start as well as knowing explicitly that the cyclists are supporting the Tube strike, information that comes as early as the super-headline 'Motorists fume over show of support for strikers'. Unlike *Evening Standard* Text 1, it is very clear that the protesters, entering LU's headquarters was in support of the Tube strike. In sentence 9, there is the modifier 'anti-car'. Use of basic-level categories such as 'cycle' and 'car' means that the *Guardian* text is more relevant with regard to superordinate goals than *Evening Standard* Text 1 since the cognitive effects with regard to reasons for the event are greater for the same amount of effort. Like the previous texts, the *Guardian* text does not attempt to conceal the fact that the cycle protest caused huge disruption. Also like the previous texts, it does not try to specify the Reclaim the Streets perceived causal consequent: that LU management has caused the extra traffic pollution. Nor does it seek to flesh this out after sentence 13 (where LU's reneging on a pay deal is mentioned). The mention of the banner 'Squeeze Cars Not Tubes' (sentence 15) again hints at the perceived causal consequent of Reclaim the Streets. But, on the basis of IR, a fuller generation of the consequence is unlikely to be forthcoming since again it is a consequent based on the perception of the campaigners. It would thus require strategic processing effort in order to produce the necessary identification.

Causal Consequence and Causal Antecedence

Compare the following two extracts:

The Guardian
Headline: Cycle Protest Adds to Tube Disruption
10. While participants said the aim was not to infuriate car drivers, an inevitable consequence was that traffic – already slower than normal because of the Tube strike – was brought to a standstill in several places.

Evening Standard Text 1
1. Protestors today smashed their way into London Underground headquarters **as a mass demonstration on the streets and the Tube strike brought central London to a standstill**.
13. The protest, ironically aimed at combating car use and supporting public transport, **caused massive knock-on effects on routes already overloaded with Tube strike traffic**. [my bold]

In *The Guardian*, there is a separation of the causal consequents of the Tube strike and the protest in the headline and so this is done very early on in the text. This is then confirmed and elaborated upon later in the text. Because of this separation, the reader is able to appreciate that the effects of the Tube strike *preceded* the effects of the cycle demonstration. In other words, the occurrence of the Tube strike meant that the traffic was slower than normal; the protest meant that the slower-than-normal traffic was brought to a standstill in several places. By comparison with the *Guardian* text, the fact that in *Evening Standard* Text 1 these consequents are not separated in the early part of the text seems to imply deliberate conflation.

We saw from Graesser et al. (1994) that readers habitually try to ascertain why something happened rather than how, where, or *when* it happened. In IR the search for causal antecedence is in line with expectations of relevance and least effort processing. On such a basis, given the information as presented in the *Evening Standard* Text 1 above, and the fact that least effort readers are unlikely to try to ascertain when actions occur, the non-critical reader would stand a good chance of perceiving that the standstill of central London was caused by the mass demonstration and the Tube strike simultaneously. Although the reader does not know at this point that the mass demonstration is a bicycle demonstration, a possible bias may be set up in the non-critical reader's mind that the mass demonstration had a similar impact to the Tube strike in terms of its effect on central London.

10.5.2 Main and Secondary Characters: Comparing *The Daily Telegraph*, *The Guardian* and *Evening Standard* Text 1

Consider these sentences of hard news text from each of the following newspapers:

Evening Standard Text 1
4. LU chairman Peter Ford said: 'I was astonished when they burst into my office.
5. I asked them what they wanted and they didn't seem too sure.
6. 'They started chanting slogans, throwing paperwork around and opening the windows and unfurling banners outside.
7. 'I was worried that they would damage my family photographs so I asked them to respect them and they did.
8. I explained I was a keen cyclist and asked them if there were any points I could clarify about the dispute.
9. 'I even told them how much Underground drivers earn.
10. Then they said they wanted to lock the doors but I told them if this was a non-violent protest they would have to play by the rules, which they did.'

The Daily Telegraph
8. The small group who reached Mr Ford's office charged past startled secretaries and hung banners out of the windows proclaiming their case.
9. 'One of them started throwing my papers around,' Mr Ford said. 'I asked them to leave my family photographs alone, which they did.
10. 'I asked them what the problem was and one said they were in favour of bicycles, so I told them I was a keen cyclist.

Cyclists' demo adds to Tube strike chaos

By David Millward

COMMUTERS forced to drive by the Tube strike yesterday found cyclists from the militant Reclaim the Streets group had blocked rush-hour routes. The cyclists also stormed London Transport's headquarters.

Peter Ford, London Transport's chairman, was confronted by about 10 protesters who reached his seventh-floor office. They were among 50 who burst into the St James's Park building shortly after 11 am as a protest by about 100 cyclists in Trafalgar Square and Parliament Square was ending.

The invasion resulted in nine arrests. A police officer and a security guard were hurt in the melee. Three other demonstrators were arrested for public order offences in the main protest.

The small group who reached Mr Ford's office charged past startled secretaries and hung banners out of the windows proclaiming their case.

"One of them started throwing my papers around," Mr Ford said. "I asked them to leave my family photographs alone, which they did.

"I asked them what the problem was and one said they were in favour of bicycles, so I told them I was a keen cyclist. Another said they were supporting the Tube drivers. A third said they were campaigning for more investment in public transport. I told them that on that issue we were on the same side."

Earlier, with traffic heavy because of the seventh one-day Tube strike, in which only six trains ran, the cyclists converged on Trafalgar Square. Frustrated motorists sat helpless as the demonstrators moved from Trafalgar Square through Whitehall to Parliament Square and then back again.

Chris Roberts, spokesman for Reclaim the Streets, said motorists had been given advance notice of the anti-car protest and should have left their vehicles at home.

The cyclists' action was condemned by the AA. "Direct action protests cause chaos, and illegal activities can cause disruption to emergency services and people having to make urgent journeys," a spokesman said.

Meanwhile, the Royal Mail has sent letters to 130,000 members of the striking Union of Communication Workers, setting out a deal accepted by union negotiators but not by union leaders. Post Office management hopes its action will lead to union members demanding a chance to vote on the offer.

Demonstrating cyclists hold up traffic during yesterday's Underground strike

Figure 10.4 'Cyclists' demo adds to Tube strike chaos', *The Daily Telegraph*, 8 August 1996, reproduced by permission of *The Daily Telegraph*

11. Another said they were supporting the Tube drivers.
12. A third said they were campaigning for more investment in public transport.
13. I told them that on that issue we were on the same side.'

The Guardian
4. An LT spokeswoman said that the chairman, Peter Ford, was in his seventh floor office when about 10 cyclists came in, started throwing papers around, and hung a banner out the window.
5. They spent 10 minutes having a 'fairly good-humoured chat', in which they all agreed public transport was under-funded, until the police arrived with bolt cutters.

Recall the information as to selective processing of narratives we looked at in section 7.4. We saw that a number of studies indicated that *main* and *secondary* characters are processed in different ways. We saw how Morrow (1985) showed that when a character (B) is perceived from the point of view of character (A), then the reader's perception of states can be bound up with the perspective of character (A). In effect, (A) becomes the main character and (B) the secondary character. With these points in mind, consider the 'character' of Peter Ford in *Evening Standard* Text 1. In *seven* sentences, the protestors are viewed from Peter Ford's perspective. It is, of course, difficult to know whether readers will inadvertently view the protestors as 'secondary characters' just because they are viewed from the perspective of Peter Ford. But in the absence on page 1 of the superordinate goals of Reclaim the Streets, and in the absence of accounts of the event from spokespeople for Reclaim the Streets, the possibility that the protestors are further downplayed in the reader's mind in reading Peter Ford's account is a real one. Morrow's (1985) psycholinguistic evidence is useful in alerting us to this possibility and thus to the prospect of continued mystification as to the purpose of the protestors. In the same way, in sentences 16 and 17 of *Evening Standard* Text 1, Edmund King is given more 'main character' status in being allowed to voice his opinion of the protestors. And so the protestors here could continue to receive the status of 'secondary characters' in the absence of spokespeople from Reclaim the Streets explicitly signalling their superordinate goals. Of course, for a reader more familiar with the nature of the protest, the 'secondary character' status of the protestors in Peter Ford's account would not be likely to lead to such mystifying discourse.

In *The Guardian*'s text, unlike those in *The Daily Telegraph* and the *Evening Standard*, Peter Ford's perspective is third-person and not first-person. This prevents the possibility of the protestors being perceived from the viewpoint of a main character and thus the possibility of the reader having an attenuated perspective on the protestors as 'secondary characters'. Although *The Daily Telegraph* includes Peter Ford's first-person description of the protestors, it nevertheless includes Ford providing information on the rationale of the protestors – they were 'supporting the Tube drivers' and 'they were in favour of bicycles'. This, then, somewhat reduces the 'secondary role status' of the protestors.

It is worthwhile including a word or two about apparent anomalies in *Evening Standard* Text 1. Peter Ford explains in sentence 8 that he is a keen cyclist and, in sentence 9, says, 'I even told them how much Underground drivers earn'. As I wrote in 10.4.1, such comments might appear anomalous given that on page 1 there is no explicit information that the protestors are cycle protestors and are supporting the Tube strike. However, both these anomalies are from Peter Ford's perspective, the main character perspective and so, on the basis of IR, the oddity of 'cyclist' could be somewhat diminished in a non-critical reader's discourse.

NEWS TEXT LIKELY TO MYSTIFY IN READING FOR GIST 245

10.5.3 Comparing Headlines and Photographs: the *Evening Standard*, *The Guardian* and *The Daily Telegraph*

Evening Standard Text 1
Headline: Protest Mob Storm Tube HQ
Sub-headline: Demonstrators fight past security men to occupy chief's office
Photograph caption: Demonstrating cyclists surround a motorist at Trafalgar Square today

The Guardian
Super-headline: Motorists fume over show of support for strikers
Headline: Cycle protest adds to Tube disruption
Photograph caption: Two wheels good, four wheels bad . . .
Cyclists get a dusty response from *FT*-reading motorists held up by yesterday's protest

The Daily Telegraph
Headline: Cyclists' demo adds to Tube strike chaos
Photograph: Demonstrating cyclists hold up traffic during yesterday's Underground strike

Let us compare *The Daily Telegraph* and *The Guardian* first. Both headlines mention the protest in the context of 'cycles' and so the pictures are easy to relate to the text. That is, the cycle protest around central London is made focal in the headlines and in the pictures. There is, then, in both broadsheets clear coherence between headlines, photographs and captions. This further highlights the aberrant absence of a coherent link between the photograph in *Evening Standard* Text 1 and its headlines, which helps to attentuate appreciation of the superordinate goals of Reclaim the Streets.

10.5.4 Text Presence Bias: Comparing the *Evening Standard* with *The Guardian* and *The Daily Telegraph*

In this analysis I have primarily focused on discourse bias which results from the rationale and so on of Reclaim the Streets being mystified. More specifically, I have tried to indicate the inadvertent bias that could potentially be generated in the discourse of a non-critical reader, that is, one who in reading for gist invests something close to minimum effort. This is why I have focused on certain text absences since, given the effort to detect them, they stand a good chance of being absent in the discourse of such a reader. As discourse bias via text absence has been my focus, I have not examined *text presence* bias (what was referred to simply as 'text bias' in 2.3). In line with what was stated in 2.3, it is more difficult to say whether a text presence bias will be taken into discourse as bias. A lexical item like 'mob' in *Evening Standard* Text 1 carries negative connotations. But since it is present in the text, it does not take much effort to notice that it carries negative connotations. A non-critical reader reading for gist may notice the protestors being described negatively, or this bias may unwittingly become part of their discourse. It is difficult to predict either way. In 10.6, I alter *Evening Standard* Text 1 so as to minimise discourse bias. But I do not alter the text to remove text presence bias for the reasons just given (besides, also in line with what was indicated in 2.3, trying to totally remove text presence bias so as to create a value-neutral text is difficult, if not impossible, to achieve). For the reader to appreciate this rationale, it will help to draw attention, at least, to some more of the text presence bias that I leave in the altered version in 10.6.

'Mob' is an example of a text presence bias that does not really need comparative analysis to identify. But other examples of text presence bias do require comparative analysis. In making this point, I am mindful of what Stubbs (1997: 107) writes about the need for comparative analysis in CDA, which I quoted in 10.1. What Stubbs says is also pertinent to discourse bias since I have tried to show the likelihood of this through comparison with an idealised model of reading as well as comparison with other news reports of the same event. But let us return to text presence bias. One type of text presence bias where it is only through comparison that revelation can occur relates to text quantity. *Evening Standard* Text 1 includes 122 words relating to Peter Ford talking about the protestors. Forty-five words in the same text relate to Edmund King providing a negative perspective on the protestors. Thus, around 40 per cent of the article is devoted to perspectives *on* the protestors in contrast to 0 per cent of the article devoted to perspectives provided *by* the protestors. *The Daily Telegraph* devotes eighty-one words to Peter Ford talking about the protestors but, unlike *Evening Standard* Text 1, includes a paragraph from a spokesperson for Reclaim the Streets. Sentence 6 of *Evening Standard* Text 1 ('they started . . . throwing paperwork around and opening the windows and unfurling banners') repeats much of sentence 3 ('There they threw papers around and unfurled banners from the windows . . .'), violating Grice's maxim of quantity. There is no similar repetition in either the *Guardian* or the *Daily Telegraph* texts. Thus, the comparative analysis helps to highlight how the superordinate goals of the protestors are further delayed in *Evening Standard* Text 1. But to come back to the point made in the previous paragraph, it is difficult to say in what way these examples affect the reader, and so they are difficult to put in terms of discourse bias. Consequently, it is better to look at them in terms of *(comparative) text presence bias*.

In line with Toolan's (1997) recommendation that CDA (see 8.2.4) prescribe non-manipulative alternatives, I now move on to indicate the following: how *Evening Standard* Text 1 could be changed so as to minimise discourse bias by minimising the potential for mystification of Reclaim the Streets. So, while removing text presence bias in order to produce a value-neutral text is difficult, if not impossible, to achieve, mystification on the basis of absences from the text can be reduced by including these absences.

10.6 ALTERING *EVENING STANDARD* TEXT 1 VIA IR SO AS TO MINIMISE DISCOURSE BIAS

The principle behind improving *Evening Standard* Text 1 is to increase its relevance through a greater yield of cognitive effects for investment of minimum effort, that is, in line with the IR framework. In addition, since the elaborative inferences I listed in 10.2.2 will not be generated by IR, information connected with these inferences is included in the text. All additions and changes to the original text are in italics. The first thing that I try to improve relates to making superordinate goals more visible in the first few sentences of the hard news text:

> *ECO*-PROTEST MOB STORM TUBE HQ
> *Cycle* Demonstrators fight past security men to occupy chief's office
> 1. *Anti-car* protestors today smashed their way into London Underground headquarters *in support of the Tube strike*.
> 2. *The* angry mob *from the protest group Reclaim the Streets* overpowered security guards at the LU head offices above St James's station and rushed up seven floors to march into the chairman's office.
> 3. There they threw papers around and unfurled banners from the windows declaring 'Don't squeeze the Tube'.

'Protest', in the headline, needs to be modified by something like 'eco' or the use of the basic-level category 'car' in 'anti-car', as in sentence 1, or the basic-level 'cycle' in the sub-headline. On the principle of cognitive economy, these basic-level categories are able to yield a larger amount of cognitive effects for little effort and, in enabling instantiation of 'protestors' and 'demonstrators', thus increase relevance. I have not, then, removed what might be regarded by some CD analysts as nominalisations, namely, 'protestors' and 'demonstration'. This is because it is not their syntactic form that is the obscuring factor but rather the lack of appropriate information to instantiate these categories. I have removed the link between mass demonstration and the Tube strike since this does not fit in with the initial focus of the article, that is, the invasion of the London Underground HQ. In removing it, I avoid the distraction of 'mass demonstration'; in any case, the mass (cycle) demonstration is referred to later. I have not removed the text presence bias of 'mob' for reasons given above. In sentence 1, I have added the prepositional phrase 'in support of the Tube strike', to provide more information as to superordinate goals. Finally, the inclusion of 'cycle' supplies the instrument of the protest.

In following a text structure of general to particular – general superordinate goals to particular superordinate goals – sentence 4 provides not only more specific rationale for Reclaim the Streets but also an understanding of the subordinate goal action (sentence 3) of 'how' their actions were supporting the Tube strikers, something which is unlikely to be generated on something close to minimum effort in reading.

> 4. *A spokesperson from Reclaim the Streets said the protest was against London Underground leaving the Tube drivers no option but to strike and thus leading to more traffic than usual on the streets and so more pollution.*

I would also recommend an alternative picture to assist processing, for example, cycle protestors being led away from the London Underground HQ by police.

We have seen that, in comparison with other newspapers, the amount of space given to Peter Ford in *Evening Standard* Text 1 indicates text presence bias. But what about a discourse bias perspective? Since I have fleshed out the Reclaim the Streets protestors with a clear rationale as well as including their perceived causal antecedent (London Underground) for the causal consequents (leaving tube drivers no option but to strike, which in turn leads to more pollution), it makes it less likely that readers will perceive the protestors in Peter Ford's report as attentuated 'secondary characters'. This is why I have left sentences 5 to 11 intact.

> 5. LU chairman Peter Ford said: 'I was astonished when they burst into my office.
> 6. I asked them what they wanted and they didn't seem too sure.

7. 'They started chanting slogans, throwing paperwork around and opening the windows and unfurling banners outside.
8. 'I was worried that they would damage my family photographs so I asked them to respect them and they did.
9. I explained I was a keen cyclist and asked them if there were any points I could clarify about the dispute.
10. 'I even told them how much Underground drivers earn.
11. Then they said they wanted to lock the doors but I told them if this was a non-violent protest they would have to play by the rules, which they did.'

I leave sentences 12 to 18 intact for similar reasons. So although Edmund King is given more 'main character' status in being allowed to voice his opinions of the protestors, the 'secondary character' status of the protestors is mitigated by the fact that the rationale of Reclaim the Streets has already been explicitly acknowledged. I leave, for reasons already given, the text presence bias of 'anarchist(s)' and so on.

12. Police were later questioning a number of the protestors.
13. At the same time, during the height of the morning rush hour, several hundred cyclists

[Page 2]
from the same group of protestors – Reclaim the Streets – converged on Trafalgar Square.

14. The protest, ironically aimed at combating car use and supporting public transport, caused massive knock-on effects on routes already overloaded with the Tube strike traffic.
15. Scuffles broke out as anarchist cyclists confronted police and angry motorists.
16. They were greeted by shouts of abuse, fist waving, and a cacophony of tooting car horns from cabbies and drivers as they deliberately dismounted and remounted and pedalled slowly around the Square.
17. Edmund King, head of campaigns for the RAC, said: 'I'm appalled by the action of a bunch of anarchists stopping the traffic.
18. It's ironic they are campaigning against pollution when they've caused 10 times more in Trafalgar Square by blocking the traffic.'

Sentences 19 to 21 below come from *The Guardian*'s article. The reader will already know generally that Reclaim the Streets hold London

Underground responsible for the events leading to the extra pollution (sentence 4 above). With sentence 21, the reader will have the information needed to understand specifically why the Tube drivers decided to strike.

> 19. *Reg Wagland, aged 62, a retired electrician, said the protest was to highlight transport problems and show solidarity.*
> 20. *'We are here to support the Tube drivers.*
> 21. *Their employers reneged on a deal.'*

I finish with the rest of the *Evening Standard* Text 1, which includes, in sentence 22, a negative causal consequent of the cycle protest. And because sentence 22 is not adjacent to Edmund King's statement, the possibility of the implicature spillage I mentioned at the end of 10.4.4 is reduced.

> 22. After an hour the cyclists peeled off down Whitehall to Parliament Square where they again slowed traffic.
> 23. Tempers rose to boiling point when several vanloads of police trapped the demonstrators in a bus lane.
> 24. A stand-off followed, with lines of officers blocking both ends of the street.

10.7 ENDPOINTS

I hope I have shown that the IR framework can be used to reveal absences from hard news text which can lead to causal mystification in non-critical reading and, in turn, to discourse bias. In my conclusion in Chapter 11, I provide an overarching contrast between previous assumptions in CDA and assumptions of text processing in IR.

NOTES

1. For a different take on the detection of absences from text see Fairclough (1995a: 104–9, 1995b: 5) and van Leeuwen (1993, 1996).
2. figures taken from http://www.dmgt.co.uk/corp_structure/associated_newspapers/evening_standard.htm
3. It should be pointed out, however, that just because a chain of events is almost a daily news focus, many people can still be unsure of the superordinate goals of participants. Recent research on TV viewers' awareness of the reasons for the

Palestinian – Israeli conflict and its origins would bear this out, for example, Philo, G. (2002) 'Missing in action: New research suggests that television news fails to inform young people about what's going on in the Occupied Territories, or why', *The Guardian*, Tuesday, 16 April 2002, at
http://education.guardian.co.uk/egweekly/story/0,5500,684671,00.html

CHAPTER 11

Conclusion

11.1 INTRODUCTION

In Chapter 2 of this book I drew attention to three types of manipulation that CDA has dealt with and where news text as data has figured prominently. These types of manipulation, intended or not, are as follows: text presence bias, mystification, and socio-cognitive. Each type of manipulation requires a different critical focus to uncover: comparative text presence bias requires critical text analysis; mystification requires critical discourse (1) analysis; and socio-cognitive requires critical discourse (2) analysis. Mystification analysis has been the main focus of this book. 'Critical' in mystification analysis means locating the absences from a text and exploring how presences in the text work to reinforce these absences. If hard news text involves mystification of one set of participants (their goals, rationale and so on) but not the other set of participants, then such absences from the text can result in *discourse bias* for a non-critical reader.

Because my focus has been mystification analysis, my conclusion deals mostly with this. Some of what follows does, however, relate to socio-cognitive manipulation (and thus critical discourse (2) analysis) as well as text presence bias manipulation (and thus critical text analysis). To begin with, I provide a comparison of a master-metaphor employed in this book – 'shallow' – and a master-metaphor often used in CDA – 'consumption' – (which I flagged up in 2.5.3) to indicate what I have tried to accomplish in this book. Then, from such a broad perspective, I move on to sum up the more specific things that I have demonstrated.

11.2 SHALLOW READING VERSUS CONSUMPTION READING

11.2.1 The Misleading Consumption Metaphor

The consumption metaphor as regards text processing is a common one in CDA. In 4.8, we saw how Halliday's thinking, a major theoretical source for CDA, implicitly endorses the consumption metaphor. But, in the light of the evidence for shallow processing I outlined in Sections B and C, it can hardly be said that everything in a text is 'consumed' in the reading process. We saw in the psycholinguistic evidence of 7.4 that for a reader of a narrative with general goals, there is more likely to be inadvertent downplaying of phenomena such as secondary characters. But the consumption metaphor would imply that main and secondary characters are processed to the same degree. The consumption metaphor would also imply that the mental representation of words in a sentence mirrors their compositionality in the sentence. However, this conflicts with the concept of accommodation which is used in cognitive linguistics and connectionism. The consumption metaphor thus reinforces the notion that sentences can be taken as a representational medium rather than serving as evokers of background knowledge. The metaphor detracts from viewing text as an external device to be interacted with. It detracts from a perspective where readers make pragmatic meaning as a fraction of the semantic potential of a text in line with expectations of relevance, their goals and so on.

11.2.2 The Consumption Metaphor as Legitimisation of CDA

The consumption metaphor can legitimise dissection of the text by the CD analyst by proxy for the non-analyst on the assumption that they consume the whole text, making a mental copy of it, and so ingesting 'encoded ideologies' and so on. One 'job description' of the CD analyst that naturally flows from this is to show readers what encoded phenomena have been ingested or would be ingested if these had not been pointed out. Since all of the text is consumed, it allows the analyst to dissect the text without any conceptual limitations, picking out anything they choose since anything could be relevant for the consumptive reader. There is the danger, however, that analysts, free to dissect any part of the text they choose, will pick out aspects of the text which they notice because of their own values at the expense of other presences which could be in tension with the interpretation they formulate. Thus, the consumption metaphor can not only lead to the erasure of inter-personal variation among readers but of the intra-personal variation based on degree of vested interest and familiarity with the text's subject matter that I have tried to highlight in this book. Since the consumption metaphor does not properly capture actual processing, this casts serious doubt upon it as a legitimating device for the above practice.

Of course, shallow processing is another metaphor. But in contrast to the use of the consumption metaphor in CDA, I have supplied a good deal of cognitive detail from four paradigms for the following: that shallow processing is a more plausible metaphor than consumption for the hard news text comprehension by a least effort reader who is largely unfamiliar with its subject matter and seeks causal (antecedent) relevance. That is, in this book 'shallow' has been an explanatory rather than constitutive metaphor in explaining processing for low effort investment rather than (misleadingly) constituting thinking as to the nature of processing (see Ungerer and Schmid (1996: 144–52) on this distinction).

The approach I have taken to text processing highlights how the degree of a reader's cognitive investment in a text affects the type of inferences generated and thus the discourse derived from the text. My approach has been explicitly interactionist. While current work in the interpretation stage of CDA accords in theory with an interactionist principle, in practice there is a tendency to assume that the text is merely mentally facsimiled by a non-analyst. In other words, there is little attempt to show how the static symbols on a page are actually dynamised in reading. As I have suggested, the drawing-upon of Hallidayan functional grammar in CDA's interpretation stage has contributed to this. Use of Hallidayan functional grammar in CDA's description stage is, however, wholly legitimate, a point I come on to later.

11.3 SPECIFIC DEMONSTRATIONS OF THE BOOK

11.3.1 Smoothing Out Tensions between Analysis of Two Different Types of Manipulation

In 2.6 I laid out a number of tensions between a number of mystification analyses and socio-cognitive analyses in the interpretation stage. Now, I repeat them and indicate how I have addressed them in this book:

1. The mystification analyses were based on readers who do not make much effort (although the reader is never properly theorised). Readers are 'non-energetic' or 'read across' and so may not notice they are being manipulated. However, in the

socio-cognitive analyses, there was an assumption that while
some inferencing will be automatic, other inferencing will
require work that readers will be prepared to invest.

We saw that Fairclough (2001: 67–8) outlines two types of inferencing: 'automatic gap-filling', which requires minimum cognitive labour, while 'inferences' are those which require higher-than-minimum cognitive labour. His assumption, emanating from Brown and Yule (1983) and adopted by Gough and Talbot (1996), was that readers are willing to work to produce inferences necessary for what he regards as the coherence of a particular text, even if the subject matter is unfamiliar. However, we have seen that if the subject matter is unfamiliar for a reader who makes minimum cognitive effort, then (1) causal consequents are unlikely to be produced or weakly at best; (2) even coherence inferences, those which are normally instituted, can be shallowly generated, with readers satisfying themselves that a text is coherent because it is cohesive. In other words, on the basis of the psycholinguistic evidence I discussed in Chapter 7, if readers are unfamiliar with the subject matter of the text and have general goals, it is unlikely that they will work to create inferences as Fairclough supposes. While Fairclough makes a distinction between automatic gap-filling and inferences, using the minimalist hypothesis of McKoon and Ratcliff (1992), my distinction has been between automatic and strategic inferences. The latter require work and so depend on the inclination and vested interest of the reader. In terms of this vocabulary, Fairclough supposes that readers will naturally seek to make the strategic inferences that Fairclough makes in line with his vested interest in a text. This may well be the case if a reader is prepared to make the necessary effort. But readers with general goals are much less likely to do so. Socio-cognitive analysis, then, needs also to be based on this notion as much as mystification analysis.

2. In the mystification analyses, inferences in reading were weak representations. In the socio-cognitive analyses, inferences were implicitly strong representations since they can lead to ideological reproduction.

I have indicated how readers of hard news text will automatically assume that the information presented to them is maximally relevant for establishing, if it is not already explicitly mentioned, the causal antecedence of an action. All other inferences can be strong if (1) background knowledge is readily available and only one obvious inference would be generated; (2) if the reader were willing to invest the necessary cognitive effort to strategically generate them. So inferences across clauses or otherwise are not weak per se. It depends on the existing conditions for their generation. Instantiations, where the background knowledge is readily available, are also likely to be strong inferences. And so on. The relationship between accessible background knowledge and strength of inference generation is one that relates to both mystification and socio-cognitive angles of analysis. Through an exploration of inferences, this book has highlighted the conditions for when inferences are likely to be strong or weak – again smoothing out tensions between the socio-cognitive and mystification angles of analysis.

3. The reader is sometimes made explicit in the mystification analyses. The reader is made more explicit in the socio-cognitive analyses.

This book has sought to theorise the reader which has implications for both angles.

4. With regard to processing, the mystification analyses are bottom-up and the socio-cognitive analyses top-down.

This book has looked at mystification analysis from both bottom-up and top-down perspectives (that is, pragmatic expectations of relevance).

11.3.2 Other Problematic Processing Assumptions in the Interpretation Stage of CDA

In Chapter 2 I listed some key processing assumptions of CDA and ones which guide how CDA highlights (predominantly) mystifying text. In this book I have shown many of these assumptions to be problematic.

A High Degree of Nominalisation in a Text Requires Extra Processing Effort

We saw in 4.4 that Hodge and Kress (1993) regard transformations as being psychologically real, and in 2.4.2 that a non-energetic reader would not process deeply enough to recover the 'original form' of a nominalisation. Hodge and Kress (1993), in effect, were detailing a form of shallow processing but it is a variety of shallow processing that is disallowed by the IR framework. We saw in Chapter 3 how the derivational theory of complexity has been discredited and so looking at nominalisation in terms of psychologically real transformations is incorrect.

Excessive Nominalisation Distances the Reader from the Events being Reported

Critical discourse analysis makes the point that since nominalisations remove participants, events are made more *distant*. However, CDA often conflates ideational distance with interpersonal distance. Ideational distance is the extent of separation between the actual event and the reader's understanding of what happened in that event via what the author provides. Interpersonal distance refers to the level of formality or intimacy that a text sets up between author and reader. Nominalisations can produce interpersonal distance: as compared with informal texts, formal written documents are often characterised by a higher degree of nominalisation, and thus deletion of participants. And interpersonal distance can be created through the absence of participants from a text. But this does not mean, as I showed in Chapters 5 and 6, that ideational distance is necessarily created by nominalisations through the absence of participants and the presence of 'object-like' nominals. Basic-level noun categories are cognitively interdependent with basic-level action categories. So just because a basic-level noun is used to describe an action, it does not follow that its nominal form leads the reader to see the action in an abstract, distant 'objectified' way. Ideational distance can be created, however, when superordinate/abstract categories, nominal or verbal, lack sufficient information in the text to lead to their instantiation (for example, sufficient basic-level categories).

The evidence in 7.4 shows that there can be ideational distance even if participants *are* present. In Chapter 7, I showed that just because participants are present in a text, it does not necessarily mean that there are no differences in the 'depth' to which different participants are processed in discourse. In the reading of narrative texts, secondary characters are more likely to be more ideationally distant than main characters in the discourse of a reader. Secondary characters are more likely to be read in a shallower way than main ones, for a reader who has little vested interest in a text, since the focus is more likely to be on main characters in relation to cause and effect.

Confusing Semantic Transitivity with Syntactic Transitivity

Following the experimental evidence of Taraban and McClelland (1988), with psycholinguistic evidence of top-down expectation overriding bottom-up processing and so on, as well as the principles of connectionism and cognitive linguistics where syntax and semantics are interactive, the IR framework prohibits the imparting of semantic transitivity – the structure *agent-process-affected* – to just any *subject-verb-object* structure.

Compositional Processing

I have tried to indicate the problems with focusing compositionally on a lexical item without considering how its co-text affects its meaning, as well as how ignoring co-text helps to facilitate an interpretation which would be at odds with that of a least effort reader.

11.3.3 Situating CDA Processing Assumptions in an Historical Context

In Chapter 4, I showed how symbolic assumptions of processing inadvertently and problematically underpin much of CDA, assumptions in line with much Anglo-American-Austrian philosophy in the twentieth century and symbolic cognitive science. This was brought into relief especially by setting them alongside assumptions of mental representation in connectionism and cognitive linguistics. The inconsistencies in CDA with regard to psycholinguistic assumptions (see 2.6) no doubt arise, in part, because CDA has been largely nescient of its cognitive foundations.

Symbolic attitudes in CDA towards inference generation are often in conflict with recent psycholinguistic research. The IR framework, rooted in empirical psycholinguistic study, enables a more plausible, comprehensive and thus consistent perspective on inference generation in reading and how this relates to mystification. Owing to their different assumptions about mental representation and cognition, where the non-symbolic IR framework detects text that can lead to mystification in reading is not necessarily coincident with where symbolic CDA detects mystification.

11.4 THE INTERPRETATION STAGE IN CDA

11.4.1 Possibility for Combining Causal-Cognitive Analysis and Socio-Cognitive Analysis

I have concentrated on causal-cognitive discourse analysis in this book with regard to the uncovering of mystification. This has been because I have been concerned with the processing principles behind how readers search for causal relevance in hard news texts, principles which can be regarded as universal since they relate to neurophysiology and not socialisation. This is not to say that socio-cognitive analysis could not be used to investigate causality in relation to hard news text. Such an investigation, for example, could be concerned with how people become socialised into accepting certain causal relations. A recent instance could be how some people regard genetically modified crops as potentially causing problems for health and the environment and how others do not regard them this way. And so a socio-cognitive analysis of a news report might involve investigation of those discourses (2) circulating with regard to such causal relations and to what extent they are active in the reading of a news article on genetic modification of crops. Indeed, it is possible that causal-cognitive analysis and socio-cognitive analysis can complement one another. We might want to investigate whether the search for causal relevance in a hard news text on GM crops leads to the activation of a particular socialised memory store of causal relations relating to health and the environment. Such a linking of causal-cognitive and socio-cognitive angles of analysis (for example, in the analysis of *Evening Standard* Text 1, 'Protest mob storm Tube HQ', in Chapter 10) has, of course, been beyond the scope of this book.

11.4.2 Making a Clearer Distinction between Interpretation and Description in CDA

As I indicated in Chapter 1, a standard framework in CDA is Fairclough's (2001) tripartite description-interpretation-explanation. Despite the tripartite nature of this framework, for Fairclough (2001: 22) the distinction between description and interpretation is quite porous:

> description is ultimately just as dependent on the analyst's 'interpretation'... What one 'sees' in a text, what one regards as worth describing, and what one chooses to emphasize in a description, are all dependent on how one interprets a text.

However, use of the IR framework necessarily reduces the subjectivity of the analyst in the interpretation stage. Moreover, an advantage of having a framework of an idealised reader with which to guide analysis means that a clearer distinction between description and interpretation can be drawn. Interpretation of a text via IR is done on behalf of a non-critical reader while description of a text is not. In addition, mystification analysis (part of the interpretation stage) via IR on behalf of a non-critical reader relates first to absences from and then presences in a text. With such a perspective, the distinction between description and interpretation becomes even more marked. Describing absences from a text forms part of the description stage of analysis. But deciding whether absences from a text may or may not be absences from discourse forms part of the interpretation stage.

11.4.3 Making a Distinction between Text Presence Bias (Description Stage) and Discourse (1) Bias (Interpretation Stage) in CDA

Where CDA has been particularly strong is in using Hallidayan functional grammar to uncover text presence bias. CDA's use of Hallidayan functional grammar in its comparative analysis of the lexico-grammatical patterns of different newspapers has been useful in systematically revealing and articulating differences in text presence bias. However, it is difficult to predict whether text presence bias might be taken into discourse. So it is best to see text presence bias from a semantico-syntactic perspective. In this respect, application of Hallidayan (semantico-syntactic) functional grammar in comparative text presence bias analysis is wholly legitimate. However, use of Hallidayan functional grammar is not legitimate for uncovering discourse (1) bias. This is because in being a grammar it can say little about how the semantic potential of text is pragmatically realised in line with considerations of relevance, reader goals and so on. Indeed, it is in the uncovering of discourse (1) bias, as this book has tried to show, where CDA has not been so strong. Seeing explicitly that there are different types of bias for CDA to uncover makes for a clearer analytical organisation in terms of Fairclough's CDA framework: text presence bias belongs to the description stage and discourse (1) bias belongs to the interpretation stage. On this organisation, there is no reason why use of the idealised reader framework in the interpretation stage (*critical discourse (1) analysis*) cannot complement use of Hallidayan functional grammar in the description stage (*critical text analysis*). Again, such complementary analysis has been beyond the scope of this book. I should say as a corollary that all this is not to say that use of Hallidayan functional grammar in the description stage of analysis will not have a bearing on mystification analysis in the interpretation stage. Such description, particularly in comparison with other texts, aids in pinpointing absences from texts. What this description cannot say is whether these absences are likely or unlikely to be absences in discourse (1).

11.4.4 IR as a Guide for Mystification Analysis

Naturally the idealised reader framework is limited in that it only focuses on causal cognition in relation to hard news text. However, hard news text has particular cultural salience and, indeed, continues to be something of a staple in CDA. The IR framework does not, of course, provide an exact mirroring of the processing of a reader with regard to causal relations in news texts. Nevertheless, it can be useful in that it maps out the limits of what a minimum effort reader is likely or unlikely to do in reading news text. As a result it can check the prospect of *over-interpretation* by the analyst on behalf of a non-critical reader. It also allows the analyst to point systematically to absences from a text which are likely to lead to absences from discourse for a non-critical reader and thus mystification of events and participants being described. In doing so, it helps to avoid intuitive/subjective isolations of absences from a text. That the prospect of such absence detection is less likely to be subjective or intuitive derives from the cognitive interdisciplinarity of the framework, its basis in empirical evidence and the fact that it only consists of compatible and thus mutually supporting aspects of its source components. Finally, in prohibiting quite problematic analysis based on symbolicism, the IR guide can help to produce more robust interpretations on behalf of the non-critical reader as to whether a text is likely to be mystifying or not.

As I have said elsewhere in this book, it is not necessary to be a critical discourse analyst to be a critical reader. Of course, non-analysts can notice absences from a news text should they wish to expend the effort to do so, although the detection of absences may be well be subjective, in line with political values and so on. I have argued in this book that there should be, however, two key differences between being 'critical' in critical discourse (1) analysis and 'critical' in critical lay-reading. The former should be much more systematic in its detection of absences from a news text as well as how the presences in a news text reinforce these absences. Creating a framework to enable such systematicity has been one of the aims of this book. 'Critical' in critical discourse (1) analysis means also seeking to overcome the prospect of subjective or intuitive detection of absences so that prediction can be made of the extent to which absences from a news text would be mystifying for non-critical readers in general. This kind of generalisability would presumably be beyond the inclination of most critical lay-reading. Creating a reader framework which can generate reasonable generalisability has been another aim of this book.

Bibliography

Altmann, G. and Steedman, M. (1988), 'Interaction with context during human sentence processing', *Cognition* 30: 191–238.
Anderson, A., Garrod, S. C. and Sanford, A. J. (1983), 'The accessibility of pronominal antecedents as a function of episode shifts in narrative discourse', *Quarterly Journal Of Experimental Psychology* 35a: 427–40.
Anderson, J. A. and Hinton, G. E. (1981), 'Models of information processing in the brain', in G. E. Hinton and J. A. Anderson (eds), *Parallel Models of Associative Memory*, Hillsdale, NJ: Erlbaum.
Aristotle (1933), *Metaphysics*, trans. H. Tredennick, London: Heinemann.
Armstrong, S. L., Gleitman, L. R. and Gleitman, H. (1983), 'What some concepts might not be', *Cognition* 13: 263–308.
Ayer, A. (1982), *Philosophy in the Twentieth Century*, London: George Wiedenfield and Nicolson Ltd.
Barsalou, L. W. (1983), 'Ad-hoc categories', *Memory and Cognition* 11: 211–27.
Barsalou, L. W. (1989), 'Intra-concept similarity and its implications for inter-concept similarity', in S. Vosniadou and A. Ortony (eds), *Similarity and Analogical Reasoning*, Cambridge: Cambridge University Press, pp. 76–121.
Barton, S. B. and Sanford, A. J. (1993), 'A case-study of pragmatic anomaly detection: relevance-driven cohesion patterns', *Memory and Cognition* 21: 477–87.
Bates, E. and MacWhinney, B. (1982), 'Functionalist approaches to grammar', in E. Wanner and L. R. Gleitman (eds), *Language Acquisition: The State of the Art*, New York: Cambridge University Press, pp. 173–218.
Bechtel, W. (1990), 'Connectionism and the philosophy of mind: an overview', in W. G. Lycan (ed.), *Mind and Cognition: A Reader*, Oxford: Blackwell, pp. 252–73.
Bechtel, W. (1996a), 'What knowledge must be in the head in order to acquire language?', in B. M. Velichkovsky and D. M. Rumbaugh (eds), *Communicating Meaning: The Evolution and Development of Language*, Mahwah, NJ: Lawrence Erlbaum Associates, pp. 45–78.
Bechtel, W. (1996b), 'What should a connectionist philosophy of science look like?', in R. N. McCauley (1996), *The Churchlands and their Critic*, Oxford: Blackwell, pp. 121–44.
Bechtel, W. and Abrahamsen, A. (1991), *Connectionism and the Mind: An Introduction to Parallel Processing in Networks*, Oxford: Blackwell.
Bechtel, W. and Abrahamsen, A. (2002), *Connectionism and the Mind: Parallel Processing, Dynamics, and Evolution in Networks*, 2nd edn, Oxford: Blackwell.
Bell, A. (1991), *The Language of News Media*, Oxford: Blackwell.
Berlin, B., Breedlove, D. and Raven, P. (1974), *Principles of Tzeltal Plant Classification*, New York: Academic Press.

Bex, T. (1996), *Variety in Written English: Texts in Society, Societies in Text*, London: Routledge.
Bierwisch, M. (1967), 'Some semantic universals of German adjectivals', *Foundations of Language* 3: 1–36.
Bierwisch, M. (1970), 'Semantics', in J. Lyons (ed.), *New Horizons in Linguistics, vol. 1*, Harmondsworth: Penguin, pp. 166–84.
Black, J. B. and Bower, G. H. (1980), 'Story understanding and problem solving', *Poetics* 9: 223–50.
Bloom, C. P., Fletcher, C. R., van den Broek, P., Reitz, L. and Shapiro, B. P. (1990), 'An on-line assessment of causal reasoning during comprehension', *Memory and Cognition* 18: 65–71.
Bower, G. H., Black, J. B. and Turner, T. J. (1979), 'Scripts in memory for text', *Cognitive Psychology* 11: 177–220.
Bransford, J. D., Barclay, J. R. and Franks, J. J. (1972), 'Sentence memory: a constructive versus interpretive approach', *Cognitive Psychology* 3: 193–209.
Bransford, J. D. and Johnson, M. K. (1973), 'Considerations of some problems of comprehension', in W. Chase (ed.), *Visual Information Processing*, New York: Academic Press, pp. 383–438.
Bredart, S. and Modolo, K. (1988), 'Moses strikes again: focalization effect on a semantic illusion', *Acta Psychologica* 67: 135–44.
Brown, E. K. (1991), 'Transformational-generative grammar', in K. Malmkjaer (ed.), *The Linguistics Encyclopedia*, London: Routledge, pp. 482–97.
Brown, G. and Yule, G. (1983), *Discourse Analysis*, Cambridge: Cambridge University Press.
Brown, R. (1958), 'How shall a thing be called?', *Psychological Review* 65: 14–21.
Brown, R. (1965), *Social Psychology*, New York: Free Press.
Bruner, J. (1973), 'Beyond the information given', in J. Anglin (ed.), *Studies in the Psychology of Knowing*, New York: W. W. Norton.
Caldas-Coulthard, C. and Coulthard, M. (1996), *Texts and Practices: Readings in Critical Discourse Analysis*, London: Routledge.
Cameron, D. (ed.) (1998), *The Feminist Critique of Language: A Reader*, 2nd edn, London: Routledge.
Cameron, D. (2001), *Working with Spoken Discourse*, London: Sage.
Carnap, R. ([1928] 1967), [Der logische Aufbau der Welt] *The Logical Structure of the World: Pseudo-Problems in Philosophy*, trans. R. A. George, London: Routledge and Kegan.
Carnap, R. (1935), *Philosophy and Logical Syntax*, London: Kegan Paul, Trench, Trubner and Co.
Carnap, R. (1937), *The Logical Syntax of Language*, London: Kegan Paul, Trench, Trubner and Co.
Charniak, E. (1983), 'Passing markers: a theory of contextual influence in language comprehension', *Cognitive Science* 7: 171–90.
Chomsky, N. (1957), *Syntactic Structures*, The Hague: Mouton.
Chomsky, N. (1959), 'A review of B. F. Skinner's *Verbal Behaviour*', *Language* 35: 26–58.
Chomsky, N. (1965), *Aspects of a Theory of Syntax*, Cambridge, MA: MIT Press.
Chomsky, N. (1986), *Knowledge of Language*, New York: Praeger.
Chomsky, N. and Halle, M. (1968), *The Sound Pattern of English*, New York: Harper and Row.
Chouliaraki, L. and Fairclough, N. (1999), *Discourse in Late Modernity: Rethinking Critical Discourse Analysis*, Edinburgh: Edinburgh University Press.
Christie, C. (1998), 'Rewriting rights: a relevance theoretical analysis of press constructions of sexual harassment and the response of readers', in *Language and Literature* 7 (3): 214–34.
Christie, C. (2000), *Gender and Language: Towards a Feminist Pragmatics*, Edinburgh: Edinburgh University Press.
Churchland, P. M. (1988), *Matter and Consciousness*, rev. edn, Cambridge, MA: MIT Press.
Churchland, P. M. and Churchland, P. S. (1996), 'Connectionism as psychology', in R. N. McCauley (ed.), *The Churchlands and Their Critics*, Oxford: Blackwell, pp. 232–8.
Churchland, P. S. (1986), *Neurophilosophy*, Cambridge, MA: MIT Press.
Clark, A. (1989), *Microcognition: Philosophy, Cognitive Science and Parallel Distributed Processing*, Cambridge, MA: MIT Press.

Clark, A. (1993), *Associative Engines: Connectionism, Concepts, and Representational Change*, Cambridge, MA: MIT Press.
Clark, A. (1996), 'Introduction', in A. Clark and P. J. R. Millican (eds), *Connectionism, Concepts, and Folk Psychology: The Legacy of Alan Turing, vol. 2*, Oxford: Clarendon Press, pp. 1–6.
Clark, K. (1992), 'The linguistics of blame', in M. J. Toolan (ed.), *Language, Text and Context*, London: Routledge, pp. 208–24.
Cook, G. (1994), *Discourse and Literature: The Interplay of Form and Mind*, Oxford: Oxford University Press.
Cook, G. (2003), *Applied Linguistics*, Oxford: Oxford University Press.
Cooper, R. (1996), 'Explanation and simulation in cognitive science', in D. W. Green (ed.), *Cognitive Science: An Introduction*, Oxford: Blackwell, pp. 23–52.
Cotter, C. A. (1984), 'Inferring indirect objects in sentences: some implications for the semantics of verbs', *Language and Speech* 27: 25–45.
Cottrell, G. W. and Small, S. L. (1983), 'A connectionist scheme for modelling word sense disambiguation', *Cognition and Brain Theory* 6: 89–120.
Crain, S. and Steedman, M. (1985), 'On not being led up the garden path: the use of context by the psychological syntax processor', in D. Dowty, L. Karttunen and A. Zwicky (eds), *Natural Language Parsing*, Cambridge: Cambridge University Press, pp. 320–54.
Cruse, D. A. (1977), 'The pragmatics of lexical specificity', *Journal of Linguistics* 13: 153–64.
Damasio, A. (1994), *Descartes' Error: Emotion, Reason, and the Human Brain*, New York: Grosset-Putnam.
Dell, G. S., McKoon, G. and Ratcliff, R. (1983), 'The activation of antecedent information during the processing of anaphoric reference in reading', *Journal of Verbal Learning and Verbal Behavior* 22: 121–32.
DeJong, G. (1979), 'Prediction and substantiation: a new approach to natural language processing', *Cognitive Science* 3: 251–73.
Dyer, M. G. (1983), *In-Depth Understanding: A Computer Model of Integrated Processing for Narrative Comprehension*, Cambridge, MA: MIT Press.
Eccles, J. C. (1977), Part II of K. Popper and J. C. Eccles, *The Self and its Brain*, Berlin: Springer-International, pp. 225–406.
Eco, U. (1995), *The Search for the Perfect Language*, London: Fontana.
Edelman, G. (1992), *Bright Air, Brilliant Fire*, London: Penguin.
Ellis, D. G. (1992), *From Language to Communication*, Hillsdale, NJ: Lawrence Erlbaum Associates.
Elman, J. L. (1990), 'Representation and structure in connectionist models' in G. T. M. Altmann (ed.), *Cognitive Models of Speech Processing: Psycholinguistic and Computational Perspectives*, Cambridge, MA: MIT Press, pp. 345–82.
Elman, J. L. (1992), 'Grammatical structure and distributed representations', in S. Davis (ed.), *Connectionism: Theory and Practice*, Oxford: Oxford University Press, pp. 138–78.
Erickson, T. A. and Mattson, M. E. (1981), 'From words to meaning: a semantic illusion', *Journal of Verbal Learning and Verbal Behaviour* 20: 540–52.
Eysenck, M. W. and Keane, M. T. (1995), *Cognitive Psychology: A Student's Handbook*, 3rd edn, Hove: Psychology Press.
Eysenck, M. W. and Keane, M. T. (2000), *Cognitive Psychology: A Student's Handbook*, 4th edn, Hove: Psychology Press.
Fairclough, N. (1989), *Language and Power*, 1st edn, London: Longman.
Fairclough, N. (1992), *Discourse and Social Change*, Oxford: Polity Press.
Fairclough, N. (1995a), *Media Discourse*, London: Edward Arnold.
Fairclough, N. (1995b), *Critical Discourse Analysis: The Critical Study of Language*, London: Longman.
Fairclough, N. (2001), *Language and Power*, 2nd edn, London: Longman.
Fairclough, N. and Wodak, R. (1997), 'Critical discourse analysis', in T. van Dijk, *Discourse as Social Interaction. Discourse Studies: A Multidisciplinary Introduction, vol. 2*, London: Sage, pp. 258–84.

Feldman, J. A. and Ballard, D. H. (1982), 'Connectionist models and their properties', *Cognitive Science* 6: 205–54.
Fletcher, C. R. (1986), 'Strategies for the allocation of short-term memory during comprehension', *Journal of Memory and Language* 27: 43–58.
Flores d'Arcais, G. B. (1987), 'Syntactic processing during reading for comprehension', in M. Coltheart *Attention and Performance XII: The Psychology of Reading*, Hillsdale, NJ: Lawrence Erlbaum Associates, pp. 619–33.
Fodor, J. A. (1975), *The Language of Thought*, New York: Crowell.
Fodor, J. A. (1983), *The Modularity of Mind*, Cambridge, MA: MIT Press.
Fodor, J. A. and Garrett, M. (1966), 'Some reflections on competence and performance', in J. Lyons and R. J. Wales, *Psycholinguistic Papers*, Edinburgh: Edinburgh University Press.
Fodor, J. A. and Garrett, M. (1967), 'Some syntactic determinants of sentential complexity', *Perception and Psychophysics* 2: 289–96.
Fodor, J. A. and Pylyshyn, Z. W. (1988), 'Connectionism and cognitive architecture: a critical analysis', *Cognition* 28: 3–71.
Fodor, J. A., Bever, T. G. and Garrett, M. F. (1974), *The Psychology of Language: An Introduction to Psycholinguistics and Generative Grammar*, New York: McGraw-Hill.
Fodor, J. D., Fodor, J. A. and Garrett, M. F. (1975), 'The psychological unreality of semantic representations', *Linguistic Inquiry* 6 (4): 515–31.
Foucault, M. (1972), *The Archaeology of Knowledge*, trans. A. M. Sheridan-Smith, London: Tavistock.
Fowler, R. (1986), *Linguistic Criticism*, 1st edn, Oxford: Oxford University Press.
Fowler, R. (1996a), 'On critical linguistics' in C. R. Caldas-Coulthard and M. Coulthard (eds), *Texts and Practices: Readings in Critical Discourse Analysis*, London: Routledge, pp. 3–14.
Fowler, R. (1996b), *Linguistic Criticism*, 2nd edn, Oxford: Oxford University Press.
Fowler, R. (1991), *Language in the News: Discourse and Ideology in the Press*, London: Routledge.
Fowler, R. and Kress, G. (1979a), 'Rules and Regulations' in R. Fowler et al., *Language and Control*, London: Routledge and Kegan Paul, pp. 26–45.
Fowler, R. and Kress, G. (1979b), 'Critical Linguistics' in R. Fowler et al., *Language and Control*, London: Routledge and Kegan Paul, pp. 185–213.
Fowler, R., Hodge, R., Kress, G. and Trew, T. (1979), *Language and Control*, London: Routledge and Kegan Paul.
Frazier, L. (1987), 'Sentence processing: a tutorial review', in M. Coltheart (ed.), *Attention and Performance XII: The Psychology of Reading*, Hillsdale, NJ: Lawrence Erlbaum Associates, pp. 559–86.
Frazier, L. and Fodor, J. D (1978), 'The sausage machine: a new two-stage parsing model', *Cognition* 6: 291–325.
Freeborn, D. (1993), *Varieties of English: An Introduction to the Study of Language*, 2nd edn, Basingstoke: Palgrave.
Gardner, H. (1987), *The Mind's New Science: A History of the Cognitive Revolution*, New York: Basic Books.
Garnham, A. (1981), 'Anaphoric reference to instances, instantiated and non-instantiated categories: a reading-time study', *British Journal of Psychology* 72: 377–84.
Garnham, A. (1985), *Psycholinguistics: Central Topics*, London: Methuen.
Garrod, S., O'Brien, E. J., Morris, R. K. and Rayner, K. (1990), 'Elaborative inferences as an active or passive process', *Journal of Experimental Psychology: Learning, Memory, and Cognition* 16: 250–7.
Garrod, S. C. and Sanford, A. J. (1982), 'Bridging inferences in the extended domain of reference', in J. Long and A. Baddeley (eds), *Attention and Performance IX*, Hillsdale, NJ: Erlbaum, pp. 331–46.
Garrod, S. C. and Sanford, A. J. (1988), 'Thematic subjecthood and cognitive constraints on discourse structure', *Journal of Pragmatics* 12: 519–34.
Gernsbacher, M. A. (1994), *Handbook of Psycholinguistics*, San Diego, CA: Academic Press.
Goatly, A. (2000), *Critical Reading and Writing: An Introductory Coursebook*, London: Routledge.

Goatly, A. (2001), 'Green grammar and grammatical metaphor, or language and myth of power, or metaphors we die by' in A. Fill and P. Mühlhäusler (eds), *The Ecolinguistics Reader: Language, Ecology and Environment*, London: Continuum, pp. 203–25.

Gough, V. and Talbot, M. (1996), '"Guilt over games boys play": coherence as a focus for examining the constitution of heterosexual subjectivity on a problem page', in C. Caldas-Coulthard and M. Coulthard (eds), *Texts and Practices: Readings in Critical Discourse Analysis*, London: Routledge, pp. 214–30.

Graddol, D., Cheshire, J. and Swann, J. (1994), *Describing Language*, 2nd edn, Buckingham: Open University Press.

Graesser, A. C. (1981), *Prose Comprehension Beyond the Word*, New York: Springer-Verlag.

Graesser, A. C. and Clark, L. F. (1985), *Structures and Procedures of Implicit Knowledge*, Norwood, NJ: Ablex.

Graesser, A. C., Millis, K. K. and Zwaan, R. A. (1997), 'Discourse comprehension', *Annual Review of Psychology* 48: 163–89.

Graesser, A. C., Singer, M. and Trabasso, T. (1994), 'Constructing inferences during narrative text comprehension', *Psychological Review* 101 (3): 371–95.

Grice, H. P. (1975), 'Logic and conversation', in P. Cole and J. Morgan (eds), *Syntax and Semantics 3: Speech Acts*, New York: Academic Press, pp. 41–58.

Gumenik, W. E. (1979), 'The advantage of specific terms over general terms as cues for sentence recall: instantiation or retrieval?' *Memory and Cognition* 7: 240–4

Hacking, I. (1975), *Why does Language Matter to Philosophy?*, Cambridge: Cambridge University Press.

Halliday, M. A. K. (1973), *Explorations in the Functions of Language*, London: Edward Arnold.

Halliday, M. A. K (1978), *Language as a Social Semiotic*, London: Edward Arnold.

Halliday, M. A. K. (1994), *An Introduction to Functional Grammar*, 2nd edn, London: Edward Arnold.

Halliday, M. A. K. (1996/1971), 'Linguistic function and literary style: an inquiry into the language of William Golding's *The Inheritors*', originally published in 1971 and reprinted in J. J. Weber (ed.) (1996), *The Stylistics Reader: From Roman Jakobson to the Present*, London: Routledge, pp. 56–86.

Hammersley, M. (1996), 'On the foundations of critical discourse analysis', Occasional Paper 42, Southampton: Centre for Language in Education, University of Southampton.

Hampton, J. A. (1981), 'An investigation of the nature of abstract concepts', *Memory and Cognition* 9: 149–56.

Harder, P. (1997), *Functional Semantics: A Theory of Meaning, Structure and Tense in English*, Berlin: Mouton de Gruyter.

Harley, T. (2001), *The Psychology of Language*, 2nd edn, Hove: Psychology Press.

Harman, G. (1986), *Change in View*, Cambridge, MA: MIT Press.

Harris, C. L. (1990), 'Connectionism and cognitive linguistics', *Connection Science* 2 (1).

Harris, Z. S. (1952), 'Discourse analysis', *Language* 28: 18–30.

Hastie, R. (1983), 'Social inference', *Annual Review of Psychology* 34: 511–42.

Hilton, D. J. (1990), 'Conversational processes and causal explanation', *Psychological Bulletin* 107: 110–19.

Hobbes, T. ([1651] 1962), *Leviathan: Or the Matter, Forme and Power of a Commonwealth Ecclesiastical and Civil*, London: Collier Books.

Hodge, R. and Kress, G. (1974), 'Transformations, models and processes: towards a useable linguistics', *Journal of Literary Semantics* 4 (1): 4–18.

Hodge, R. and Kress, G. (1993), *Language as Ideology*, 2nd edn, London: Routledge.

Hopper, P. J. and Thompson, S. A. (1985), 'The iconicity of the universal categories "noun" and "verb"', in J. Haiman (ed.), *Iconicity in Syntax*, Amsterdam: John Benjamins, pp. 151–83.

Johnson, K. E and Mervis, C. B. (1997), 'Effects of varying levels of expertise on the basic level of categorization', *Journal of Experimental Psychology: General* 126: 248–77.

Johnson-Laird, P. N. (1980), 'Mental models in cognitive science', *Cognitive Science* 4: 71–115.

Johnson-Laird, P. N. (1983), *Mental Models*, Cambridge, MA: Harvard University Press.

Just, M. A. and Carpenter, P. A. (1980), 'A theory of reading: from eye fixations to comprehension', *Psychological Review* 87: 329–54.
Katz, J. J. and Fodor, J. A. (1963), 'The structure of a semantic theory', *Language* 39: 170–210.
Katz, J. J. and Postal, P. M. (1964), *An Integrated Theory of Linguistic Descriptions*, Cambridge, MA: MIT Press.
Kay, P. (1971), 'Taxonomy and semantic contrast', *Language* 47: 866–87.
Keefe, D. E. and McDaniel, M. A. (1993), 'The time course and durability of predictive inferences', *Journal of Memory and Language* 32: 446–63.
Keenan, J. M., MacWhinney, B. and Mayhew, D. (1977), 'Pragmatics in memory: a study of natural conversation', *Journal of Verbal Learning and Verbal Behaviour* 16: 549–60.
Keenan, J. M., Baillet, S. D. and Brown, P. (1984), 'The effects of causal cohesion on comprehension and memory', *Journal of Verbal Learning and Verbal Behavior* 23: 115–26.
Kempson, R. (1996), 'Semantics, pragmatics and deduction' in S. Lappin (ed.), *Handbook of Contemporary Semantic Theory*, Oxford: Blackwell, pp. 561–98.
Kimball, J. (1973), 'Seven principles of surface structure parsing in natural language', *Cognition* 2: 15–47.
Kintsch, W. (1988), 'The role of knowledge in discourse comprehension: a constructive–integration model', *Psychological Review* 95: 163–82.
Kress, G. (1989), *Linguistic Processes in Sociocultural Practice*, Victoria: Deakin University Press.
Kress, G. (1993), 'Against arbitrariness: the social production of the sign as a foundational issue in critical discourse analysis', *Discourse and Society* 4(2): 169–91.
Kress, G. and Hodge, R. (1979), *Language as Ideology*, London: Routledge and Kegan Paul.
Kuipers, B. (1985), 'Commonsense reasoning about causality: deriving behavior from structure' in D. G. Bobrow (ed.), *Qualitative Reasoning about Physical Systems*, Cambridge, MA: MIT Press, pp. 169–204.
Lakoff, G. (1987a), *Women, Fire and Dangerous Things*, Chicago: University of Chicago Press.
Lakoff, G. (1987b), 'Cognitive models and prototype theory', in U. Neisser (ed.), *Concepts and Conceptual Development: Ecological and Intellectual Factors in Categorization*, Cambridge: Cambridge University Press, pp. 63–100.
Lakoff, G. and Johnson, M. (1980), *Metaphors We Live By*, Chicago: University of Chicago Press.
Lakoff, G. and Johnson, M. (1999), *Philosophy in the Flesh: The Embodied Mind and its Challenge to Western Thought*, New York, NY: Basic Books.
Langacker, R. W. (1987a), *Foundations of Cognitive Grammar, vol. I*, Stanford, CA: Stanford University Press.
Langacker, R. W. (1987b), 'The cognitive perspective', *Centre for Research in Language Newsletter, University of California, San Diego* 1 (3): 3–15.
Langacker, R. W. (1997), 'The contextual basis of cognitive semantics', in J. Nuyts and E. Pederson (eds), *Language and Conceptualisation*, Cambridge: Cambridge University Press, pp. 229–52.
Lee, D. (1992), *Competing Discourses: Perspective and Ideology in Language*, London: Longman.
Leech, G. N. and Short, M. H. (1981), *Style in Fiction: A Linguistic Introduction to English Fictional Prose*, London: Longman.
Levinson, S. (1983), *Pragmatics*, Cambridge: Cambridge University Press.
Levinson, S. (2000), *Presumptive Meanings: The Theory of Generalized Conversational Implicature*, Cambridge, MA: MIT Press,
Lucas, M. M., Tanenhaus, M. K. and Carlson, G. N. (1990), 'Levels of representation in the interpretation of anaphoric reference and instrument inference', *Memory and Cognition* 18 (6): 611–31.
MacDonald, C. and MacDonald, G. (1995), *Connectionism: Debates on Psychological Explanation, vol. 2*, Oxford: Blackwell.
McClelland, J. L. and Kawamoto, A. H. (1986), 'Mechanisms of sentence processing: assigning roles to constituents of sentences', in J. L. McClelland et al. *Parallel Distributed Processing*, Cambridge, MA: MIT Press, pp. 272–325.

McClelland, J. L, Rumelhart, D. E. and the PDP Research Group (eds) (1986), *Parallel Distributed Processing: Explorations in the Microstructure of Cognition, Vol. 2: Psychological and Biological Models*, Cambridge, MA: MIT Press.

McClelland, J. L., St. John, M. F. and Taraban, R. (1989), 'Sentence comprehension: a parallel distributed processing approach', *Language and Cognitive Processes* 4: 287–335.

McKoon, G. and Ratcliff, R. (1981), 'The comprehension processes and memory structures involved in instrumental inference', *Journal of Verbal Learning and Verbal Behaviour* 20: 671–82.

McKoon, G. and Ratcliff, R. (1986), 'Inferences about predictable events', *Journal of Experimental Psychology: Learning, Memory and Cognition* 12: 82–91.

McKoon, G. and Ratcliff, R. (1989a), 'Semantic associations and elaborative inference', *Journal of Experimental Psychology: Learning, Memory and Cognition* 15 (2): 326–38.

McKoon, G. and Ratcliff, R. (1989b), 'Inferences about contextually defined categories, *Journal of Experimental Psychology: Learning, Memory and Cognition* 15 (6): 1,134–46.

McKoon, G. and Ratcliff, R. (1992), 'Inference during reading', *Psychological Review* 99: 440–66.

McLaughlin, M. L. (1990), 'Explanatory discourse and causal attribution', *Text* 10: 63–8.

Marslen-Wilson, W. and Tyler, L. K. (1980), 'The temporal structure of spoken language understanding', *Cognition* 8: 1–71.

Martin, J. R. (1989), *Factual Writing: Exploring and Challenging Social Reality*, 2nd edn, Oxford: Oxford University Press.

Meinhof, U. and Richardson, K. (eds) (1994), *Text, Discourse and Context: Representations of Poverty in Britain*, London: Routledge.

Miikkulainen, R. (1993), *Subsymbolic Natural Language Processing*, Cambridge, MA: MIT Press.

Miller, G. A. (1956), 'The magical number seven, plus or minus two: some limits on our capacity for processing information', *Psychological Review* 63: 81–97.

Miller, G. A. (1962), 'Some psychological studies of grammar', *American Psychologist* 1: 748–62.

Miller, G. A. and McKean, K. (1964), 'A chronometric study of some relations between sentences', *Quarterly Journal of Experimental Psychology* 16: 297–308.

Montgomery, M. (1995), *An Introduction to Language and Society*, 2nd edn, London: Routledge.

Montgomery, M., Durant, A., Fabb, N., Furniss, T. and Mills, S. (2000), *Ways of Reading: Advanced Reading Skills for Students of English Literature*, 2nd edn, London: Routledge.

Montgomery, M., Tolson, A. and Garton, G. (1989), 'Media discourse in the 1987 general election: ideology, scripts and metaphors', *English Language Research* 3: 173–204.

Mooney, R. J. (1990), *A General Explanation-Based Learning Mechanism and its Application to Narrative Understanding*, San Mateo, CA: Morgan Kaufman.

Morris, N. (ed.) (1986), *The Baby Book*, London: Newbourne Publications.

Morrow, D. G. (1985), 'Prominent characters and events organize narrative understanding', *Journal of Memory and Language* 24: 304–19.

Myers, J. L., Shinjo, M. and Duffy, S. A. (1987), 'Degree of causal relatedness and memory', *Journal of Memory and Language* 26: 453–65.

Newell, A. and Simon, H. A. (1972), *Human Problem Solving*, Englewood Cliffs, NJ: Prentice Hall.

Nisbett, R. E and Wilson, T. D. (1977), 'Telling more than we can know: verbal reports on mental processes', *Psychological Review* 84: 231–79.

O'Brien, E. J., Shank, D. M, Myers, J. L. and Rayner, K. (1988), 'Elaborative inferences during reading: do they occur on-line?', *Journal of Experimental Psychology: Learning, Memory and Cognition* 14: 410–20.

Ogborn, J., Kress, G., Martins, I. and McGillicuddy, K. (1996), *Explaining Science in the Classroom*, Buckingham: Open University Press.

O'Halloran, K. A. (1997), 'Why Whorf has been misconstrued in stylistics and critical linguistics', *Language and Literature* 6 (3).

Outhwaite, W. (1987), *New Philosophies of Social Science: Realism, Hermeneutics and Critical Theory*, Basingstoke: Macmillan.

Pennington, N. and Hastie, R. (1986), 'Evidence evaluation in complex decision making', *Journal of Personality and Social Psychology* 51: 242–58.

Popper, K. R. and Eccles, J. C. (1977), *The Self and its Brain, Pts I and II*, Berlin: Springer International.
Potts, G. R., Keenan, J. M. and Golding, J. M. (1988), 'Assessing the occurrence of elaborative inferences: lexical decision versus naming', *Journal of Memory and Language* 27: 399–415.
Putnam, H. (1975), *Philosophical Papers, vol. 2, Mind, Language and Reality*, Cambridge: Cambridge University Press.
Quine, W. (1953), 'Two dogmas of empiricism', in W. Quine, *From a Logical Point of View*, Cambridge, MA: Harvard University Press.
Quine, W. (1960), *Word and Object*, Cambridge, MA: MIT Press.
Rayner, K., Carlson, M. and Frazier, L. (1983), 'The interaction of syntax and semantics during sentence processing: eye movements in the analysis of semantically biased sentences', *Journal of Verbal Learning and Verbal Behaviour* 22: 358–74.
Read, S. J. (1987), 'Constructing causal scenarios: a knowledge structure approach to causal reasoning', *Journal of Personality and Social Psychology* 52: 288–302.
Read, S. J. and Marcus-Newhall, A. (1993), 'Explanatory coherence in social explanations: a parallel distributed processing account', *Journal of Personality and Social Psychology* 65: 429–47.
Reder, L. M. and Kusbit, G. W. (1991), 'Locus of the Moses illusion: imperfect encoding, retrieval, or match?', *Journal of Memory and Language* 30: 385–406.
Regier, T. (1996), *The Human Semantic Potential: Spatial Language and Constrained Connectionism*, Cambridge, MA: MIT Press.
Reiger, C. (1975), *Conceptual Memory and Inference: Conceptual Information Processing*, Amsterdam: North-Holland.
Renkema, J. (1984), 'Text linguistics and media: an experimental inquiry into coloured news reporting', in W. van Peer and J. Renkema, *Pragmatics and Stylistics*, Leuven, Belgium: Acco, pp. 317–71.
Richardson, K. (1987), 'Critical linguistics and textual diagnosis', *Text* 7 (2): 145–63.
Rifkin, A. (1985), 'Evidence for a basic level in event taxonomies', *Memory and Cognition* 13: 538–56.
Roberts, R. M. and Kreuz, R. J. (1993), 'Nonstandard discourse and its coherence', *Discourse Processes* 16: 451–64.
Rorty, R. (1980), *Philosophy and the Mirror of Nature*, Oxford: Blackwell.
Rosch, E. (1975a), 'Cognitive reference points', *Cognitive Psychology* 7: 532–47.
Rosch, E. (1975b), 'Cognitive representations of semantic categories', *Journal of Experimental Psychology, General* 104: 193–233.
Rosch, E. (1978), 'Principles of categorization' in E. Rosch and B. B. Lloyd, *Cognition and Categorization*, Hillsdale, NJ: Lawrence Erlbaum Associates, pp. 27–48.
Rosch, E. (1981), 'Prototype classification and logical classification: the two systems' in E. Scholnick (ed.), *New Trends in Cognitive Representation: Challenges to Piaget's Theory*, Hillsdale, NJ: Lawrence Erlbaum Associates, pp. 73–86.
Rosch, E., Mervis, C. B., Gray, W. D., Johnson, D. M. and Boyes-Braem, P. (1976), 'Basic objects in natural categories', *Cognitive Psychology* 8: 382–439.
Roth, E. M. and Shoben, E. J. (1983), 'The effect of context on the structure of categories', *Cognitive Psychology* 15: 346–78.
Rumelhart, D. E. (1975), 'Notes on a schema for stories' in D. G. Bobrow and A. M. Collins (eds), *Representation and Understanding: Studies in Cognitive Science*, San Diego, CA: Academic Press, pp. 211–36.
Rumelhart, D. E. and McClelland, J. L. (1986), 'PDP models and general issues in cognitive science' in D. E. Rumelhart et al. (eds), *Parallel Distributed Processing*, Cambridge, MA: MIT Press, pp. 110–46.
Rumelhart, D. E, McClelland, J. L. and the PDP Research Group (eds) (1986), *Parallel Distributed Processing: Explorations in the Microstructure of Cognition, vol. 1: Foundations*, Cambridge, MA: MIT Press.
Rumelhart, D. E. and Norman, D. A. (1982), 'Simulating a skilled typist: a study of skilled cognitive-motor performance', *Cognitive Science* 6: 1–36.

Russell, B. and Whitehead, A. N. (1910), *Principia Mathematica*, Cambridge: Cambridge University Press.
St John, M. F. (1992), 'The story Gestalt: a model of knowledge intensive processes in text comprehension', *Cognitive Science* 16: 271–306.
St John, M. F. and McClelland, J. L. (1992), 'Parallel constraint satisfaction as a comprehension mechanism', in R. G. Reilly and N. E. Sharkey (eds), *Connectionist Approaches to Natural Language Processing*, Hillsdale, NJ: Lawrence Erlbaum Associates, pp. 97–136.
Sanford, A. J. (1990), 'On the nature of text-driven inference', in D. A. Balota, G. B. Flores D'Arcais and K. Rayner (eds), *Comprehension Processes in Reading*, Hillsdale, NJ: Lawrence Erlbaum Associates, pp. 515–35.
Sanford, A. J. and Garrod, S. C. (1981), *Understanding Written Language: Explorations of Comprehension Beyond the Sentence*, Chichester: John Wiley and Sons.
Sanford, A. J. and Garrod, S. C. (1994), 'Selective processing in text understanding', in M. A. Gernsbacher, *Handbook of Psycholinguistics*, San Diego, CA: Academic Press, pp. 699–719.
Sanford, A. J., Moar, K. and Garrod, S. C. (1988), 'Proper names as controllers of discourse focus', *Language and Speech* 31: 43–56.
Savin, H. and Perchonock, E. (1965), 'Grammatical structure and the immediate recall of English sentences', *Journal of Verbal Learning and Verbal Behaviour* 4: 348–53.
Schank, R. C. (1980), 'An artificial intelligence perspective on Chomsky's view of language', *The Behavioral and Brain Sciences* 3: 35–7.
Schank, R. C. (1986), *Explanation Patterns: Understanding Mechanically and Creatively*, Hillsdale, NJ: Erlbaum.
Schank, R. C. and Abelson, R. (1977), *Scripts, Plans, Goals and Understanding*, Hillsdale, NJ: Lawrence Erlbaum.
Schopman, J. and Shawky, A. (1996), 'Remarks on the impact of connectionism on our thinking about concepts', in A. Clark and P. J. R. Millican (eds), *Connectionism, Concepts, and Folk Psychology: The Legacy of Alan Turing*, vol. 2, Oxford: Clarendon Press, pp. 67–74.
Searle, J. (1995), *The Construction of Social Reality*, London: The Penguin Press.
Sejnowski, T. J. and Rosenberg, C. R. (1987), 'Parallel networks that learn to pronounce English text', *Complex Systems* 1: 145–68.
Sharrock, W. W. and Anderson, D. C. (1981), 'Language, thought and reality, again', *Sociology* 15: 287–93.
Simpson, P. (1993), *Language, Ideology, and Point of View*, London: Routledge.
Singer, M. (1979a), 'Processes of inference in sentence encoding', *Memory and Cognition* 7: 192–200.
Singer, M. (1979b), 'Temporal locus of inference in the comprehension of brief passages: recognizing and verifying implications about instruments', *Perceptual and Motor Skills* 49: 539–50.
Singer, M. (1980), 'The role of case-filling inferences in the coherence of brief passages', *Discourse Processes* 3: 185–201.
Singer, M. (1990), *Psychology of Language: An Introduction to Sentence and Discourse Processes*, Hillsdale, NJ: Erlbaum.
Singer, M. (1994), 'Discourse inference processes' in M. A. Gernsbacher, *Handbook of Psycholinguistics*, San Diego, CA: Academic Press, pp. 479–515.
Skinner, B. F. (1957), *Verbal Behaviour*, New York: Appleton-Century-Crofts.
Skinner, B. F. (1976), *About Behaviourism*, New York: Knopf.
Slobin, D. (1982), 'Universal and particular in the acquisition of language', in E. Wanner and L. R. Gleitman (eds), *Language Acquisition: The State of the Art*, Cambridge: Cambridge University Press, pp. 128–70.
Smolensky, P. (1987), 'Connectionist AI, and the brain', *Artificial Intelligence Review* 1: 95–109.
Smolensky, P. (1995/1988), 'On the proper treatment of connectionism', originally published in 1988 and reprinted in C. MacDonald and G. MacDonald (eds) (1995), *Connectionism: Debates on Psychological Explanation*, vol. 2, Oxford: Blackwell, pp. 28–89.
Southgate, V. (no date), *The Enormous Turnip*, Loughborough: Wills and Hepworth.

Sperber, D. and Wilson, D. (1986), *Relevance: Communication and Cognition*, 1st edn, Oxford: Blackwell.
Sperber, D. and Wilson, D. (1995), *Relevance: Communication and Cognition*, 2nd edn, Oxford: Blackwell.
Stevenson, R. J. (1993), *Language, Thought and Representation*, Chichester: John Wiley and Sons.
Stillings, N. A., Weisler, S. E., Chase, C. H., Feinstein, M. H., Garfield, J. L. and Rissland, E. L. (1995), *Cognitive Science: An Introduction*, 2nd edn, Cambridge, MA: MIT Press.
Stockwell, P. (2002), *Sociolinguistics: A Resource Book for Students*, London: Routledge.
Stubbs, M. (1997), 'Whorf's children: critical comments on critical discourse analysis', in A. Ryan and A. Wray (eds), *Evolving Models of Language: British Studies in Applied Linguistics* 12: 100–16.
Swinburne, R. (1986), *The Evolution of the Soul*, Oxford: Oxford University Press.
Taraban, R. and McClelland, J. L. (1988), 'Constituent attachment and thematic role assignment in sentence processing: influences of content-based expectations', *Journal of Memory and Language* 27: 597–632.
Taylor, J. (1995), *Linguistic Categorisation*, 2nd edn, Oxford: Oxford University Press.
Thomason, R. (ed.) (1974), *Formal Philosophy: Selected Papers of Richard Montague*, New Haven: Yale University Press.
Toolan, M. J. (1997), 'What is critical discourse analysis and why are people saying such terrible things about it?' *Language and Literature* 6 (2): 83–103.
Toolan, M. J. (2001), *Narrative: A Critical Linguistic Introduction*, 2nd edn, London: Routledge.
Touretzky, D. S. and Geva, S. (1987), 'A distributed connectionist representation for concept structures', paper presented to the 9th annual conference of the Cognitive Science Society, Seattle.
Trabasso, T. and Sperry, L. (1985), 'Causal relatedness and importance of story events', *Journal of Memory and Language* 24: 595–611.
Trabasso, T., van den Broek, P. and Suh, S. Y. (1989), 'Logical necessity and transitivity of causal relations in stories', *Discourse Processes* 12: 1–26.
Trask, L. (1999), *Key Concepts in Language and Linguistics*, London: Routledge.
Trew, T. (1979), 'Theory and ideology at work', in R. Fowler et al., *Language and Control*, London: Routledge and Kegan Paul, pp. 94–116.
Turing, A. M. (1950), 'Computing machinery and intelligence', *Mind* 59: 433–60.
Ungerer, F. and Schmid, H.-J. (1996), *An Introduction to Cognitive Linguistics*, London: Longman.
van den Broek, P. (1990), 'Causal inferences and the comprehension of narrative text' in A. C. Graesser and G. H. Bower (eds), *Inferences and Text Comprehension*, San Diego, CA: Academic Press, pp. 175–96.
van den Broek, P. (1994), 'Comprehension and memory of narrative texts: inferences and coherence' in M. A. Gernsbacher, *Handbook of Psycholinguistics*, San Diego, CA: Academic Press, pp. 539–88.
van Dijk, T. (ed.) (1997a), *Discourse as Structure and Process. Discourse Studies: A Multidisciplinary Introduction, vol. 1*, London: Sage.
van Dijk, T. (1997b), *Discourse as Social Interaction. Discourse Studies: A Multidisciplinary Introduction, vol. 2*, London: Sage.
van Dijk, T. (2001), 'Critical discourse analysis' in D. Tannen, D. Schiffrin and H. Hamilton (eds), *The Handbook of Discourse Analysis*, Oxford: Blackwell, pp. 352–71.
van Dijk, T. and Kintsch, W. (1983), *Strategies of Discourse Comprehension*, New York: Academic Press.
van Leeuwen, T. (1993), 'Genre and field in critical discourse analysis: a synopsis', *Discourse and Society* 4(2): 193–223.
van Leeuwen, T. (1996), 'The representation of social actors' in C. R. Caldas-Coulthard and M. Coulthard (eds), *Texts and Practices: Readings in Critical Discourse Analysis*, London: Routledge, pp. 32–70.
Varela, F. J., Thompson, E. and Rosch, E. (1991), *The Embodied Mind: Cognitive Science and Human Experience*, Cambridge, MA: MIT Press.

von Neumann, J. (1947), 'Preliminary discussion of the logical design of an electronic computing instrument', US Army Ordnance Report.
Vonk, W. and Noordman, L. (1990), 'On the control of inferences in text understanding' in D. A. Balota, G. B. Flores d'Arcais and K. Rayner (eds), *Comprehension Processes in Reading*, Hillsdale, NJ: Lawrence Erlbaum Associates, pp. 447–64.
Wales, K. (2001), *A Dictionary of Stylistics*, London: Longman.
Waltz, D. L. (1989), 'Connectionist models: not just a notational variant, not a panacea', in Y. Wilks, *Theoretical Issues in Natural Language Processing*, Hillsdale, NJ: Lawrence Erlbaum Associates, pp. 56–63.
West, C., Lazar, M. M. and Kramarae, C. (1997), 'Gender in discourse' in T. van Dijk (ed.), *Discourse as Social Interaction: Discourse Studies, A Multidisciplinary Introduction, vol. 2*, London: Sage, pp. 119–43.
Whorf, B. L. (1956), *Language, Thought and Reality*, ed. J. B. Carroll, Cambridge, MA: MIT Press.
Widdowson, H. G. (1995a), 'Discourse analysis: a critical view', in *Language and Literature* 4 (3): 157–72.
Widdowson, H. G. (1995b), 'Review of Fairclough's *Discourse and Social Change*', *Applied Linguistics* 16 (4).
Widdowson, H. G. (1996), 'Reply to Fairclough: discourse and interpretation: conjectures and refutations', *Language and Literature* 5 (1): 57–69.
Widdowson, H. G. (1997), 'The use of grammar; the grammar of use', *Functions of Language* 4 (2): 145–68
Widdowson, H. G. (1998), 'Review article: the theory and practice of critical discourse analysis', *Applied Linguistics* 19 (1): 136–51.
Widdowson, H. G. (2000), 'On the limitations of linguistics applied', *Applied Linguistics* 21 (1): 3–25.
Wilensky, R. (1983), *Planning and Understanding: A Computational Approach to Human Reasoning*, Reading, MA: Addison Wesley.
Wilson, D. and Sperber, D. (1986), 'Inference and implicature', in C. Travis (ed.), *Meaning and Interpretation*, Oxford: Blackwell, pp. 45–75.
Wilson, D. and Sperber, D. (2004), 'Relevance theory', in G. Ward and L. Horn (eds), *Handbook of Pragmatics*, Oxford: Blackwell.
Wittgenstein, L. ([1921] 1961), *Tractatus Logico-Philosophicus*, trans. D. F. Pears and B. F. McGuinness, London: Routledge and Kegan Paul.
Wittgenstein, L. ([1953] 1967), *Philosophical Investigations*, trans. G. E. M. Anscombe, 3rd edn, Oxford: Basil Blackwell.
Wolpert, L. (1992), *The Unnatural Nature of Science*, London: Faber and Faber.

Index

Abelson, R., 77–8, 80, 161, 185
Abrahamsen, A., 73, 107
absences
    from discourse, 172, 229, 233, 234–5, 259, 260
    from text, 1, 3, 10–11, 58, 163, 171, 194, 245, 252, 259, 260, 261; detecting, 33–4, 224–7, 261: causal consequent, 233–5; of instrument, 232; and mystification 192, 223, 230–1, 247, 250; of subordinate goal-action, 232–3; of superordinate goal, 230–1
accidents, 44–5
accommodation, 174–6, 253
action categories
    basic-level, 124–5
    superordinate, 128–30
actionals, 59–61; *see also* transactives
advertisements, 75
agency, 22, 154–5
algorithms, 36, 37, 38, 47
Althusser, Louis, 11
Anderson, A., 151
Anderson, D. C., 31, 224
animals, 89
Aristotle, 44–5
artificial intelligence, 48

Ballard, D. H., 88
Barsalou, L. W., 113–14, 175–6, 205
Barton, S. B., 147–8, 150
Bechtel, W., 73, 103–4, 107, 109–10, 176
behaviourism, 46
Bell, A., 194–5
Bex, T., 221

bias
    discourse, 235–6, 238–42, 245–6, 247–50, 252, 260
    partiality, in interpretation, 31, 163
    text, 1, 20–1, 33, 252, 260; text presence bias, 245–7, 248–9, 260
brain, 37, 38, 87, 88
    neurophysiology, 38, 87–93, 111, 258
    see also cognition; memory; mind
Bransford, J. D., 129, 130, 136–7, 179
'Breadline Britain' (TV series), 219
Brown, E. K., 49
Brown, G., 160, 169
Brown, R., 117

Cameron, D., 57, 219
canonical sentence structure (CSS), 51–2, 67–8
Carnap, Rudolph, 38, 41, 42, 43, 61–3
case (semantic) roles, 95–6, 98–102
categories and categorisation, 111
    basic-level, 116–27, 129–30, 131–2, 191, 257; action, 124–5, 257; cognitive economy, 118–19; and context, 120–1; event, 125–7; nouns, 124–7
    classical theory, 44–6, 72–4, 111
    parasitic, 127
    and prototypicality, 112–16, 121–4
    and relevance theory, 205
    subordinate, 118–19
    superordinate *see separate entry*
    syntactic, 115–16
Catholicism, 12
causality, 76–7, 153, 155–8, 161, 217
    causal antecedent inferences, 136, 140–2, 155, 156, 157, 188, 190, 207–8, 211, 212,

causality (*cont.*)
   causal antecedent inferences (*cont.*)
      215, 255; and hard news texts, 208–11, 226, 242; and Widdowson's criticism, 226
   causal cognition, 218–19, 258–61
   causal consequent inferences, 142, 161, 181, 185, 190, 207, 208, 211, 225–6, 238, 255; absences, 233–5
   as interaction, 122–4
   scientific, 61–3
characters
   emotional reaction inferences, 213
   main and secondary, 151–2, 157, 242–4, 253, 257
Chomsky, Noam, 43, 51, 55n, 60, 80, 104, 120, 221
   and CDA, 64–6
   and symbolicism, 46–50
Churchland, P. M., 38, 89, 100, 174
Clark, K., 56–9, 75–6, 105–6, 132, 156–7, 210
classification
   chunking, 43
   taxonomy, 117
   see also categories and categorisation
closure, late, 52–3
cognition, 2–4, 11, 13–14, 21, 30, 31, 36, 37, 69, 70
   causal, 218–19, 258–61
   see also socio-cognitive analysis
cognitive economy, 119
cognitive interdependence, 124–7
cognitive linguistics, 111–32
   and compounds, 130–1
   and connectionism, 173–8; accommodation, 174–6; functionalism, 176–7
   and relevance theory, 204
   and shallow processing, 179–81
cognitive science, 2, 4, 37–8, 42, 48
coherence, 184, 231
   coherent (backward) inferences, 28, 136, 186–7, 189, 255
compositionality, 36–7, 41–2, 69–71, 98, 150, 161–2, 258
compounds, 130–1, 133n
computation, 37, 149
computers, 36, 37, 88
Comte, Auguste, 55n
connectionism, 60–1, 80, 85–110
   and cognitive linguistics, 173–8; accommodation, 174–6; functionalism, 176–7
   and inference generation, 102–6
   and mental representation, 106–10
   and prototype theory, 178

   and relevance theory, 204
   sentence processing, 95–102
   and shallow processing, 182–9
constructionist position, 136–7, 161, 211, 212
consumption of texts, 29, 79, 252–4
   and shallow processing, 252–4
context and co-text, 114–15, 129
   and basic level, 120–1
Cooper, R., 36
co-operative principle, 198–9, 201
co-operative text, 149
Cotter, C. A., 145
Critical Discourse Analysis (CDA), 1–6
   analysts, 3, 10, 162–3, 194, 253, 259–60; compared with readers, 170–1
   'critical' in, 33, 261
   definitions, 11
   explanation, 215–17
   interpretation stage, 9–81
   and language cognition, 83–165
   and manipulative news text, 9–34
   symbolicism of, 56–81
   tenets, 12
Critical Linguistics, 14–16, 30–1, 80
critical text analysis, 20–1

Daily Express, 25–6, 68
Daily Mail, 19–20, 27–8
Daily Telegraph, 238, 242–3, 244–5, 246
Derivational Theory of Complexity (DTC), 50–1, 66, 67, 256
Descartes, René, 37
description, 9, 33, 259–60
   scientific, 61–2, 73–4, 109–10
descriptivism, gross, 106, 132
discourse
   absences from, 172, 229, 233, 234–5, 259, 260
   bias, 235–6, 238–42, 245–6, 247–50, 252, 260
   type (1), 10–11, 12–13
   type (2) (Foucauldian), 10, 11–14
discourse analysis, 1, 10–11, 13, 32; *see also* Critical Discourse Analysis
discourse practice, 10, 12
distance
   ideational, 17–18, 130, 257
   interpersonal, 257
dualism, 37–8

Eccles, J. C., 37
Ellis, D. G., 58–9
Elman, J. L., 104, 175
empiricism *see* logical empiricism

enactment, 109
epistemology, 108
Erickson, T. A., 148–9, 150
essence, 44–5, 119–20
Evening Standard, 223
　'Crawl to work is the worst yet', 236, 237–8
　'Protest mob storm tube HQ', 226–36, 240, 241–2, 244, 245, 246, 247–9, 250, 259
experientialism, 120
explanation, 2, 4, 9–10
explicatures, 204, 205, 206
Eysenck, M. W., 212

Fairclough, Norman, 12–13, 15, 27–9, 32, 34n, 76–7, 78, 79, 98, 115, 130, 194, 255, 259
　on *The Baby Book*, 74–5
　Language and Power, 5n
　on TV programme on the poor, 69–70, 157–60, 161–2
Feldman, J. A., 88
feminist discourse, 57
Flores d'Arcais, G. B., 149, 155
Fodor, J. A., 36–7, 43–4, 51–2, 54–5, 66, 67, 221
Foucault, Michel, 11–13
Fowler, R., 14, 21, 24, 25, 31, 64, 70–1, 80, 100, 116, 223
　on university regulations, 67–8
Frazier, L., 52–3
Frege, Gottlob, 39, 40

garden-path sentences, 53, 67
Gardner, H., 43, 48, 55n
Garnham, A., 143–4, 149, 231
Garrett, M., 51–2, 54–5, 66, 67
Garrod, S., 145, 151, 152–3, 180, 184, 188, 206, 231
　primary processing principle, 146–8
Goatly, A., 9, 25, 213–15
Gough, V., 28–9, 160–1
Graesser, A. C., 142, 192, 193–4, 209, 210, 211, 212–13, 220, 241
grammar, 46–50, 78–9
　form, 73
　functional, 16, 18, 21, 254, 260
　generative/transformational, 46–50
　lexico-, 20
　transitivity, 17
Gramsci, Antonio, 11
Grice, H. P., 198–9, 201, 246
gross descriptivism, 106, 132
gross internalism, 106–7, 132
Guardian, The, 21

'Cycle protest adds to tube disruption', 233, 238–41, 243, 244, 245, 246, 249–50
　on picketing, 23–4, 72
Gumenik, W. E., 125

Habermas, Jürgen, 11
Habitat, 24–5
Hacking, I., 48
Halle, M., 49
Halliday, Michael, 15, 16, 17, 21, 78–80, 102, 107, 253, 254, 260
Hammersley, M., 34n
Hampton, J. A., 127
Harder, P., 43
Harley, T., 120–1, 178
Harris, Zellig, 47
heuristics, perceptual, 51–2, 67–8
Hobbes, Thomas, 37
Hodge, R., 31, 46, 74, 80, 116, 123, 256
　on children's story, 61–2, 156
　on *Guardian* editorial, 23–4, 72–3
　Language as Ideology, 2, 5, 14, 21, 22, 64–6
　and psychological realism, 66–7
　on scientific language, 110
　and simple, 59–64
　on transformations, 64–5
Hopi language, 15
Horizon (TV programme), 'A New Green Revolution?', 69–70, 157–60
human understander, 42, 46, 62, 63–4, 155
Hume, David, 37

idealised reader (IR)
　causal cognition, 218–19
　empirical testing, 171, 219–20
　framework, 189–96, 225–6, 229–32, 235, 240–1, 242, 258, 259, 260–1
　and interpretation, 170–3
　in mystification analysis, 226–9, 230–8
　and news texts, 192–5
　processing principles, 189–91
　and relevance theory, 203–4, 211–15
ideational distance, 17–18, 130, 257
ideational function of language, 16–19
ideology, 14, 15, 253
implicatures, 199, 202, 203–4, 206–8, 235–6
inference generation 3, 4, 32, 188, 258
　vs. automatic gap-filling, 28–9, 145–6, 160, 255
　and connectionism, 102–6
　and IR framework, 212
　in mystification analysis, 74
　psycholinguistic evidence for, 134–50, 162–3, 184–6; likelihood, 135–46

inference generation (cont.)
  in socio-cognitive analysis, 27–9
  and symbolism, 74–8
  and syntax processing, 54–5
inferences, 189, 191
  anaphoric, 164n
  automatic, 145–6, 189, 190
  character emotional reaction, 213
  elaborative (forward/prediction), 142, 144–5, 179, 189, 190, 207, 211; vs. coherence, 135–6; likelihood of generation, 136–40; shallow generation of, 184–8; *see also* instantiation
  psycholinguistic, 206–8
  referential, 136, 211
  relevance theory, 206–8; less relevant, 211–15
  role assignment, 136, 211
  strategic, 139, 160–2, 163, 193, 255
  strong, 27–8, 255–6
  subordinate goal-action, 211, 217, 225, 238
  superordinate goal, 211–12, 225, 238, 247–8
  and symbolism, 74–8
  thematic, 213, 215
  weak representations, 21–2, 30, 191, 255–6
  see also causal antecedent inferences; causal consequent inferences; coherence (backward) inferences; implicatures; instrument inferences
instantiation, 142–4, 156, 179–80, 190, 196n, 225, 247–8, 256
  and likelihood of inference generation, 142–4
  and prototypicality, 196n
  and shallow processing, 179–80
instrument inferences, 86–7, 190, 211, 217, 225, 237
  absence, 232
  likelihood of generation, 144–5, 180–1
  and shallow processing, 180–1
internalism, 106, 116
  gross, 106–7, 132
  modest, 106, 132
International Express, 213–14
International Wildlife, 24–5
interpretation, 2, 3, 6n, 9–11, 30–2, 33, 258–60
  developing, 31–2
  and IR framework, 170–3
  over-, 3, 261; in socio-cognitive analysis, 157–62, 164
  partiality, 31, 163
  in short text processing, 104–5

Johnson, M., 42, 48, 119, 129, 130, 131, 179, 209

Katz, J. J., 45, 49
Kawamoto, A. H., 94, 107, 175, 177
  'Mechanisms of sentence processing', 95–6, 98–101
Keane, M. T., 212
Keefe, D. E., 181
Keenan, J. M., 141, 154, 188, 207, 212
Kress, Gunther, 31, 46, 74, 80, 100, 116, 120, 123, 224, 256
  on children's story, 61–2, 156
  on *Daily Express*, 25–6
  on *Guardian* editorial, 23–4, 72–3
  Language as Ideology, 2, 5, 14, 21, 22, 64–6
  Linguistic Processes in Sociocultural Practice, 183
  and psychological realism, 66–7
  on scientific language, 110
  and simple, 59–64
  on transformations, 64–5
  on university regulations, 67–8
Kusbit, G. W., 149, 150

Lakoff, George, 42, 44, 48, 112, 174, 177, 209, 232
  on basic level, 117–18, 121–5
  on compounds, 130–1
  on objectivism, 119, 120
  on symbolic paradigm, 45–6
  Women, Fire and Dangerous Things, 111, 113, 114, 115
Lancaster Guardian, 76–7
Langacker, R. W., 48, 69, 173–4, 175
language
  function, 63–4, 176–7
  processing; symbolic approaches to, 66–72
  see also grammar; linguistics; scientific discourse/language
Language and Control, 2
late closure, 52–3, 67
law of contradiction, 45
law of excluded middle, 45
learning, 46, 92, 95, 108
Leech, G. N., 71
Leibniz, G. W., 37, 50
lexical decision task, 138
lexicalisation, 24
lexico-grammar, 20
linguistics *see* cognitive linguistics; Critical Linguistics; psycholinguistics
Locke, John, 37
logic, 37, 39–41, 44, 88

logical empiricism, 38–44, 58–9, 63, 74, 75, 77, 107–9, 131
logical positivism, 43, 55n

McClelland, J. L.
  1988 experiments, 86–7
  on connectionism, 94, 102–3, 107, 175, 177, 196n, 257
  'Mechanisms of sentence processing', 94, 95–6, 98–101
  Parallel Distributed Processing, 94
  shallow processing, 182–3, 184, 185
  short-text processing, 104–5, 187–8
McDaniel, M. A., 181
MacDonald, C. and G., 85
McKoon, G., 137–9, 142, 143, 144, 180, 185, 188, 193
manipulation
  linguistic, 1–2, 11, 14–16, 33, 252
  symbolic, 35–6, 37
  see also bias; mystification
Martin, J. R., 24–5, 60, 126, 128, 131
materialism, 37–8
mathematics, 39, 48, 49, 88
Mattson, M. E., 148–9, 150
meaning, 1, 37, 40–2, 44–6
  ideational *see* transitivity
  shading of, 97–8
Meinhof, U., 219
memory, 137, 138, 141, 149, 155, 156, 165n, 176
microfeatures, 93–4, 95–7, 178
Miller, G. A., 50–1
mind, 46, 87–8, 89
  -body problem, 37–8
  modelling, 35–7
  see also brain; reason; representation, mental; thought
minimal attachment principle, 53–4, 86–7
minimalist hypothesis, 142, 145, 146, 156, 179, 193–4, 212–13
  and elaborative inference generation, 137–9
  and shallow generation of forward elaborative inferences, 184–8
modest internalism, 106, 132
modularity hypothesis, 52, 54, 86
Montague, Richard, 43
Montgomery, M., 19, 22, 57, 217
Morning Star, 19–20
Morrow, D. G., 151–2, 243–4
Moses Illusion, 148–9, 164n, 182
mystification analysis, 1–3, 9–11, 254–6
  in CDA, 33, 56, 59, 64, 78
  and cognition, 21–5
  and Critical Linguistics, 14–16

  IR and, 230–8, 260–1
  key concepts, 16–21
  and nominalisation, 72–3
  and socio-cognitive analysis, 30
  transformations, 64–6, 69
mystifying text, 1, 9, 154–7, 252
  detecting, 223–51

narratives, processing, 151–3, 208–10; *see also* news texts
Neurath, Otto, 38
neurophysiology, 37–8, 111, 258
  neural networks, 87–93
news texts (reports), 1–3, 21–9, 33–4, 157, 165n, 215–17, 251n
  and causal relations, 208–15
  detecting mystifying text, 223–50; absences, 223–6
  and idealised reader, 191–5, 230–8, 260–1
  manipulative, 9–34, 252
  nominalisation, 18–19, 23–5
  reporting both sides, 235–7
newspapers, 9, 19–20, 223, 260; *see also titles*
nominals and nominalisation, 100, 115–16, 130
  distancing, 257
  high degree of, 23–5
  ideational, 18–21
  and objectification, 24, 72–4, 75
  processing, 256
Noordman, L., 139–40, 141, 159, 160, 189, 213
nouns, 72, 115–16
  basic-level, 124–6
  in sentence processing, 86–7, 95–6
  superordinate, 127
  see also nominals and nominalisation

objectification, 24, 72–3, 75, 115
objectivism, 111, 116
  challenging, 119–20
O'Brien, E. J., 144–5, 180
O'Halloran, K. A., 34n
ostension, 199–200
over-interpretation, 3, 261
  in socio-cognitive analysis, 157–62, 164

partiality in interpretation, 31, 163; *see also* bias
passives, 17–18, 22, 50–1, 154, 165n
passivisation, ideational, 17–18
perceptual heuristics, 51–2, 67–8
philosophy, 39–41, 108
  and symbolic modelling, 37–8
  see also logical empiricism
phonemes, 49, 91–3
phonology, 49

physicalism, 61–3
Plato, 37
Postal, P. M., 45
primary processing principle, 146–8, 160, 164n
   and relevance theory, 206
   and shallow processing, 184
   and short text processing, 188
primitiveness, 60–2
processing, 231, 258
   compositional, 69–72, 258
   IR and, 189–91
   language, and symbolicism, 66–8
   of narratives, 151–3, 208–10
   parallel distributed (PDP), 87
   sentence, 50–5, 67–8, 87–9, 94–102; and CSS, 51–2; and DTC, 50–1; and instantiation, 142–4; syntax-first, 54–5
   shallow (weak), 68, 134, 154, 256; and cognitive linguistics, 179–81; and connectionism, 182–9; vs. consumption reading, 252–4; top-down, 146–50, 155
   short text, 185–8
   see also primary processing principle; reading
prototypes, 127, 177–8, 196n
   and basic-level, 121–4
   and categories, 112–16; effects, 112–15, 132n; syntactic categories, 115–16
psycholinguistics, 2, 32, 258
   evidence for inference generation, 134–64, 204; and relevance theory, 204, 206–8, 210
Putnam, H., 37
Pylyshyn, Z. W., 36–7, 43–4

Quine, W., 37–8, 62–3

Ratcliff, R., 137–9, 142, 143, 144, 180, 185, 188, 293
rationalism, 38
Rayner, K., 53, 54
readers, 140, 149, 160–2, 163, 255–6
   vs. analysts, 170–1
   compliant, 160
   critical, 14, 261
   framework, 3, 5, 31, 32, 34, 170–3
   ideal, 27–8
   idealised (IR) *see separate entry*
   inference-making, 169–70
   lay-, 31
   non-critical/complicit, 10–11, 29, 33–4, 167, 169–70, 192, 261
   non-energetic, 24, 30, 254, 256
   resistant or non-resistant, 154, 159

reading, 134–5, 140
   as consumption, 29, 52, 79, 225; shallow vs., 253–4
   goals, 191–4, 213, 225
   and relevance, 197–8
   time, 51, 87, 143–5, 152–3
reason, 37, 44, 45, 48, 209–10
Reder, L. M., 149, 150
relevance theory, 198–204
   and category type, 205
   cognitive principle, 199
   communicative principle, 199–201
   and connectionism, 204–8
   vs. co-operative principle, 201
   and explicatures, 205
   and idealised reader, 197–217
   inferences, 206–8
   and news texts, 208–15
   and non-symbolicism, 204
   optimal, 199–201
   and primary processing principle, 206
religion, 12
Renkema, J., 15
representation, mental, 65, 94, 116, 132
   and connectionism, 106–10
   vs. enactment, 107–9
   of language, 80; *see also* thought
   in neural networks, 91–3
representations, 36–7, 88
   case-frame, 95–101
   distributed, sub-symbols (microfeatures), 93–4, 95–7, 178
   scientific, 109–10
   sentences as, 63–4
   strong, 27–8, 255–6
   weak, 21–2, 74, 191, 255–6
   see also symbolicism
Richardson, K., 14, 31, 219, 220
Rifkin, A., 125–6
Rorty, R., 108
Rosch, Eleanor, 111–13, 114, 121, 129, 174, 178, 179
Rumelhart, D. E., 88, 94
Russell, Bertrand, 39–40, 42, 43, 48

St John, M. F., 94, 101, 102–3, 104–5, 107, 182–3, 184, 185–8
Sanford, A. J., 134, 145, 146–8, 150, 151, 152–3, 164n, 180–1, 184, 188, 206, 231
Sapir, Edward, 34n
Schank, R. C., 77–8, 80, 161, 185
Schlick, Moritz, 38
Schmid, H.-J., 111, 114, 119, 121, 125, 126, 127, 128, 254

Schopman, J., 85, 108–9
scientific discourse/language, 12, 18, 41, 61–3
  and connectionism, 73–4
  and nominals, 109–10
scripts, 77–8
Searle, J., 120
semantic roles, 17
semantic transitivity, 25–6
semantic value, 148
sentence-crunching, 87–8, 89
sentences, 46–7, 50–3, 60–4
  atmosphere or target, 151–3
  comprehension, 86–7
  garden-path, 53, 67
  kernel, 47, 60–1
  primitive, 61
  processing *see under* processing
  structure, 39–42, 63–4, 155, 156–7;
    canonical, 51–2, 67–8; surface and deep,
    47–8, 65
  see also compositionality
Sharrock, W. W., 31, 224
Shawky, A., 85, 108–9
Short, M. H., 71
simples (propositions), 40–1, 47–8
  explicit acknowledgement of, 59–64
  implicit acknowledgement of, 56–9
Simpson, P., 22, 29, 56, 57–9, 74, 105, 126,
    156, 157, 210–11
Singer, M., 143, 144, 145, 180–1
Skinner, B. F., 37, 46
Slobin, D., 63
Smolensky, P., 93–4, 189
socio-cognitive analysis, 13, 26, 32, 33, 76, 154,
    219–20, 252, 256
  and causal cognitive analysis, 258–9
  cognition, 27–9
  and mystification analysis, 30
  over-interpretation, 157–62, 164
sociocultural analysis, 3, 13
speech, formal and material, 41
Sperber, D., 198, 199–203, 205, 206, 207, 208,
    209, 210, 221, 231
Stubbs, M., 30–1, 32, 171, 223, 246
Sun, The, 56–9, 75–6, 105
Sunday Mirror, 28–9
superordinate categories, 127–30, 191, 217, 257
  action, 128–30
  goal inferences, 211–13, 225; absences,
    230–1, 233
  and instantiation, 142–4, 179–80
  noun, 127
  translating into basic level, 129–30
Swinburne, R., 37

symbolicism, 2–3, 35–55, 261
  of CDA, 56–80, 163–4; and Halliday, 78–80;
    and inferences, 74–8
  Chomsky and, 46–50
  and language processing, 66–9
  modelling, 35–7
  and philosophy, 37–8
  symbolic paradigm, 48–9, 94; and classical
    theory of categories, 45–6; and logical
    empiricism, 43–4; sub-symbols, 93–4
syntax, 50–5, 68, 86–7, 173
  syntactic categories, 115–16

Talbot, M., 28–9, 160–1
Taraban, R., 86–7, 101, 177, 182–3, 184, 257
text, 110
  analysis, 197; critical, 20–1
  bias, 1, 20–1, 33, 245–7, 252, 260
  comprehension, 134–5, 146, 184–5
  consumption, 29, 79, 252–4
  co-operative, 149
  inferences in, 135–46
  mystifying, 1, 9, 94, 154–7, 252; detecting
    mystification, 94, 223–51
  production, 6n
  shallow processing of, 146–50
  short, processing, 104–5, 185–8
  see also news texts; reading
thought, 31, 36–7, 44, 50, 65
  Whorfian hypothesis, 15, 16, 34n, 71
  see also representation, mental
Times, The, on riot in Africa, 21–2, 101–2,
    123–4, 163, 215–17
Toolan, M. J., 22, 172, 247
topicalisation, 164n
transactives, 26, 59–64, 65–6, 68, 81n, 107, 123,
    132, 156
transformations, 47–51, 66, 256
  and mystification, 64–6
transitivity, 16–20, 23, 25–6, 257
Trew, T., 21–2, 57, 74, 101–2, 105, 123–4, 155,
    163, 215–16
truth, 39, 42
Turing, Alan, 36
Turing machine, 36, 37, 49
Tzeltal community, 117

understander, human, 42, 46, 62, 63–4, 155
Ungerer, F., 111, 114, 119, 121, 125, 126, 127,
    128, 254

values, 224
van den Broek, P., 140, 141
van Dijk, Teun, 11, 13, 57

van Leeuwen, T., 163
Varela, F. J., 94
verificationism, 38
Vienna Circle, 38, 55n
von Neumann, John, 36, 48, 88
Vonk, W., 139–40, 141, 159, 160, 189, 213

Whitehead, Alfred North, 39
Whorf, Benjamin Lee, 15, 34n, 65

Whorfian hypothesis, 15, 16, 34n, 71
Widdowson, H. G., 31, 32, 78–9, 81n, 170–1, 194, 197, 222n, 223–4, 226
Wilson, D., 198–203, 205, 206–10, 221, 231
Wittgenstein, Ludwig, 39, 40–1, 127
Wodak, R., 12–13, 15
Wolpert, Lewis, 63

Yule, G., 160, 169